MAFIA HITS, MISSES, WARS, AND PROSECUTIONS

MAFIA HITS, MISSES, WARS, AND PROSECUTIONS

JEFFREY SUSSMAN

BLOOMSBURY ACADEMIC
NEW YORK • LONDON • OXFORD • NEW DELHI • SYDNEY

BLOOMSBURY ACADEMIC

Bloomsbury Publishing Inc, 1385 Broadway, New York, NY 10018, USA
Bloomsbury Publishing Plc, 50 Bedford Square, London, WC1B 3DP, UK
Bloomsbury Publishing Ireland, 29 Earlsfort Terrace, Dublin 2, D02 AY28, Ireland

BLOOMSBURY, BLOOMSBURY ACADEMIC and the Diana logo are trademarks of
Bloomsbury Publishing Plc

First published in the United States of America 2026

Copyright © Jeffrey Sussman, 2026

Cover design: Sally Rinehart
Cover image © iStock.com/sengerg

All rights reserved. No part of this publication may be: i) reproduced or transmitted in any form, electronic or mechanical, including photocopying, recording or by means of any information storage or retrieval system without prior permission in writing from the publishers; or ii) used or reproduced in any way for the training, development or operation of artificial intelligence (AI) technologies, including generative AI technologies. The rights holders expressly reserve this publication from the text and data mining exception as per Article 4(3) of the Digital Single Market Directive (EU) 2019/790.

Bloomsbury Publishing Inc does not have any control over, or responsibility for, any third-party websites referred to or in this book. All internet addresses given in this book were correct at the time of going to press. The author and publisher regret any inconvenience caused if addresses have changed or sites have ceased to exist, but can accept no responsibility for any such changes.

Library of Congress Cataloging-in-Publication Data

ISBN: HB: 979-8-8818-0479-4
eBook: 979-8-8818-0534-0
ePDF: 979-8-8818-6785-0

Typeset by Deanta Global Publishing Services, Chennai, India

For product safety related questions contact productsafety@bloomsbury.com.

To find out more about our authors and books visit www.bloomsbury.com
and sign up for our newsletters.

To Barbara, my wife and best friend.

CONTENTS

Acknowledgments ix

Introduction 1

1 A Bullet in the Gut Ends an Era 13

2 No Love Lost on Valentine's Day 23

3 The Castellammarese Wars and the Emergence of the New Mafia 33

4 Jews and Italians 43

5 Lansky and Luciano: Brothers in Crime 49

6 The Business of Murder 57

7 Little Man against the Mob 65

8 The Only Mob Boss Fried in Old Sparky 73

9 Deportations 81

10 The Biggest Hit on Television 97

11 Another Committee Hearing 105

12 Unseating the Lord High Executioner 119

13 The Apalachin Disaster 127

14 The Canary Sang 135

15 Robert F. Kennedy, Mafia Nemesis 145

16 The Gallo Wars 157

17 The Colombos Go to War Again 173

18 The Banana Wars 185

19 Flippers, Informants, Rats, Explainers 197

20 Friends of the FBI 215

21 Decapitation 235

About the Author 247
Bibliography 248
Index 250

ACKNOWLEDGMENTS

There are numerous people whose understanding and knowledge have helped me achieve my goals as an author. In particular I am grateful to my editors, Becca Beurer and Sarah Rinehart. In addition, Steven Spataro, reference librarian extraordinaire, has been diligent in helping me obtain old newspaper and magazine articles for my research. And my wife, Barbara, continues to be my first reader, offering helpful suggestions.

Introduction

I have written several books about organized crime that exposed realms where the mob has operated, including boxing, Las Vegas, rock music, Hollywood, and New York City. Unlike those books, this book focuses on pivotal events that caused the mob to adapt to new circumstances so that it could continue thriving.

Though there are many books about organized crime, this is the only book that focuses on how the mob adapted to the murders of its bosses, to failed hits, to internecine wars, and to prosecutions. (Throughout this book, I use the word "Mafia" only when referring to Italian organized crime; I use the word "mob" when referring to all organized crime groups).

The notorious murders and wars that the mob engaged in throughout much of the twentieth century occurred mostly in New York and Chicago. The most famous pivotal prosecutions of mobsters also took place in New York and Chicago, though many originated in Washington, D.C. The prosecutors who built successful political careers following noteworthy mob convictions were Thomas Dewey, William O'Dwyer, Burton Turkus, Robert F. Kennedy, and Rudolph Giuliani. This book covers their most far-reaching prosecutions. In addition, the book describes how a host of murders and wars ended the careers of Mafia bosses while opening doors for new Mafia bosses to change the way their crime families operated and altered their targets of opportunity.

Here are several brief descriptions of pivotal events that dramatically changed the way the mob did business.

The St. Valentine's Day Massacre

On February 14, 1929, the most sensational Mafia massacre occurred in Chicago. It quickly became known as the St. Valentine's Day Massacre. It was ordered by Al Capone, boss of the South Side Gang and of the Chicago Outfit, so that he could eliminate competition from George "Bugs" Moran, leader of the Northside Gang. The two bosses had attempted to kill each other several times, and each time failure was the result.

Capone decided that ambushes and on-site street killings would likely fail, so he organized a clever plan. He had a liquor dealer offer to sell Moran a truckload of whiskey at a steep discount. It would be delivered at 10:30 a.m. to the S.M.C. Cartage garage where Moran kept his fleet of trucks. The garage was located on North Clark Street and was a hangout for Moran's men and a few gangster wannabes. Shortly after 10:30 in the morning, four men drove up to the garage in what looked like a genuine police car; two uniformed fake cops and two plainclothes fake cops emerged from the car and ordered all seven men in the garage up against a wall. There, they were told they would be frisked for weapons. The ersatz cops then brought out tommy guns and 12-gauge shotguns that had been concealed in their overcoats. All of Bugs' men, but one, died instantly. The one who survived for only minutes was Frank Gusenberg. Keeping to the gangsters' standard code of silence, he refused to say who had killed his cohorts. He took a few painful breaths, then died, his body full of bloody holes.

Just prior to the shooting, Moran was walking to his garage; he saw the cop car arrive and decided to wait in a nearby café for its departure. To say that he was shocked and consumed with fear after what happened would be an understatement. In fact, he was so frightened that he would soon be killed by Capone later that day, he publicly accused his nemesis of planning the massacre and demanded that Capone be arrested. Capone, smiling and shrugging his shoulders when confronted by reporters at his Florida estate, exclaimed, "Moran who?" Because Capone was in Florida when the massacre took place, he had an alibi that many believed was tissue thin. It proved to be unbreakable.

While Capone had successfully eliminated his rival, the ensuing publicity and notoriety of the massacre made Capone the foremost gangster in America. He now had a target on his career, and the government moved diligently to nail him. He was arrested, tried, and convicted for tax evasion; while in prison he drifted into insanity from untreated syphilis.

The government's use of the IRS in the Capone case had warned every gangster in America to have credible legal income and expenses unless they wanted to follow Capone into prison.

With the elimination of its competitors and Big Al knocked off his throne, the Outfit became not only the dominant gang in Chicago; it dominated the entire state of Illinois. And like most growing local corporations, it grew to be a national syndicate, extending its reach wherever it could do business. It opened operations in Hollywood, St. Louis, Kansas City, Cleveland, and by the early 1970s, it controlled four major casinos in Las Vegas. Al Capone's absence had created a vacuum for the Outfit, which became the largest multi-ethnic organized crime organization in America.

The Castellamarese War

From February 26, 1930, to April 15, 1931, the Castellamarese War raged in New York. The war was a result of two Mafia bosses, Joe "the Boss" Masseria and Salvatore Maranzano, each attempting to control illegal activities in New York. The press named the war after the region of Sicily where Maranzano had been born: Castellammare del Golfo. Many of his gunmen were also from Sicily.

The war was a result of the two bosses running their Mafia families like ancient tribes: they would only partner with other Italians, in some cases only with Sicilians. The two bosses intensely disliked other ethnicities, especially Jews and Irish Americans. Lucky Luciano, who worked for Masseria and secretly partnered with Jewish gangsters Meyer Lansky and Bugsy Siegel, believed that if the Mafia were to grow and significantly increase its power, its reach, and its income, it had to be open-minded about dealing with others. If not, it would be a small enterprise, largely confined to Italian immigrant neighborhoods in Brooklyn and Manhattan. In addition to Luciano, the Masseria gang included others who wanted to expand the gang's territory and businesses: Frank Costello (formerly Francesco Castiglia), Joe Adonis (formerly Antonio Doto), Albert "Mad Hatter" Anastasia, Vito Genovese, and Willie Moretti, among various other future Mafia powerhouses.

Luciano convinced the young Turks in the Masseria gang that they had to get rid of their boss or they would be tied to his old-world ways and their gang would not thrive to its full potential. Next, he met with Maranzano, who agreed that if Luciano and his cohorts killed Masseria, the war would come to an end. So, Luciano lured Masseria to lunch at Nuova Villa Tammaro, an Italian restaurant in Coney Island. After Masseria stuffed himself on a big meal, primarily of spaghetti with meat sauce and a bottle of Chianti, he and Luciano relaxed over a game of cards and a pair of double espressos. Luciano excused himself to go to the restroom. Masseria's bodyguards quietly departed as four gunmen rushed into the restaurant. They were Bugsy Siegel, Albert Anastasia, Vito Genovese, and Joe Adonis; they fired bullets from .32 and .38 caliber revolvers into Masseria's head and back. The deed done, the four men ran from the restaurant and got into a waiting stolen getaway car. The driver, Ciro "The Artichoke King" Terranova, was shaking like a dying leaf in a hurricane. Siegel pushed Terranova aside, took the wheel, and the car sped to safety. None of the killers was ever prosecuted for Masseria's death.

The war now over, Maranzano, as surviving boss, divided the Mafia into five families, positioning himself as boss of bosses (capo di tutti capi). The Five Families would be led by Luciano, Joe Bonanno, Joseph Profaci, Vincent Mangano, and Thomas Gagliano. Profaci and Bonanno would figure in three of the bloodiest wars of the 1960s and 1970s: the Profaci-Colombo Gallo Wars.

Luciano was not happy with Maranzano, who was authoritarian and greedy, demanding substantial tributes from all members of the five families. In addition, Maranzano proved as old-worldly as Masseria, refusing to deal with Jews and promoting only Italians, often just Sicilians, to positions as underbosses, consiglieris, capos, soldiers. Luciano decided that Maranzano would have the same fate as his former rival. Oddly, Maranzano did not trust Luciano, perhaps because he had betrayed Masseria. Maranzano decided it was time to get rid of Luciano, lest he betray his new boss. Offering $25,000, Maranzano hired Vincent "Mad Dog" Coll, an Irish gangster, to kill Luciano. Since Maranzano disliked Jews and refused to partner with them, Luciano arranged with Meyer Lansky for four Jewish hitmen to kill Maranzano. They were Red Levine, a member of Murder Incorporated; Bo Weinberg, a member of the Dutch Shultz gang, and two others whose identities remain a mystery. Posing as IRS agents, they arrived at Maranzano's office at 230 Park Avenue, the New York Central Building, which overlooked Park Avenue to the north and Grand Central Terminal to the south. Maranzano was prepared to show the ersatz agents one set of carefully edited books; however, the hitmen pulled out switchblades and hunting knives and fell upon Maranzano, stabbing him multiple times. He was finished off with a shot to the head. As the hitmen were departing, they passed Coll in a hallway, who was on his way to receive payment from Maranzano to kill Luciano. The hitmen told him that Maranzano had been killed, so Coll hastily departed. (He would later be machine-gunned to death in a drugstore phone booth). As with Masseria's murder, no one was ever indicted for the Maranzano hit.

Luciano's next move was to form the commission, which would oversee and mediate all Mafia actions going forward. He even offered Lansky, his boyhood pal, a position as a boss on the commission. Lansky, however, demurred, for he said that he didn't believe that Italians would be happy taking orders from him. In the future, however, his word was like a command from god: next to Luciano, Lansky was the most powerful gangster in America. Luciano and Lansky formed what the press called the National Crime Syndicate, which was multi-ethnic, and ruled from coast to coast, controlling vast amounts of illegal activities for decades. If it hadn't been for the war and the death of the two old-time bosses, the Mafia would not have become the corporate behemoth that it would be. (In a bugged telephone conversation, Meyer Lansky was recorded saying that his syndicate was bigger than US Steel).

Murder Incorporated

As organized crime's leaders grew in sophistication, they realized that they needed a subsidiary business that would meticulously carry out murders. So, they formed an organization they called the combination or combo, but which the press named Murder Incorporated. It developed from the Bug(s) and Meyer Gang, which had moved onto more sophisticated crime than murder for hire. Murder Inc's leaders were Lepke Buchalter, the only mob boss sent to the electric chair, and his partner Albert "Mad Hatter" Anastasia, who was assassinated in 1957. From 1930 to 1941, prosecutors estimated that the organization had murdered between 400 to 1,000 individuals, most of whom had been killed by Italian American and Jewish gangsters, who had been recruited from poor neighborhoods in Brooklyn (primarily Brownsville) and in Manhattan (primarily the Lower East Side and Little Italy). The killers received regular salaries, plus additional fees for each murder, ranging from $500 to $1,000. Harry Strauss (aka Pittsburgh Phil), the most ambitious of the killers, was reported to have killed as many as 500 people, thus making him the richest of the killers. Had he not been executed by the state, he could have continued investing his money in real estate. He and his cohorts used Rosie Gold's candy store (aka Midnight Rose) on the corner of Saratoga and Livonia Avenues in Brooklyn as their hangout; the public phone rang frequently, providing killers with the names and addresses of their next victims. Whether Rosie received commissions or year-end bonuses remains unknown.

Even more ambitious than Strauss was prosecutor William O'Dwyer, who would use the publicity generated by his crime-fighting prosecutions to become mayor of New York. As D.A., he won first-degree murder indictments against many members of Murder Inc., including Abe "Kid Twist" Reles, who was flung out of a window of the Half Moon Hotel in Coney Island before he could testify against Murder Inc.'s bosses. O'Dwyer was more successful when he obtained convictions against Martin "Buggsy" Goldstein, Anthony Maffetore, Frank "the Dasher" Abbandano, and Harry "Happy" Maione, all of whom were sentenced to meet their ends in the electric chair, aka Old Sparky, in Sing Sing Prison. O'Dwyer wasn't the only one riding high on Murder Inc. convictions; there was Assistant Brooklyn District Attorney Burton Turkus, who not only prosecuted seven members of M.I. but then went on to write a best-selling book about his exploits and host a television show in the 1950s.

While Turkus became a media celebrity, O'Dwyer won acclaim after being elected mayor for helping to bring the United Nations to New York and establishing the first Israel Day Parade. He also appointed Robert Moses as the city's Construction Coordinator, resulting in an abundance of new buildings as well as parks, recreation centers, beaches, and parkways that were transformational for the city and state.

For many politicians, there is an upside as well as a downside: shortly after O'Dwyer was re-elected mayor in 1949, he woke one morning to headlines that he was involved in a police corruption scandal. Though he declared his innocence, he resigned on August 31, 1950, still a loyal party man. And

Harry Truman, who placed loyalty on a higher plane than most politicians, appointed O'Dwyer as ambassador to Mexico. (Truman's political career had been engineered by Tom Pendergast, the political boss and mob fixer of Kansas City, Missouri, who spent time in prison for income tax evasion. When Pendergast died, Truman, against the advice of political cronies, attended Pendergast's funeral. He commented to reporters: "He was always my friend and I have always been his." [1]

Mexico for O'Dwyer was a lovely place to avoid knife-in-the-back political attacks. However, the knives reappeared in 1951, when O'Dwyer was called back to New York to defend himself against accusations that he did business with members of organized crime. Again, he resigned from a prestigious office, then turned his back on the city that seemed out to get him. He returned to his tranquil life in Mexico, where he lived until 1960.

The fallout from the demise of Murder Inc. not only had an effect on politics, but it also taught the mob that too many murders, too many bodies littering the streets were bad public relations that significantly hurt business. The threat of murder could be just as effective as an actual murder. But even if a murder had to be committed, it should be done in the shadows and the victim's body should be buried where no one would find it.

Kill the President

Perhaps the most devastating result of prosecuting the mob may have led to the assassination of President Kennedy. At least, that's what Attorney General Robert Kennedy said to a confidant. Robert Kennedy had prosecuted hundreds of members of organized crime, and they hated him and certainly wanted the prosecutions to end. G. Robert Blakey, who had worked for Kennedy in the Justice Department, wrote the RICO Act and was chief counsel to the United States House of Representatives Select Committee on Assassinations. He believed that two Mafiosi, Carlos Marcello and Santo Trafficante, arranged for the assassination of President Kennedy. This was backed up by Ed Becker, a business colleague of Carlos Marcello: "According to the testimony of Edward Becker later given to government investigators, the New Orleans godfather made an ominous threat in fall 1962. 'Don't worry about that little Bobby son of a bitch,' said Marcello. He said he would make sure the 'dog' stopped biting, not by cutting off its tail—Bobby—but its head, the president. Marcello also spoke of taking out 'insurance' for the president's assassination by 'setting up a nut to take the blame . . . the way they do it all the time in Sicily.'"

"Blakey's theory about the two Mafia leaders was given significant corroboration in 1994 when Frank Ragano, the long-time attorney for Santo Trafficante (and Jimmy Hoffa), published an eye-opening memoir, 'Mob Lawyer,' with the assistance of veteran *New York Times* organized crime reporter Selwyn Raab. Ragano revealed that in March, 1987, a seriously ill Trafficante, facing emergency heart bypass surgery that he would not survive, told him that he and Marcello were responsible for JFK's murder. 'That Bobby made life miserable for me and my friends,' Trafficante told his trusted lawyer. 'Who would have thought that someday (John Kennedy) would be president and he would name his goddam brother attorney general? Goddam Bobby. I think Carlos fucked up in getting rid of Giovanni (John)—maybe it should have been Bobby.' Blakey, who talked with the now-deceased Ragano before he published his book, finds the account persuasive, as have other organized crime experts like Raab and journalist Nicholas Pileggi." [2]

In 1979, the Assassinations Committee issued its report, which concluded that President Kennedy was "probably assassinated as a result of a conspiracy." [3]

In addition, the use of a scientific acoustical investigation provided evidence of a high probability that at least two gunmen had fired at the president.

"The Committee believes, on the basis of the evidence available to it, that the national syndicate of organized crime, as a group, was not involved in the assassination of President Kennedy, *but the available evidence does not preclude the possibility that individual members may have been included."* [4]

In addition, the report claims that a fourth shot was fired from the grassy knoll by a second gunman, but the bullet did not hit the president. The claim was based on the Dallas Police Department's Dictabelt recording, plus eyewitness testimony that there was suspicious activity on the knoll.

One of the great paradoxes and enigmas of American history is why Robert F. Kennedy, in his role as attorney general, would prosecute hundreds of mobsters, knowing that his father, Joseph Kennedy, did business with them. In addition, Papa Kennedy had arranged with the Chicago Outfit to make sure that John F. Kennedy carried the state of Illinois in the 1960 presidential election. The great unanswered question is why did RFK pursue and prosecute the mobsters who had helped his brother become president by delivering the necessary votes in Illinois?

Other events that changed the way the mob did business are included in chapters about the Gallo Wars and the Bonanno War (aka Banana War); prosecutions conducted by Thomas Dewey, Robert Kennedy, and Rudolph Giuliani; the shattering McClellan and Kefauver Hearings, where mobsters were held up to ridicule and public disgrace; how rats and confidential informants destroyed Mafia families; perhaps the most infamous of informers was Whitey Bulger, who helped to decimate the Patriarca crime family of New England. Then there were former Mafiosi whose testimony awakened the public to the depth of Mafia control of businesses: they were Joseph Valachi and Sammy "The Bull" Gravano. Their testimony made for riveting television and caused many gangsters to scurry into the anonymity of shadows. There's also a chapter about how the Apalachin Conference of 1957 shook up the FBI, resulting in J. Edgar Hoover finally admitting, after decades of denial, that a Mafia existed and was a national menace.

Taken together, all the chapters in this book demonstrate that the Mafia refuses to die by being as adaptive as the most progressive companies that have survived for generations. And those companies, along with the Mafia, will be with us for the imaginable future.

Notes

1 David M. Oshinsky, Allan Brinkley, and Davis Dyer, "Harry Truman," in *The American Presidency*, ed. Alan Brinkley and Davis Dyer (Boston, MA: Houghton Mifflin, 2004), 365–80.

2 David Talbot, https://www.salon.com/2003/11/22/conspiracy_6/

3 https://www.nytimes.com/1978/12/31/archives/text-of-report-summary-issued-by-committee-on-assassinations.html

4 https://www.nytimes.com/1978/12/31/archives/text-of-report-summary-issued-by-committee-on-assassinations.html

1

A Bullet in the Gut Ends an Era

Arnold Rothstein was the octopus of organized crime. His tentacles stretched in every direction and his ambitions were like suction cups attached to every possible criminal enterprise. Though born into an upper-middle-class Jewish family, whose paterfamilias was known as Abraham the Just, for his incorruptible honesty, young Arnold was attracted to the underworld. And not as an observer or a reader of crime books, but as an aspiring participant. As a young man, he hung around pool halls, gambling dens, and cafés that were hangouts for criminals. He breathed in the milieu as if it were an aphrodisiac. He not only wanted to be part of the world of criminals; he wanted to be king of the underworld. And in time, he became known as the Big Bankroll, the Brain, the Man Uptown.

Well into his career as a major criminal, Rothstein met a young Meyer Lansky at a bar mitzvah in Brooklyn. The older man was impressed by the young man's intelligence, chutzpah, and criminal creativity. He soon thereafter became Lansky's mentor, and the young man would bring along his pals: Lucky Luciano, Frank Costello, and Bugsy Siegel. Rothstein would mentor them all, teaching them not only how to dress and which fork to use, but more importantly how to organize criminal activities into corporate business enterprises. He would help to finance their activities for a generous portion of the take.

Rothstein, as a visionary, would prove to be the father of organized crime in America. His four proteges would shape and control the National Crime Syndicate for decades.

No one who knew Rothstein denies his brilliance, craftiness, and amorality. Had he gone legit, he would have been a titan of industry, whose visage would have been on a US postage stamp and his name chiseled into hospital and university buildings. Instead, as a criminal genius he could have declaimed to judges, police, prosecutors, and political reformers: "Look on my Works, ye Mighty, and despair!"

To launch his proteges onto the road of becoming multi-millionaire gangsters, he financed every aspect of their bootlegging operations during Prohibition. That included trucks, garages for the trucks, boats bringing booze into the United States, warehouses, speakeasies, and bottling companies. Whatever was needed, Rothstein underwrote the costs. He quickly understood that Prohibition lent itself to the development of a corporate structure that would control all the elements of illegal activities. Gangs fighting against each other would only endanger otherwise successful corporations and significantly reduce profits. If small gangs or independent operators didn't fall in line with Rothstein's vision, he conspired for their elimination. And since Bugsy Siegel and Meyer Lansky operated the most vicious, murderous gang in New York, the Bug and Meyer Gang, they easily and quickly eliminated recalcitrant competitors. None of their numerous murders resulted in indictments.

Though Rothstein preferred to operate in the shadows, or as someone noted, a rat in a dark doorway waiting to pounce on his cheese, he had gained unwelcome notoriety after being accused of fixing the 1919 World Series. It became known as the Black Sox Scandal. Rothstein's alleged bagman was world boxing champion Abe Attell, who convinced players to throw the game for $100,000, little of which was actually paid to the players. When brought to trial, Attell, who was known for his chutzpah, proved to be as agile in front of a jury as he was in a boxing ring: he convinced the jurors that he was the wrong Abe Attell; there was another scoundrel with the same name who was the real guilty party. Right after his acquittal, he nearly skipped out of the courtroom, a big smile on his bony, boxer's face.

Rothstein, too, escaped legal culpability, denying he had anything to do with fixing the series: "The whole thing started when Attell and some other cheap gamblers decided to frame the Series and make a killing. The world knows I was asked in on the deal and my friends know how I turned it down flat. I don't doubt that Attell used my name to put it over. That's been done by smarter men than Abe. But I wasn't in on it, wouldn't have gone into it under any circumstances and didn't bet a cent on the Series after I found out what was under way. My idea was that whatever way things turned out, it would be a crooked Series anyhow and that only a sucker would bet on it." [1] Following the indictment of the players, all of their grand jury testimony vanished. Poof! Thereafter, the fixed players refused to repeat their initial confessions, citing their Fifth Amendment constitutional rights against self-incrimination. Though they avoided jail, they were banished from baseball by the sport's first appointed commissioner, Kenesaw Mountain Landis. Never again would those eight Chicago White Sox players be permitted to thrill fans with their outstanding athletic prowess.

Leo Katcher, a Rothstein biographer, wrote: "While Rothstein won the Series, he won a small sum. He always maintained it was less than $100,000. It actually was about $350,000. It could have been much—very much—more. It wasn't because Rothstein chickened out. A World Series fix was too good to be true—even if it was true." [2] In other words, Rothstein cleaned up from the fixed series, placing blame on his former bagman Abe Attell. The two never spoke again.

Rothstein went on to make millions of dollars in fixed horse races and the importation, distribution, and sale of liquor and drugs. In fact, he became the biggest drug dealer in the United States. His ravenous appetite for money-generating illegal activities was never satiated. The more, the better; but better was never enough.

He became such a power broker, bribing politicians and judges, that the Democratically controlled Tammany Hall became his plaything. Whatever Rothstein wanted, he got. As a young man, he had learned the political bribe from his mentor Big Tim Sullivan, a Tammany Hall political boss and a congressman representing the Lower East Side of Manhattan. Sullivan gained lasting political fame by creating the Sullivan Act, which controls the ownership of guns in New York City. In addition to owning theaters, racetracks, racehorses, and professional boxers, he also owned gambling casinos and brothels. Sullivan realized that Rothstein's talents could be used to increase the take in his casinos and on racetracks. He put the young man to work, and sure enough, receipts in one of Sullivan's casinos doubled, then tripled, then quadrupled. Rothstein also fixed horse races, either by paying off jockeys or by placing a sponge in a horse's nostrils to reduce its intake of oxygen. To ensure that the law would not interfere with his actions, he regularly paid off politicians, judges, prosecutors, and police precinct captains.

However, Rothstein did something that no other gangster at that time had attempted: he would get politicians to work for him, rather than working for them. Earlier gangs, such as the Plug Uglies, the Hudson Dusters, and the Gophers, were paid by politicians to deliver votes and eliminate enemies. Rothstein, instead, used politicians to pass laws and regulations that would benefit him and his various enterprises. He may have set the pattern for future lobbyists. Sullivan was so impressed by Rothstein's accomplishments that he once jokingly asked his protégé if, in time, their roles would become reversed and Sullivan would work for the Big Bankroll.

As a young man, a budding criminal, Rothstein became so wealthy working for Sullivan that he purchased his own gambling casino, then expanded to opening brothels, stock brokerages, saloons, and an insurance company.

While Rothstein was growing his power and wealth, Sullivan was spiraling downward. He suffered from tertiary syphilis. As his mind turned to mush, he became less and less able to manage his own affairs. Rothstein gave money to his former mentor, but no amount of money could help the increasingly disabled Sullivan. In 1912, Sullivan was committed to a sanitarium after being found incompetent to handle his affairs; he had also become highly paranoid, believing that others were trying to poison him. His brother took pity on him and brought Sullivan into his home. But poor Sullivan imagined all sorts of enemies were lurking nearby, just waiting to murder him. Unable to deal with his fear of imagined enemies, Sullivan stole away from his brother's house. Several hours later, his body was found lying across railroad tracks in Eastchester in the Bronx. It was found by police officer Peter Purfield, but not identified as Sullivan because it was without any identification. The body was thought to be that of a vagrant and scheduled to be buried in Potter's Field. However, just before being shipped off for burial, the body's shirt was seen to have a pair of diamond-inlaid, solid gold cufflinks. Each was inscribed with Sullivan's initials: TDS. *The New York Times* speculated that Sullivan may have been murdered and his body dumped on the tracks. *The Times* also noted that the Bronx coroner, a Tammany Hall appointee, had not recognized Sullivan, though the two were good friends. After the public learned of Sullivan's fate, a huge wake was held at his political clubhouse at 207 Bowery. There was not enough room to accommodate all those who came to pay their respects. And at his funeral in St. Patrick's Old Cathedral on Mulberry Street, more than 25,000 mourners showed up and were part of the procession that buried Sullivan in Calvary Cemetery in Queens, New York.

As Sullivan may have predicted, Rothstein had become an untouchable power in New York. No police, no judges, no DAs ever laid a hand on him. There were others, however, whom Rothstein had not paid off. Dozens of gamblers were owed money from bets that Rothstein had lost. Though he was quick to demand payment from those who owed him money, he was worse than dilatory in paying his own debts. The longer he could string creditors along, the more he did so.

On November 4, 1928, at 10:15 pm, Rothstein received a phone call from George "Hump" McManus, to whom Rothstein owed money. Rothstein had been sitting at his regular table in Lindy's Restaurant on Broadway, doing deals, lending money, and receiving tips on fixed sporting events when the call came in. McManus asked Rothstein to meet him in room 349 at the Park Sheraton Hotel on Seventh Avenue. Though Rothstein knew that McManus could be impulsive, had a hair-trigger temper, and was angry that Rothstein hadn't paid him the money he was owed, Rothstein decided to go unarmed to the hotel. He handed his pearl-handled revolver to his associate James Meehan, saying, "I won't need this tonight."

In the hotel room, Rothstein engaged in a high-stakes poker game with McManus, Titanic Thompson, Nigger Nate Raymond, and Hyman Biller. The game went on for three days. Much to Rothstein's shock, he was the big loser, down about $320,000. As his losses increased, he convinced himself that Raymond and Thompson were cheating him. His frustration and anger were like a consuming fire, destroying his rational approach to gambling. Indeed, he played like a man on fire. He had become a stereotypical loser: a victim of his own delusions, believing that the next hand would be a winning one. But the next hand, the next hand, and the ones that followed were losing ones. His bluffs failed; his bets were foolhardy. When he should have folded, he played on. Then, nervous that he might have overplayed a losing hand, he folded while holding a winning one. The Brain was in a state of panic; he played compulsively, obsessively, desperately fighting against insurmountable losses. No wonder he thought he was being cheated. This was not the octopus who controlled every gambling event and scam he participated in.

Having declared the game fixed, he would not pay anyone. That declaration caused the other players to threaten Rothstein. He realized that he had gone too far and attempted to cool the hot tempers of his enraged opponents. He said he would pay them all, plus a small interest, if they would only wait for the outcome of the election. He had bet that Roosevelt would win the governor's race, and Herbert Hoover the presidential one. If that happened, Rothstein assured the players that he would collect $550,000 and pay what they were owed. Either they didn't believe him, or they didn't believe that he had bet on the race. In addition, he was known as a welcher. Though quick to collect on a debt, he was slow to pay off his own debts. If he owed money to someone he regarded as powerless, a nobody, Rothstein might never pay that person. Rothstein may have been the richest deadbeat gambler in the Big Apple.

Deadbeat or not, he gambled on his fate and got a bullet in the gut. Who pulled the trigger was a question asked over and over again. Much speculation followed as Rothstein lay in Polyclinic Hospital, where he died two days after being shot. Initially, Nigger Nate Raymond was thought to have been the shooter, but there was no evidence against him. So speculation settled on Titanic Thompson, but no evidence could be found against him. Both men had reputations for being dishonest gamblers, swindlers, cheats, and liars, though only Titanic was known as a killer.

Raymond, not as widely known in gambling circles as Thompson, had such a notorious reputation as a cheater that any honest gambler would have avoided him. Years after Rothstein's death, he was convicted of stock fraud and sentenced to five to ten years in prison. Many disenchanted suckers waited for his release in order to recover money they had lent or invested with Raymond. Their wait was a waste of time.

Thompson was far cleverer than Raymond and capable of every kind of imaginable deceit. To say he was completely without a conscience would not be an overstatement. New York Fats, the world-renowned pool player, claimed that Thompson was given the name Titanic after bragging that he had avoided going down with the Titanic by dressing as a woman and getting into a lifeboat reserved for women and children. Only a man proud of his shameless craftiness would brag about how he avoided drowning while others perished.

In addition to being a gambler, Titanic was also a killer; he had murdered five men and managed never to be indicted for any of the murders. Though he was well-known for cheating at cards, he also had a reputation for cheating at golf, billiards, craps, and even horseshoes. A man who had avoided being indicted for five murders was not about to be indicted for shooting Rothstein. That dishonor fell to McManus, a well-known Broadway bookmaker and gambler. Cops were told that McManus had pulled a gun on Rothstein, threatened to kill him if he didn't pay, and accidentally shot him. The gun was tossed out of a window, landing on the roof of a taxi. It bounced off the car's roof, landed on Seventh Avenue, and the curious taxi driver hit his brakes. He got out of his taxi, found the gun, and soon turned it over to the police. The only fingerprints on it were those of the taxi driver. As Rothstein lingered at death's door in the hospital, cops repeatedly questioned him about the identity of the shooter. He told the cops, "You stick to your trade, I'll stick to mine." [3] He maintained the gangster tradition of omerta, never ratting on friends or enemies. Finally, Rothstein succumbed to his wound and was taken to the mortuary. The charge against McManus was changed from attempted murder to murder. McManus, however, had high-ranking friends at Tammany Hall. He owed some of them large sums of money; they would not let him sink without payment. McManus now had a new hand to play, and he played it with all the confidence of a gambler who only bets on sure things. Of course, he was acquitted. There was no evidence that would have resulted in a conviction.

His death, twelve years later, resulted in the following headline in *The New York Times*: M'MANUS, GAMBLER, DIES IN NEW JERSEY; When a Broadway Figure He Was Acquitted of the Rothstein Murder. IN POOR HEALTH 2 YEARS Was Last in Limelight When Named by Police as Head of Gambling Syndicate. [4]

Shortly after Rothstein died, his personal papers were stolen from a safe in his apartment. Then, after waiting three weeks, police initiated an investigation into his murder. Thomas Rice, a member of the New York State

Crime Commission, wrote a blistering editorial that appeared in the *Brooklyn Eagle* newspaper on March 31, 1929. In it, he accused the police and a district attorney of slow-walking a careless and inept investigation into Rothstein's murder. And no wonder, for Rothstein's attorney, William Hyman, stated that once Rothstein's safe deposit boxes were opened there would be a lot of suicides and men suddenly taking long cruises to distant countries.

Rothstein's murder resulted, within a few years, of his proteges taking over his manifold operations, forming the National Crime Syndicate, and creating the five Mafia families of New York. As a result of Rothstein's role as the biggest drug dealer in New York, the federal government decided it needed an official organization that would control the spread of illicit drugs while arresting and indicting known drug dealers. The Federal Bureau of Narcotics was born in 1930 and headed by tough guy Harry J. Anslinger, who declared a war on drugs, including marijuana. He remained as director for thirty-two years and served Presidents Hoover, Roosevelt, Truman, Eisenhower, and Kennedy. Editorialists now blasted away at Tammany Hall, a corrupt organization populated by dishonest politicians, all of whom could be bought. That led in 1933 to New York electing a reformer named Fiorello La Guardia as mayor. He became known as the Little Flower, an Italian Jew who was a member of the Episcopal Church and made it his mission to drive the gangsters out of New York.

Notes

1 Leo Katcher, *The Big Bankroll* (New York: Da Capo Press, 1994), 144–5.
2 Katcher, *The Big Bankroll*, 148.
3 Jeffrey Sussman, *Big Apple Gangsters: The Rise and Decline of the Mob in New York* (Lanham, MD: Rowman & Littlefield, 2020), 8.
4 https://www.nytimes.com/1940/08/30/archives/mmanus-gambler-dies-in-new-jersey-when-a-broadway-figure-he-was.html

2

No Love Lost on Valentine's Day

The murder of Arnold Rothstein in 1928, while a pivotal event in the history of organized crime, has not lent itself to numerous books, movies, and TV dramas as has the 1929 St. Valentine's Day Massacre. The massacre would lead to a single organized crime group controlling crime in Chicago and cities in the Midwest, the West, and the Southwest. The organized crime group, the Outfit, became a multi-ethnic organization, primarily run by Italian Americans and comprising hundreds of gangsters centered in Chicago, but with subsidiaries in Detroit, Milwaukee, Cleveland, Phoenix, Las Vegas, and Kansas City, among several others.

The Outfit started its notorious reign in 1910 under the control of Big Jim Colosimo, who built a criminal empire by developing a chain of brothels. Prior to opening his first brothel, Big Jim married Victoria Moresco, a Chicago madam; with their combined drive, his love of prostitutes, and her knowledge, the duo embarked on building a chain of brothels, eventually numbering more than 200. Their enterprise generated tens of thousands of dollars a month in 1920s money. To maintain control of the prostitution racket, Big Jim hired tough guy criminals, such as Johnny Torrio of New York, who would threaten competitors to sell their operations or be killed. How many died by gunshot, garroting, knifing is unknown, but few resisted the entreaties and threats of

Torrio. As the prostitution racket grew, Big Jim expanded into gambling and loan sharking and brought in Jewish, Irish, and Polish gangsters. Unlike the all-Italian Mafia families of New York, the Outfit relied on a wide variety of gangsters of different ethnicities; skill and talent were more important than heritage, which may be why the Outfit became more powerful than its East Coast Mafia brethren.

By 1919, Colosimo and Torrio had become partners and opened a brothel named the Four Deuces. Torrio brought in his Brooklyn protégé, Al Capone, to be the brothel's bartender and bouncer. The Colosimo-Torrio partnership proved to be short-lived, for in 1920 at the start of Prohibition, Colosimo refused to venture into bootlegging. To reject such an opportunity to make millions was the curse that doomed Big Jim. An angry Torrio imported Al Capone's former boss, gunman Frankie Yale, from Brooklyn.

"At 4:30 PM on May 11, 1920, Colosimo arrived at the nearly deserted café and walked to the rear office, where his secretary, Frank Camilla, sat. 'Hello Frank. What's doing ?' the Kingpin said cheerfully. 'Nothing,' came the reply. A few moments later, he went alone to the front. When he reached the lobby, a dark figure emerged from the shadows. Two shots rang out. One splintered a glass pane, the other struck Colosimo in the head. He fell face down on the porcelain floor, dead at age 49." [1]

Torrio now led the Outfit into the highly profitable business of bootlegging. To celebrate, Torrio ordered an ostentatious funeral for his former boss and invited thousands of attendees. No one refused the new boss' invitations. Yale was questioned by police but (as is said on TV crime shows), he had an "airtight alibi."

Years later, back in Brooklyn, Yale had been hijacking Capone's bootlegging trucks. After a series of meetings in Chicago between the two crime bosses to negotiate a settlement, Yale returned to Brooklyn, convinced that his dispute with Capone had been resolved. Not long afterward, while enjoying a card game at the Sunrise Club in Brooklyn, Yale received a panicked phone call. The caller told him his wife was in trouble. Yale rushed out of the club and got into his new bulletproof Lincoln; the car dealer had never told Yale that only the glass on the car was not bulletproof. A large Buick sedan pulled up alongside the Lincoln, cut it off, and forced it to the curb. Immediately, five men opened fire on the Lincoln. The rapid rat-tat-tat of gunfire from a Thompson submachine gun made mush of Yale's brain, and blasts from a shotgun blew off a piece of Yale's skull. As if that were not sufficient, barrages of .38 and .45 caliber bullets drilled holes in his upper torso. Mission accomplished, the killers sped away. The killers, who were never caught, were Tony Accardo, Gus Winkler, Fred "the Killer" Burke, George "Shotgun" Ziegler, and Louis Campagna, known as Little New York.

Yale's bloody body was patched and cosmetized by artisan undertakers in preparation for the biggest, most ostentatious funeral that Brooklyn had ever seen. Few subsequent gangster funerals have matched the Yale extravaganza. To begin, following facial repairs, Yale's body was clad in an elegant tuxedo, then placed into a $15,000 silver coffin; his hands wore soft leather, pearl gray gloves and held a gold rosary. The coffin was slid into an elegant black hearse, which was then followed on the funeral route by thirty-eight flower cars, which were followed by 250 Cadillac limousines. All of it was observed by more than 10,000 Brooklynites who lined the route of the funeral. At Holy Cross Cemetery, 112 mourners tossed long-stem roses onto Yale's coffin. Two of those mourners caused a minor commotion when each of them announced she was the dead man's wife. *The New York Daily News* wrote that Yale's funeral provided a bigger and better show than any Chicago gangster funeral. In fact, Yale's funeral became the prototype for many extravagant gangster funerals not only in the real world but also in movies.

Yale had been a vital instrument for Torrio and Capone, helping them get rid of competitors and those who threatened to disrupt their bootlegging operations. Not only had Yale disposed of Colosimo, but he also eliminated Dion O'Banion, head of the North Side gangsters and a much bigger threat to the Outfit than any other gang leader. Before his demise, O'Banion's trucks were being hijacked by the Genna brothers, who ran a gang that operated often in association with the Outfit. Some of the booze they hijacked was sold to the Outfit. When O'Banion learned that the Gennas were the ones stealing his booze, he set up a meeting with Torrio, who subsequently agreed to get the Gennas to cease their hijacking. He never did so, and the hijacking continued. As a result, O'Banion's mob hijacked the Genna trucks.

Though Torrio was known as the Fox, O'Banion proved the foxier of the two. He told Torrio he had decided to retire, leave Chicago, and settle in Colorado. He wanted to sell his Sieben brewery to Torrio for $500,000. Torrio agreed to buy it. But just as the two were signing off on the deal, the police raided the brewery and arrested Torrio, O'Banion, and a few others. O'Banion got off because he had no prior bootlegging conviction, but Torrio had a prison record and faced a jail sentence. He had been conned out of the brewery and $500,000; his blood boiled with revenge. However, he was told to postpone any retaliation by Mike Merlo, head of the Unione Siciliana, a Mafia-run Italian fraternal organization. Merlo wanted to keep the gangs from fighting each other and disrupting the status quo of illegal activities. In 1924, Merlo died of cancer and his place was taken by of all people, Bloody Angelo Genna, the youngest of the six vicious Genna brothers. Though he and his brothers popped champagne corks in celebration of Angelo becoming president, they had no idea what lay ahead. The North Side gang was not finished with their treachery, and a year later Angelo was gunned down. It was now time for the Outfit to seek its revenge. O'Banion's days were numbered in single digits.

O'Banion didn't think his life was in danger and so didn't hide in his flower shop; he believed he didn't have to. After he had extorted the original owners of Schofield Flowers Shop into turning over the store's deed to him, he paid off cops for protection. He also had an extra layer of protection, for his gang's hangout was on the floor above the store. He loved flowers and didn't care that some of the Outfit gangsters sneered at his love of flowers and made snide remarks about his masculinity. What kind of guy spends hours doing flower arrangements? It didn't matter: Schofield's was the de facto florist for all gang funerals in Chicago, and since it was right across the street from Holy Name Church, it provided flowers for funerals, weddings, and christenings at the church.

On November 10, 1924, a cold Chicago day, O'Banion was busy in the back room of his flower shop preparing an arrangement of chrysanthemums. He heard the chimes of the front door opening, placed his shears on a table and went to the store's counter. There, he greeted Frankie Yale, the last time the two would meet. Yale reached out and gripped O'Banion's right hand. He shook it hard and wouldn't release his grip. Just at that moment, John Scalise and Albert Anselmi strode into the store. "Hiya doing, Dion?" one of the men called out, then both men drew their pistols and fired bullets into O'Banion's neck and torso. The florist-gangster fell to the floor. The hitmen fired more bullets into the back of O'Banion's skull.

His murder, like many gang murders, lit a fuse that exploded in five years of gang warfare, during which the Tommy gun became the weapon of choice. As hundreds of bullets sprayed the streets of Chicago, pedestrians ducked into stores or fell onto sidewalks. Chicago had become the wild west of gangsterism: Gangland, U.S.A.

During this time, leaders and members of the Outfit were targeted by the new rulers of the North Side Gang: Hymie Weiss, Bugs Moran, and Vincent Drucci. First on their hit list was Capone, also known as the Big Man, Big Al, and Scarface. In 1925, the North Siders ambushed him, but their bullets went wild and missed. Thereafter, Capone was as cautious as a fox. He was determined to destroy his trio of enemies. Twelve days after the attempted rubout, the North Siders ambushed Torrio, shooting him several times. Torrio, badly wounded, was rushed to a hospital and slowly recovered. It was one thing to order a hit on an enemy; it was quite another to be targeted. He turned over the Outfit to Capone. You're now the boss. And he departed Chicago for retirement in Italy.

Capone was not one to walk away from a fight. He would be cautious, but his men would execute brazen attacks on his behalf. On October 27, 1925, the assassinations began. Weiss and two colleagues left the Schofield Flower Shop. On State Street, the three men turned a corner and walked into a hail of bullets: two gunmen had concealed themselves in a rooming house. One gunman, firing a Tommy gun, cut down Weiss. Another concealed gunman opened fire with a shotgun. Weiss's two companions took off like a pair of rabbits, but Weiss lay dead in a pool of his blood. Next on the hit list were Moran and Ducci.

Shortly after the shooting, police stated that Machine Gun Jack McGurn had fired the Tommy gun, and Sam "Golf Bag" Hunt had blasted away with his shotgun. Though the police never specified what evidence they had that identified McGurn as one of the shooters, the police had no doubt that Hunt was the other shooter, for he had left behind his golf bag with a hot shotgun inside it.

Drucci met his end not by the Outfit, but by the actions of a brutal cop named Dan Healy, who was known for his hatred of gangsters. By the time he encountered Drucci, Healy had beaten several gangsters so severely that they were left to recover in hospitals. On April 24, 1927, Healy arrested Drucci for carrying a concealed .45 caliber pistol. While waiting to be placed in a police car, Drucci insulted Healy, who responded to the insult with a swift smack to Drucci's face. Healy cuffed Drucci, then shoved the cursing gangster onto the backseat of the police car. Once inside the car, Healy shoved Drucci against the opposite back door. Though Drucci's wrists were cuffed, he raised both fists and attempted to bring them down on Healy's head. Healy yelled at the driver to stop the car. It came to an abrupt halt. Healy got out, pulled out his pistol, and shot Drucci in his gut, one leg, and one arm. The last two shots were gratuitous, for the first one killed Drucci. Newspapers celebrated Healy as an anti-gangster paladin.

That left George "Bugs" Moran, who was as slippery as an eel. He would become known as the man who slithered away from being killed in the infamous St. Valentine's Day Massacre. It was February 14, 1929, the day that Capone would finally vanquish the North Side Gang, headed by Moran. The Purple Gang of Detroit, working with the Outfit, had planned to lure Moran and members of his gang to the SMC Garage at 2122 North Clark Street. The gang was offered a large quantity of stolen whiskey at an irresistible price. Seven members of the gang showed up at 10:30 a.m., but Moran wasn't one of them. He had left his Parkway Hotel apartment late and was on his way to the garage. As he and one of his lieutenants rounded a corner, they spotted a police car arriving at the garage. Shit, muttered Moran. A police raid would screw up the deal to buy the stolen whiskey. The two men walked back around a corner and entered a coffee shop, waiting for the cops to depart. Four men, two of them dressed as cops, emerged from the police car and walked into the garage. The ersatz cops told the assembled gangsters to get up against a wall for a frisk. Once the men were against the wall, their backs to the cops, two men who accompanied the fake cops pulled Tommy guns out from under their overcoats. A deafening roar of gunfire followed. The seven men collapsed onto the floor. To make sure that none survived, each one was shotgunned.

To throw off possible witnesses, the men not dressed as cops marched out of the garage, their hands in the air. With their pistols drawn, the cops prodded the two others into the police car. With its siren screaming, the police car sped off. Two blocks away, the siren was silenced. The car was soon abandoned.

The seven dead men were identified as Peter Gusenberg; his brother Frank Gusenberg; Albert Kachellek; Adam Heyer, the gang's bookkeeper; Reinhardt Schwimmer, an optometrist and gangster wannabe; Albert Weinshank, (whom the killers initially had mistaken for Moran); and John May, whose dog, Highball, survived the attack but seemed to suffer a nervous breakdown.

Cops euthanized the dog. Al Capone, though suspected of ordering the attack, was in Florida. One of the alleged shooters, Machine Gun Jack McGurn, was charged in the crime, but he claimed to have spent Valentine's Day with his loving wife, Louise Rolfe, in a hotel room. She confirmed his alibi, which became known as the blonde alibi (a prototype used by numerous gangsters in the years that followed). No one was ever prosecuted for the massacre.

Following the massacre and without his gang, Moran was a severely diminished figure. He continued to operate in a much circumscribed area of the North Side, but he was now considered small potatoes, not a threat to anyone. He eventually left the area and became a small-time criminal, indulging in petty thefts. He was arrested numerous times, once for attempting to cash in a large amount of stolen American Express checks. Other times, he held up gas stations and taverns. He even attempted, with a pair of inept robbers, to hold up a bank. Throughout the 1940s and 1950s, he spent years in jail and emerged a pauper. His last sentence was for ten years to be served in Leavenworth Prison, where he died of lung cancer eleven days after Valentine's Day in 1957 at age sixty-three.

Capone profited from the massacre, becoming the undisputed crime boss of Chicago. But in 1932, following a trial for income tax evasion, he was sent to prison. Shortly after his arrival, he was diagnosed with syphilis and gonorrhea. He suffered from neurosyphilis, which caused the deterioration of his brain, leaving him with the intelligence of a twelve-year-old. He spent much of his time in a prison hospital ward and was finally paroled in 1939. Following his release, some friendly newspaper reporters did stories about how kindhearted Capone operated soup kitchens for unemployed and destitute men and women during the Great Depression. The stories would often quote early beneficiaries of Capone's largess, saying that Big Al did more for the citizens of Chicago than the politicians. He supposedly served more than 120,000 hot meals. A free man, he was in no condition to do anything for or against anyone. The ex-boss of the Outfit was succeeded by Frank Nitti, who guided the organization in its successful strategy of gaining unchallenged control of crime in Chicago, and not in the flamboyant manner of Big Al and Johnny "the Fox" Torrio. The shoot-'em-up years of Prohibition were over.

Torrio lived in peaceful retirement in Italy until Mussolini began prosecuting the Mafia. Torrio's reputation had put him on a fascist wanted list. Not wishing to be thrown into prison or executed while resisting arrest, Torrio returned to Brooklyn only to be charged with tax evasion. *The St. Petersburg Tribune* reported: "JOHNNY TORRIO PLEADS GUILTY Johnny (the immune) Torrio, deciding he wasn't immune to relentless government prosecution, pleaded guilty yesterday in federal court to a charge of $85,000 tax evasion." He was sentenced to a two-year prison sentence. [2] *The New York Daily News* added: "Twenty-eight acres of St. Petersburg real estate owned in part by Al Capone were sold at auction today to satisfy federal tax delinquencies on 19,894 barrels of Capone beer which flowed during Prohibition. Other owners of the land were Johnny Torrio, Jack Cusick, and Robert Vanella." [3]

Torrio died of a heart attack on April 16, 1957, at age seventy-five. His protégé Capone had died nearly a decade earlier on January 25, 1947. They had brought Chicago into the forefront of organized crime, and they left the Outfit as one of the most powerful organized crime organizations in America. By the 1970s, the Outfit owned numerous casinos in Las Vegas, office buildings in Chicago, and resorts. Its tentacles reached into real estate, gambling, labor relations, trucking, prostitution, drugs, the entertainment industry, and anything else that would make them money. Like many Mafia families, the Chicago Outfit had mastered the arts of survival with the skills of magicians.

Notes

1 www.newspapers.com/image/388881574/?clipping_id=103,733733,013&fcfToken=eyJ hbGciOiJIUzI1NiIsInR5cCI6IkpXVCJ9.eyJmcmVlLXZpZXctaWQiOjM4ODg4MTU 3NCwiaWF0IjoxNzIwOTA5MDk3LCJleHAiOjE3MjA5OTU0OTd9.7V2gQISKsYd

ZVZzYRY18GP6qGH79zPR-zL1QEBjojB0Way We Were by June Sawyers. *Chicago Tribune*, 163. "The Vice Lord Who Fell in Love with Choir Singer."

2 *St. Petersburg Times*, April 11, 1939, Associated Press.

3 *New York Daily News*, St. Petersburg, Florida, March 29, 1940, p. 81, United Press.

3

The Castellammarese Wars and the Emergence of the New Mafia

While the Outfit was extending its reach and amplifying its power in Chicago, the New York Mafia was about to undergo a revolution in 1931 that would change the way the Mafia operated for the next fifty years.

But earlier than 1931, two men had risen to power in the Mafia jungle of New York. They were Joe "The Boss" Masseria and Salvatore Maranzano. Masseria, a short and short-tempered, corpulent man, gave orders with a mouth full of pasta. He made it clear to his minions that he and they would only deal with Italians. All other ethnicities were verboten. He was determined to wipe out all of Maranzano's men and then go after their boss. Maranzano, known as Little Caesar, was just as determined to wipe out Masseria and his men. Compared to Masseria, Maranzano was a beau Brummell: he dressed well and kept an office in a classy Manhattan office building. However, he was just as greedy and bloodthirsty as his nemesis. The two men were like scorpions locked in a bottle. Their destructive war was hurting business. Cops, for example, hoped that the two antagonists would kill each other so that business, such as payoffs, would return to normal.

The warfare the two men engaged in was known as the Castellammarese War, named after the Sicilian town where Maranzano had been born. The war, which erupted on February 26, 1930, did not end until April 15, 1931. It ended only because a group of young Turks, led by Lucky Luciano, decided the war not only needlessly resulted in too many bleeding bodies, but even worse in coffers bleeding millions of dollars. A self-destructive war could not go on and on and on. It was time for a new generation to kill off the old Mafia chieftains.

Gangsters in the Masseria crime families were eager to get rid of their boss, and plans to do so were soon afoot. Two of them, Joe Profaci and Tommy "Three Fingers Brown" Lucchese, had defected to Maranzano's crime family, and in the years to come would become powerful leaders of their own crime families. Though hated by his underlings, Masseria had more of the Mafia's future crime bosses in his family than Maranzano had in his. They were Lucky Luciano, Vito Genovese, Joe Adonis, Frank Costello, Willie Moretti, Albert Anastasia, and Carlo Gambino, all of whom were in favor of killing their boss.

Initially, Luciano and his co-conspirators had believed that they could work for Maranzano, after Masseria had been killed, and still make more money than they had during the war. However, they would soon be disabused of their inklings.

Maranzano turned out to be as xenophobic, greedy, and power-hungry as Masseria. His attitude incensed Luciano and Frank Costello, who had proposed including Jewish and Irish gangsters in their operations. But Maranzano, like Masseria, said no. It didn't seem to matter to the old bosses that the Jewish and Irish gangsters in New York were taking in a large share of profits from illegal business that could be shared. Luciano sensibly believed that money did not have a religion or race. He wanted a crime family that would grab as much money as possible. The best way to do so, he said, was to form cartels with other mobs.

However, before the young generation of gangsters understood Maranzano's shortcomings as boss, Luciano had invited Vito Genovese to join him in a plot to end the war by killing off Masseria; they had naively assumed that Maranzano, once free of threats from Masseria, would become more flexible and practical. So they contacted Maranzano and laid out their plan to kill Masseria if Marranzano would agree to end the war, make Luciano his underboss, and give Luciano some of Masseria's rackets. Maranzano agreed but insisted that as the only remaining boss he should be declared boss of all bosses, capo di tutti capi. He would also take some of Masseria's rackets for himself. It was agreed.

Luciano, saying he had a plan for defeating Maranzano, lured Masseria into accepting a lunch date. On April 15, 1931, the two men met for lunch at the Nuova Villa Tammaro restaurant in Coney Island. It was a congenial get-together, where the two men engaged in plans to take over Maranzano's rackets. After they had consumed their meals, Luciano brought out a deck of cards, and the two played a leisurely game; some said it was pinochle, others that it was gin rummy. After playing a few hands, Luciano excused himself to use the men's room. Following his departure, Masseria's bodyguards left the restaurant, and a group of gunmen rushed in; their .38 and .32 caliber pistols blasting away. Masseria fell to the floor, a pool of blood surrounding his head, and a Tally-Ho ace of spades scissored between two of his fingers. It became known as the death card. The killers were Joe Adonis, Bugsy Siegel, Ciro "The Artichoke King" Terranova, and Albert "Mad Hatter" Anastasia. Terranova was supposed to drive the getaway car, but he was shaking like the last leaf of autumn in a whirling winter wind. Siegel pushed him aside, grabbed the steering wheel, and floored the gas pedal. Tires squealed, and the big, black sedan was never seen again. When pedestrians were questioned, none of them said they saw the getaway car. And certainly, no one saw the killers, none of whom were ever indicted for the murder. Back in the restaurant, Luciano remained, casually puffing on a cigarette, waiting to be questioned by cops. When asked what happened and where he was at the time of the shooting, he calmly said he had been in the bathroom when he heard a fusillade of gunfire. He added: "I was in the can taking a leak. I always take a long leak." [1] According to *The New York Times*, "[A]fter that, the police have been unable to learn definitely [what happened]." Reputedly Masseria was "seated at a table playing cards with two or three unknown men [sic]" when he was fired upon from behind. He died from gunshot wounds to his head, back, and chest. [2]

Following the shooting, Maranzano proudly declared himself the ultimate ruler, the boss of all bosses, rather like Napoleon crowning himself emperor. He next dictated that there would be five Mafia families, each with a boss who would report to him. Each family, in addition to having a boss, would have an underboss, a consigliere, numerous capos and soldiers, plus associates. Maranzano appointed the heads of the five families; they would be Luciano (now the Genovese crime family), Profaci (now the Colombo crime family), Gagliano (now the Lucchese crime family), Frank Scalice (now the Gambino crime family), and Maranzano himself (now the Bonanno crime family). To bring everyone on board and spell out the new rules, he called a meeting in Wappingers Falls, New York. While reiterating that he was capo di tutti capi, he remained unaware of the resentments of his chosen bosses. If they were bosses, why did they need a boss? While the five bosses and their underbosses sat schemingly, Maranzano then let it be known he was carving out pieces of each family's business and taking a large share of their profits for himself. This was too much for the bosses to tolerate, though no one said anything. Luciano smiled a serpent's smile, seeming to accept everything that Maranzano had dictated. But like a poisonous snake waiting in concealment to strike, Luciano would strike when Maranzano was vulnerable. The more the bosses heard, the more their anger burned; they looked as if they had swallowed mouthfuls of vinegar. To them, Maranzano seemed even worse than Masseria had been: greedier and more power-hungry. Each boss left the meeting knowing that Maranzano's days were numbered.

Yet, like any narcissist, Maranzano lived in a bubble of his own ego, ignorant that he had antagonized those he most needed. Little Caesar Maranzano had acted too much as if he were truly a Caesar. He had attempted to model the five families as if they were part of the Roman Empire with a military chain of command whose emperor was Maranzano himself. But it was his insatiable greed and rapacious appetite for power, his narrow-minded attitude toward Jewish partners, which sealed his fate. Luciano, the smartest and wiliest of gangsters, put a murderous plan into effect, and not a minute too late, for Maranzano (his paranoia outweighing his narcissism) had come to distrust Luciano. His underling was too ambitious and might attempt to take over and become the new boss of all bosses. Better to get rid of the ambitious young gangster. Maranzano hired Irish gangster Vincent "Mad Dog" Coll for $25,000 to kill Luciano. However, learning of the planned hit, Tommy Lucchese alerted Luciano that Maranzano had hired Mad Dog to kill him.

On September 10, Maranzano ordered Luciano and Genovese to come to his office at the New York Central Building located at 230 Park Avenue in Manhattan. Convinced that Maranzano planned to murder him, Luciano decided to act first. According to his book *Boardwalk Gangster: The Real Lucky Luciano*, Tim Newark writes, "Word of the [contract on Luciano's life] got to Luciano and he prepared his response with a degree of irony. If Maranzano so undervalued the importance of Jewish gangsters then it was they who would deal with him. Luciano recruited a crew of Jewish gunmen from out of town led by Samuel 'Red' Levine. "An observant Jew from Toledo Ohio, Levine saw no conflict between his faith and his job; if he had to carry out a hit on the Sabbath he would simply wear a yarmulke under his hat." [3] (Red Levine, who had been a member of Murder Inc., lived out his later life in shadows. After the demise of Murder Inc., he worked for a funeral company (an apt job for a killer), then became an important participant in the activities of the Newspaper and Mail Deliveres Union. He was a frequent and welcome guest at John Gotti's Ravenite Social Club on Mulberry Street in New York's Little Italy.)

Levine, pretending to be an IRS agent, contacted Maranzano, telling him that several agents would be coming to his office to examine his books. "I have nothing to hide," Maranzano assured Levine. The day before the examination, Maranzano informed his bodyguards that IRS agents were coming to his office and they should leave their guns at home. And when his bodyguards showed up gun-less the next morning, Maranzano told them they should make themselves scarce. They would not be needed for a few hours. Shortly afterward, four ersatz IRS agents arrived at Maranzano's office on the morning of September 10, 1931. They were relieved that no bodyguards were around. Maranzano invited the four agents into his office. Before he could direct them to the ledgers on his desk, a sudden look of shock came over his face, for the four killers had pulled out switchblades and hunting knives. Maranzano attempted to run to the door of his office, but the four gangsters fell upon him like a pride of ravenous lions on an overpowered gazelle. Maranzano's yells brought no help. He was stabbed multiple times, then shot for good measure. Before departing, one of the killers leaned over Little Caesar and slit his throat.

In the outer hallway, the killers ran into Mad Dog. Levine warned him to take off because cops were on their way. Mad Dog muttered thank you and took off running down flights of stairs, not realizing that he had been warned to leave by the men who had just killed the guy who had paid him $25,000 to kill Luciano. On February 8, 1932, 23-year old Mad Dog would be machine-gunned to death in a drug store's telephone booth by one of Maranzano's killers.

Following Maranzano's murder, a number of his loyal soldiers were killed over the next few days. Their murders were known as the Night of the Sicilian Vespers. After all the killings, it was time for Luciano to assume the mantle of boss. He was smart enough not to crown himself capo di tutti capi, for he knew that it was unnecessary: his word carried a great deal of authority, and he was perceived as fair-minded by the other bosses. He wanted each boss and not just the Italians to be part of a democratic voting bloc, a board of directors for a national crime syndicate. Luciano maintained the structure of the five families and formed what became known as the Commission, which would vote to settle disputes, order murders, and decide who would be accepted as made men. Luciano would serve as the Commission's informal CEO. And as if thumbing his nose at the prejudices of Maranzano and Masseria, he let it be known that Meyer Lansky served with him.

Luciano immediately got to work. The Mafia had to operate like any major American corporation. There would be fewer murders than during the war years; there would be price fixing among the families. The bottom line, as with any corporation, would determine their actions. In addition, unlike the two dead bosses, the families were free to operate with any group that could increase power and profits. Jews, Irish, Germans; it didn't matter. In Joe Bonanno's autobiography *A Man of Honor*, he states: "We revised the old custom of looking toward one man, one supreme leader for advice and the settling of disputes. We replaced leadership by one man with leadership by committee. We opted for a parliamentary arrangement whereby a group of the most important men in our world would assume the function formerly performed by one man." [4]

Once established, the Commission members invited Jewish gangsters, Meyer Lansky, Bugsy Siegel, Lepke Buchalter, Dutch Schultz, and Longy Zwillman, among others, to participate in Mafia activities and attend many Commission meetings, which were intended to take place every five years. More than anything else, the goal of the Mafia was profits before anything else. This was the start of the modern corporate Mafia, which the bosses thought would lead to a golden age.

Yet, the golden age would become tarnished. One of the most seminal events that would have unforeseen consequences for several Commission members was the board's vote to execute Dutch Schultz, who had proposed murdering Special Prosecutor Thomas Dewey. The special prosecutor had been relentlessly going after Schultz, and the gangster wanted him dead. The Commission believed that if Schultz succeeded, the murder would cause a complete disruption of the Mafia's activities, for police would close down their operations and drive them out of New York. When Schultz said he didn't care what the Commission members decreed and that he would go ahead with his planned assassination, he sealed his own fate. Lepke Buchalter, head of Murder Inc., gave the contract to kill the Dutchman to Charlie "The Bug" Workman and Emanuel "Mendy" Weiss.

On October 23, 1935, the two gunmen found Schultz and his confederates, Abe Landau, Bernard "Lulu" Rosencrantz, and Otto "Abbadabba" Berman at the Palace Chop House in Newark, New Jersey. Schultz had excused himself to visit the men's room just before the gunmen burst into the restaurant. A wild gun battle ensued during which Berman was repeatedly shot. Rosencrantz and Landau rose from their seats, firing wildly at the two hitmen, their shots going wild. Workman, not seeing Schultz in the restaurant, found him in the men's room and fired several bullets into his torso. Schultz fell in front of a urinal, where he had been standing. Rosencrantz, though bleeding from a sieve of wounds, crawled to the bar, where he demanded that the bartender give him change for a quarter. He managed to stand long enough to deposit a dime into a public phone and call for an ambulance. He passed out after giving the address of the Chop House. Weiss had already run out of the restaurant, and Workman soon followed with Landau running behind him, wildly shooting at him. Landau and Workman traded gunfire, but Landau could hardly hold onto his pistol, never mind hitting his target, for he was gushing blood from a severed carotid artery and soon lost consciousness, toppling onto a metal garbage can. Meanwhile, Weiss had jumped into a getaway car and told the driver to speed the hell away. He left a furious Workman stranded, who then trudged his way through vacant lots and swamps to the Hudson River, where he found a ferry that took him back to Manhattan. Later that night in a local hospital, Berman died at 2:20 a.m. Landau died from a loss of blood at 6:00 a.m. And Rosencrantz was shot so full of holes that doctors didn't know where to begin an operation to save his life. It took him twenty-nine hours from the time he was shot to die. Doctors were amazed that he lasted as long as he did. Following surgery, Schultz appeared to respond; however, he fell into a coma, became delirious, and died of peritonitis a day after the shooting. In addition to his notoriety as a gangster and killer, Schultz achieved additional fame for his deathbed monologue, which reminded literary scholars and novelists of a Joycean stream of consciousness. Here are some of the more mysterious words uttered by the dying Schultz: "A boy has never wept . . . nor dashed a thousand kim. You can play jacks, and girls do that with a soft ball and do tricks with it. Oh, Oh, dog Biscuit, and when he is happy he doesn't get snappy."

Beat writer William Burroughs was fascinated by Schultz's monologue and wrote a novel in the form of a screenplay titled *The Last Words of Dutch Schultz*. Though born and raised as a Jew, Schultz converted to Catholicism while in hospital and is buried in Gate of Heaven Cemetery in Hawthorne, New York. Luciano and the Commission members breathed a sigh of relief that they had prevented drawing down the wrath of law enforcement on all their operations. They would come to have second thoughts about their decision, for Dewey went on to indict Luciano for ninety-two counts of compulsory prostitution; having been found guilty, Luciano was given a sentence of from thirty to fifty years in prison on June 18, 1936. After being found guilty of murder, Lepke Buchalter was sentenced to death and died in the electric chair at Sing Sing prison on March 4, 1944, the only mob boss to be executed in New York. Had the Commission permitted Schultz to kill Dewey, those devasting prosecutions might never have happened. A worse blow to the Mafia was to happen four decades later: a trial of Commission members began on February 25, 1985, and ran until November 19, 1986. Eleven gangsters, including the bosses of the five families, were indicted by United States Attorney Rudolph Giuliani under the Racketeer Influenced and Corrupt Organizations Act (RICO) on charges including extortion, labor racketeering, and murder. Eight of them were convicted, and all but one were sentenced to 100 years in prison on January 13, 1987.

Notes

1 Carl Sifakis, *The Mafia Encyclopedia* (New York: Checkmark Books, 1999), 73.

2 David Critchley, *The Origin of Organized Crime in America: The New York City Mafia, 1891–1931.* (New York: Routledge, 2008), 165.

3 Tim Newark, *Boardwalk Gangster: The Real Lucky Luciano* (New York: Thomas Dunne Books, Imprint of St. Martin's Press, 2010), 62–3.

4 Joseph Bonanno, *A Man of Honor* (New York: St. Martin's paperback edition, 2003), 141.

4

Jews and Italians

The Lower East Side, in the early years of the twentieth century, was a neighborhood of tenements and immigrants. The tenements had no hot water, and a single bathroom on each floor served the needs of the tenants. Cold in winter, hot in summer, the tenements were a breeding ground for disease and crime. The immigrants came from Italy, Russia, and eastern Europe. They all struggled to earn decent wages. They worked hard, often at menial jobs, for low pay. Some had their own businesses: pushcarts filled with fruits and vegetables or clothes. Some could afford a wagon and an old broken-down horse that pulled their wares as they meandered across cobblestone streets. The clump-clump sound of hooves on the stones was a signal to women to come out and bargain for some vegetables for that night's dinner.

As they grew into their teenage years, the children of immigrants either strove to achieve academic excellence in school and in settlement houses or sought quick and easy ways to make money. Some joined small gangs that mugged other kids and extorted peddlers with threats of violence and destruction of their merchandise. If a peddler refused to pay for protection, his horse would be stolen, tied up miles away, and held for ransom. The owners always paid. Recalcitrant peddlers, without horses, had their pushcarts turned over and their fruits and vegetables trampled to mush; if the wagon carried piles of clothing, the whole lot would be set on fire: one kid would pour kerosene on the garments, and two other kids would set it all ablaze.

Those who finally had saved enough money to open a newsstand were also vulnerable to the teenage gangs. If the operators didn't pay up, their stands would be burned to the ground. The furiously aggrieved operators would be driven out of business.

Who were the gangs that roamed the cobblestone streets and alleys of the Lower East Side? They were primarily Italian, Jewish, and some Irish kids, though the latter congregated in Hell's Kitchen on the West Side. They were aspiring gangsters who showed no sympathy for their victims.

Because the Jews and Italian kids lived in sweaty proximity to one another, they often battled for territory. Kids were knifed, shot, bludgeoned. Some died. When cops arrived, the gangs scattered like feral cats at the sight of growling guard dogs. Some kids ran up the stairs of tenements and dropped bricks on the heads of cops. Dodge City was a safer environ than the Lower East Side.

Though the Jews and Italians had grown up fighting one another, they eventually found it profitable to form partnerships. By the time Prohibition became the law, there was enough money from bootlegging to make young gangsters millionaires. Prohibition was the single most important reason for the gangs to organize and work together. The partnerships would continue throughout much of the twentieth century.

Following the murders of Masseria and Maranzano, Luciano and Lansky organized the gangs into a great syndicate that they called the Combination. Lansky had reached out to Jewish gangsters across the country: Moe Dalitz, Robert Tucker, Morris Kleinman, Shondor Birns, Red Levine, Harry Rosen, Lou Rothkopf, Longy Zwillman, Davey Berman, and the Purple Gang in Detroit. Lansky invited them all to a convention that was held on November 11, 1931, at the Franconia Hotel in New York City. In addition to the Jews from the Midwest, local Jewish gangsters attended the confab; they included Lepke Buchalter, Doc Stacher, Jacob "Gurrah" Shapiro, Bugsy Siegel, Curly Holtz, Louis Kravits, Harry "Big Greenie" Greenberg, Harry Teitlebaum, Sam

Tucker, and Philip Kovalick. At the conclusion of the meeting, Bugsy Siegel commented that "The yids and dagos would no longer fight with one another."[1]

If you were a big-time gangster, you had to join. There would be no conscientious objectors. You either joined or you were put out of business. Waxey Gordon became an example for other gangsters who refused to join. Gordon saw no point in joining in an alliance with the Italians. He not only refused to join the syndicate, he went to war with some of its members, stealing trucks, hijacking bootleg shipments, and threatening the syndicate's customers. Lansky decided the best way to shelve Gordon was to feed information to the IRS about Gordon's taxable income from bootlegging and drug trafficking, on which he paid no taxes. Gordon was arrested, tried, convicted, and served ten years in prison. That left room for two more agreeable gangsters, so Gordon was replaced by Nig Rosen and Boo Boo Hoff.

There were also a few Italians who didn't want to join a syndicate populated by Jews. One such recalcitrant gangster was Jack Dragna, head of his own eponymous family in Los Angeles that was so *inept* it was known as the Mickey Mouse Mafia. He commented about the Jews: "Meyer's got a Jewish family built along the same lines as our thing [our thing is English for Cosa Nostra]. But his family's all over the country. He's got guys like Lou Rhody and [Moe] Dalitz, Doc Stacher, Gus Greenbaum, sharp fucking guys, businessmen, and they know better than to fuck with us." [2] Dragna was wrong about his threat to the Jews: it was Bugsy Siegel, who after moving to Beverly Hills, put a gun to Dragna's head and warned him not to fuck around. Dragna became an obedient subsidiary of the National Crime Syndicate. He did as he was told, knowing that if he didn't obey, he would be killed.

After getting rid of Waxey Gordon, Lansky and Luciano decided that Charles "King" Solomon would also have to go. Solomon controlled all the bootlegging, drug distribution, and gambling in Boston. After the end of Prohibition, Solomon refused to let Lansky and his associates participate in the flow of legal liquor across the Canadian border. On January 23, 1933, Solomon was shot and killed in the men's room of Boston's Cotton Club. His operations were taken over by Hyman Abrams, Joseph Linsey (né Linsky), and Max and Louis Fox. Abrams would later work with Lansky in the financing of numerous Las Vegas casinos as well as ones in Havana. Linsey not only worked closely with Lansky, but during Prohibition, he had partnered with Joseph Kennedy and the Bronfmans. The Syndicate reached such a high level of success that Lansky was able to declare, "We're bigger than U.S. Steel." [3]

Almost, as if in response, an FBI agent commented: "[Lansky] would have been chairman of the board of General Motors if he'd gone into legitimate business." [4] It's no wonder that after Luciano was deported to Italy, following World War II, he told his Italian confederates: Always listen to Lansky and you'll never go wrong. And they listened, because they all made money doing what Lansky suggested. So close were Lansky and Luciano, as emblematic of the alliance between Jews and Italians, that Luciano said that Lansky understood the Italian brain better than he, Luciano, did. Luciano added that Lansky, though he had a Jewish mother, must have been wet-nursed by a Sicilian.

Though he regarded Luciano almost as a brother, Lansky remained loyal to his Jewish roots. He may not have been a religious Jew, but he bore the psychic scars from his family having been targets of anti-Semitism. Beginning in 1936, Lansky began taking some time off from his illegal activities. He was deeply incensed by the rise of Nazism, and when the German–American Bund was generating publicity for its virulent anti-Semitism and pro-Nazi sentiments, Lansky decided the group had to be attacked. In New York City, the Bund was located in the Yorkville section on the Upper East Side of Manhattan. Its headquarters were at 178 East 85 Street, a block of brownstones and small apartment buildings. One block north, on East 86 Street, there were numerous German restaurants and German-run stores. Some New Yorkers referred to it as Sauerkraut Boulevard. Among the more popular restaurants and gathering places on the street were Maxi's Brauhaus, Lorelei Dance Hall, Kleine

Konditorei, Café Geiger, and Café Wienecke. All of it was a rich battleground for Jewish gangsters out to pummel the Nazis.

In 1938, Lansky contacted Judge Nathan Perlman with a proposal to attack members of the Bund. The judge nodded his approval with the proviso that no one be killed. The Jews, all members of Murder Incorporated, would face no legal sanctions. On April 20, 1938, the Bund was holding a large celebration in honor of Hitler's birthday. Fifteen Jewish gangsters rushed in like a pack of wild lions and began assaulting the Bund members. The Jews battered the Bund members with baseball bats and pickax handles, slugged them with brass knuckles and blackjacks. Those they didn't beat into a bloody heap, they threw out of windows. Though the Jews sent numerous Nazis to a hospital with fractured skulls, none of the wounded died. Lansky, who was normally motivated by opportunities to make large sums of money, acted on behalf of his fellow Jews without considering payment. He said, "I am a Jew, and I feel for the Jews in Europe who are suffering. They are my brothers." [5]

The Bund, which tried to influence America's foreign policy, issued a statement by its leader Fritz Kuhn, who said that Nazism was as American as apple pie. In 1939, Kuhn held a rally of 20,000 supporters in Madison Square Garden. It was picketed by hundreds of Jews who could not gain entrance to the Garden. News of the event was published in all the city's newspapers, including the German language *New York Staats-Zeitung*, which had a circulation of 80,000. During the rally, Kuhn—an American Hitler wannabe—was upstaged by a Jewish plumber from Williamsburg named Isadore Greenbaum, who jumped onstage, pulled the plug on Kuhn's microphone in the middle of his speech, and was roughed up by Kuhn's bodyguards. "When I heard persecution against my religion, I lost my head," [6] Greenbaum later said.

Lansky admired the plumber's chutzpah, but believed the best way to deal with the Bund was to employ the tactics of gangsters: beat your opponents into submission. Many Italian members of the Combination joined forces with their Jewish comrades not only in fighting homegrown Nazism, but also in 1948 by raising money and selling arms to Israel during its war of independence. Two who did so were Mickey Cohen and a reluctant Jimmy, "The Weasel" Fratianno. The strongest bonds between the Italians and Jews, however, were in Murder Incorporated, which comprised nearly equal numbers of the two groups.

Notes

1. Carl Sifakis, *The Mafia Encyclopedia* (New York: Checkmark Books, 1999), 19.
2. Sifakis, *Mafia Encyclopedia*, 191.
3. https://www.pbs.org/wgbh/americanexperience/features/lasvegas-syndicate/
4. Sifakis, *Mafia Encyclopedia*, 202.
5. www.jta.org/2022/06/06culturebefore-wwii-jewish-mobsters-kept-nazis-at-bay-with-their-fists
6. www.jta.org/2022/06/06culturebefore-wwii-jewish-mobsters-kept-nazis-at-bay-with-their-fists

5

Lansky and Luciano
Brothers in Crime

According to legend, Luciano and Lansky met when teenagers. The story has been around for decades. It has gone from being merely verisimilar to being considered veracious. Here's the tale: Lansky was on his way home from school one afternoon, taking a shortcut through an alley on the Lower East Side. As he was about to emerge from the shadows of the alley, a gang of young Italian hoods rushed at him, pushing him against a brick wall, and demanded money from Lansky, a skinny kid not yet even five feet tall. Lansky's response was immediate, intense, and angry: "Go fuck yourself." One kid, the seeming leader of the gang, did not respond with a violent rebuke. He smiled and told his gang to leave the kid alone. The kid giving orders was Salvatore Lucania (better known later on as Lucky Luciano). He was impressed by the little guy's defiance. He smiled and had his gang release Lansky. Lucania admired tough guys who would stand up to threats, never letting others push them around. Little Lansky (later known as the Little Man) regarded himself as too tough to ever take shit from anyone. It was there in an alley that a friendship was born that would change organized crime in America. It was a friendship that grew so close over time that people who knew both men said they could finish each other's sentences; they were like brothers born of the same mother.

Lansky introduced Lucania to another tough teenager: Benjamin "Bugsy" Siegel. (He was known as Bugsy because his violent reaction to provocations caused him to act as crazy as a bed bug.) Lansky had come across Siegel on his way home from school. Lansky always took the same shortcut through an alley, and as he emerged, he spotted a noisy crap game. One handsome kid seemed to be in control of the game. A nearby shopkeeper had called the cops because the kids had recently robbed his store, and he was worried they might strike again. The cops came swooping down, swinging their billy clubs at heads, arms, and legs. Kids scattered like a flock of frightened birds. One boy dropped a revolver, and Siegel grabbed it. He cocked the hammer and aimed at one of the cops. Before he could pull the trigger, Lansky grabbed Siegel's hand, causing the revolver to clatter onto the cobblestones. Siegel was furious that he had to take off running without the pistol. After they ran to safety, Lansky asked Siegel if he would like to partner with him in running crap games. Lansky had recently lost a nickel in an alley crap game, after which he understood the only way to make money from gambling was to control the game. Siegel could supply the muscle, intimidation, and threats—if necessary—to keep everyone in line. Lansky would control the dice. The two not only controlled local crap games, they formed a gang that terrorized local shopkeepers, newsstand operators, and peddlers, threatening them with violence and destruction of their businesses if they didn't pay for protection. Such a racket would not have worked if Lansky alone operated it, but with Siegel as his intimidating partner, no victim ever refused to cooperate. The partnership of Lansky and Siegel, which lasted until Siegel was assassinated in 1947, grew into a national gambling empire. It was only Siegel's thefts from the Flamingo Hotel and Casino that (according to gangland lore) led to Lansky's condoning the assassination of his boyhood pal.

But back in the 1920s after the two friends had formed the Bugs and Meyer Gang, they affiliated with Luciano's gang and Joe Adonis's Broadway Mob. The Lansky and Siegel mob consisted of a crew of young career criminals, many of whom would become notorious wanted men: they were Abner "Longy" Zwillman (later known as the Al Capone of New Jersey); Sam "Red" Levine (killer of Salvatore Maranzano); Joseph "Doc" Stacher (Vegas casino owner and manager); Moe Sedway (Bugsy's replacement at the Flamingo); and Louis "Lepke" Buchalter (co-boss of Murder Incorporated and the only mob boss to die in the electric chair at Sing Sing Prison). Former New York City detective Ralph Salerno told the author that "the Bugs and Meyer Gang was the most vicious in New York City. Lansky was the brains, Siegel was the muscle."[1] By the 1930s, the gang had evolved into the Italian and Jewish mob known as Murder Incorporated, co-headed by Lepke's partner, Albert "Mad Hatter" Anastasia. For his role in Murder Incorporated, Anastasia was given an additional nickname: the Lord High Executioner. Lepke and Anastasia delivered orders to their underlings who carried out hits exclusively for the National Crime Syndicate and received a monthly retainer, plus a bonus for each hit.

Rather than devoting himself to the activities of Murder Incorporated, Lansky's primary focus was gambling. He opened casinos in Saratoga, New York, and other locales. Siegel, though also involved with gambling, still enjoyed being in on murders. When carrying out a hit, he often partnered with Frankie Carbo, the man who—according to Mafia boss Ralph Natale—assassinated Siegel. Lansky, unlike Siegel, liked to think of himself as a businessman and operated several legitimate businesses, including a jukebox distribution company. Luciano, as Lansky's closest associate, seemed to replace Siegel.

Though thinking of themselves as businessmen, Lansky and Luciano, when necessary, hired Murder Inc. hitmen to carry out murders. When, for example, Abe "Kid Twist" Reles began ratting on his fellow hitmen in Murder Inc., including Siegel, he had to be eliminated. The Brooklyn DA had stashed Reles in the Half Moon Hotel in Coney Island, where six cops guarded him around the clock. Reles was a time bomb whose explosive testimony could have destroyed the lives of dozens of hitmen and their bosses; before the DA could light the fuse, the bomb had to be dismantled. The six cops guarding Reles were easily corrupted; they flung Reles out of a six-story window. "Lansky and Luciano reported to associates that Costello had spent $100,000 to bribe the five policemen who had been guarding Reles. All five were subsequently demoted, but they each deposited $20,000 into their individual safe deposit boxes. That was considerably more than their salaries, which were no more than $3,000 annually." [2] The joke amongst gangsters was "the canary could sing, but he couldn't fly." [3] The line was used years later in the movie *On the Waterfront*.

Perhaps the most extraordinary example of the friendship of Lansky and Luciano occurred following Luciano's arrest for pimping and pandering. Luciano, who was prosecuted by Thomas Dewey, was sentenced to thirty to fifty years in prison. Dewey was celebrated as America's foremost crime buster. His celebrity would carry him first into the New York governor's mansion and then to the top of the Republican Party as its presidential candidate. He served three terms as governor, followed by two campaigns for the presidency of the United States, first against Franklin Roosevelt, then against Harry Truman. He lost both times.

Putting the head of the Commission in prison could create a power vacuum and result in murderous battles to succeed Luciano. Nothing happened because Luciano relied on Genovese to carry out his orders while he was appealing his conviction. On October 10, 1938, all of Luciano's appeals came to nothing: the US Supreme Court refused to review his case. To avoid warfare within his own Mafia family, Luciano retired as boss and appointed Frank Costello as permanent boss. Genovese was not in the running to be boss because he fled to Italy in 1937 to avoid being arrested for the murder of gangster Ferdinand Boccia. Genovese carried a suitcase containing $750,000.

As much as Lansky admired Costello, his primary allegiance was to Luciano. Lansky had to do something to get his friend out of prison, where he had been since his sentencing on June 18, 1936. It would take years for Lansky to figure out a way to spring Luciano. Thanks to the Second World War, an opportunity arose, and Lansky put a plan into effect. There had been fear among politicians and military men that saboteurs could sink vessels docked at American ports. That fear had to be magnified. One of the most beautiful ocean liners, SS Normandie, was docked in the Hudson River. It was tied up like a goat waiting to be attacked by a tiger. The ship had been acclaimed as the fastest and largest ship to sail the oceans.

One day, fire broke out on the ship, flames consumed all that was flammable. No one seemed able to put out the fire: its flames spread as quickly as a nightmare. While still aflame, the burning hulk rolled over and died like a large animal. The ship had been designated as a troop carrier to bring thousands of GIs to England. Government and military officials declaimed their anger and stated that the fire must have been the work of saboteurs. Two supposedly patriotic gangsters, Tough Tony Anastasio, who controlled the longshoremen's union, and Socks Lanza, who controlled ships that brought their catches into the Fulton Fish Market, had volunteered to keep saboteurs off the docks of New York City. No one suspected that the two, under the direction of Lansky and Costello, had arranged for the Normandie fire. [4] [5] Lansky contacted Naval intelligence and convinced them that the only person who could prevent further acts of sabotage on the docks was Charles Luciano. Naval intelligence swung into action and had Luciano removed from the bleak Clinton Correctional Facility located in Dannemora, New York, to the Great Meadow Correctional Facility in Comstock, New York. It was much closer to New York City than Dannemora. Luciano and the navy negotiated a deal, approved by Dewey, that Luciano would receive commutation of his sentence in exchange for preventing further acts of sabotage. He would have his Mafia family patrol the docks and piers, make sure that no acts of sabotage occurred, and report all suspicious individuals to the appropriate authorities.

At Great Meadow, Luciano was treated better than a trustee: when Lansky and Costello visited him and wanted to have a private conference, the warden turned over his office to the mobsters. As America's invasion of Italy approached, the government called upon Luciano for further help. Just before troops landed in Sicily, the military asked Luciano for the names of local Mafioso who could assist them. Luciano provided a small book with all the names, addresses, and phone numbers that the invading forces would need. It was called Operation Underworld. Luciano was regarded as a key to the invaders' success.

After the allied victory, Lansky called upon Governor Dewey to release Luciano from prison. On January 3, 1946, Dewey commuted Luciano's prison sentence. A new year and a new life for the mobster. It would be a new life that Luciano had to live in Italy, for his commutation was dependent on his agreement that he would not contest Dewey's order of deportation. Luciano agreed.

On February 2, Luciano was escorted by immigration agents from prison to Ellis Island. He was parked there for seven days and then escorted onto a freight boat headed for Italy. The night before his departure, he was given a festive bon voyage party on board the ship by six of his closest mob associates, including Lansky, Costello, and Anastasia. Food and liquor were bountiful, as were several stunning high-class hookers. The following year, those same mobsters agreed that Siegel had to be killed for skimming millions of dollars from the construction of the Flamingo Hotel and Casino in Las Vegas. The hit could not be carried out without the concurrence of Lansky, Siegel's boyhood pal.

Luciano and Lansky continued doing business, each having points in numerous casinos. Lansky also surreptitiously aided Luciano's effort to export heroin from Italy and France into the United States and Canada. On January 26, 1962, Luciano dropped dead of a heart attack while waiting at the Naples International Airport for a film producer who wanted to make a movie of his life. Without his brothers in crime, Lansky continued to thrive, making money for himself and his mob associates. It was taken as absolute truth what Luciano had said: "Always listen to Meyer, and you'll always make money." Nothing else Luciano could have said would have been so accurate a tribute.

Notes

1 Salerno taped an interview with the author in 1991.
2 Jeffrey Sussman, *Big Apple Gangsters: The Rise and Decline of the Mob in New York* (Lanham, MD: Roman and Littlefield, 2020), 37.
3 https://web.archive.org/web/20211019034759/https://www.nysun.com/arts/excess-of-burnses-keep-a-case-open/20104/
4 Peter E. Bondanella, *Hollywood Italians: Dagos, Palookas, Romeos, Wise Guys, and Sopranos* (New York: Continuum International Publishing Group, 2004), 200.
5 Martin A. Gosch and Richard Hammer, *The Last Testament of Lucky Luciano* (Boston: Little, Brown and Company, 1974), 260–2.

6

The Business of Murder

Murder without a motive was a clever concept. Send a killer into a city with a contract to kill a stranger. There would be no known connection between the killer and his victim, no fingerprints, no evidence, and no motive. The crime would be unsolvable. It was the modus operandi of Murder Incorporated (Murder Inc.), which grew out of the Bugs and Meyer Mob. The difference was that the killers of the Bugs and Meyer Mob may have known their victims and only escaped prosecution by killing off witnesses, bribing corrupt cops and prosecutors, and/or developing credible alibis.

Murder Inc. was run like a legitimate business. Its CEOs were Louis "Lepke" Buchalter and Albert "The Lord High Executioner" Anastasia. Jacob "Gurrah" Shapiro was second in command to Lepke. Shapiro and Lepke had started as partners in crime in the early 1920s. In addition to the three, the organization had managers, and instead of workers, it had killers. Orders for murders came from the top. A killer was given a contract based on his skills with a gun, a knife, a garrote, a blunt instrument, or the ever-popular ice pick. In addition to his monthly retainer, he received a separate payment for carrying out the hit. The payments ranged from $1,000 to $5,000, depending on the difficulty of carrying out the hit and based on how much money the hit generated. Harry Strauss, one of the more prolific killers of the organization, proved to be the most ambitious of his colleagues. Prosecutors estimated that he may have killed 500 victims or one quarter of all those that Murder Incorporated had killed from 1929 to its demise in 1941.

Murder Inc. had begun by recruiting the sons of poor Italian and Jewish immigrants as well as a smattering of Irish men. They were from Brownsville, Brooklyn, and the Lower East Side of Manhattan, as well as a few other enclaves of poverty. Murder Inc. was a subsidiary of the National Crime Syndicate, and its killers were not permitted to kill anyone without getting orders to do so. It was a business, and there would be no freebies. Each killing was ordered, paid for, and carried out. There would be no murders of politicians, judges, and reporters. Since the National Crime Syndicate relied upon its beneficial relations with figures in those professions, it didn't want to alienate them or lose their compliance. When Dutch Schultz, for example, decided to kill prosecutor Thomas Dewey, he signed his own death warrant. Two members of Murder Inc., Charlie "The Bug" Workman and Mendy Weiss, were assigned to kill Schultz. Workman was eventually caught, indicted, and then agreed to plead no contest to the assassination and so was spared the death penalty. In prison, he kept his mouth shut, and the mob supported his family for twenty-three years until he was released from prison. Weiss was convicted of another murder, that of Joe Rosen, and was sentenced in 1941 to die in the electric chair at Sing Sing prison. He was executed on March 4, 1944. His final words before Old Sparky electrified his body were "I'm here on a framed-up case. And Governor Dewey knows it. I want to thank Judge Lehman. He knows me because I am a Jew. Give my love to my family and everything." [1]

Weiss and Workman had become affluent hit men by the time they were arrested. In fact, the killers of Murder Inc. regularly fattened their bank accounts and could have afforded to rent fancy offices as their bosses had; instead, they chose to operate out of Rose's candy store in Brooklyn, which was on the corner of Saratoga and Livonia Avenues in Brownsville, Brooklyn, and called Midnight Rose.

"During the 1930s and 40s, the Midnight Rose Candy Store, located under the elevated portion of the [number] 3 subway train, was run by a little old lady in her 60s, Mrs. Rosie Gold. It's hard to imagine a more innocuous and unoffending picture. But all was not as it seemed at the Midnight Rose, for this was the secret headquarters of one of the most infamous and deadly groups in the history of organized crime: Murder, Inc. . . . Rosie Gold kept a wall of pay phones along the back wall of the candy store; the members of Murder Inc., would pass the time at the Midnight Rose, sipping on Rosie's malted milks until one of the phones rang, giving the details of the hit." [2]

And the orders for hits came as regularly as the dawn of each new murderous day. And it wasn't only Weiss and Workman who were on hand to carry out murders; there was Abe "Kid Twist" Reles, Allie "Tick Tock" Tannenbaum, Marty "Buggsy" Goldstein, Louis Capone and James Feraco, Vito "Socko" Gurino, Jack "The Dandy" Parisi, Sidney "Fats" Brown, Irving Nitzberg and Frankie Carbo, Aniello Dellacroce and Philip "Little Farvel" Cohen, Harry "Happy" Maione, Frank "The Dasher" Abbandando, and Seymour "Blue Jaw" Magoon. There were others, but none of them became such big marquee names in newspaper headlines as those scary killers. Those who got screaming bold headlines on the front pages of New York's tabloids did so as they were sentenced to death in Sing Sing's electric chair. The men who were strapped onto Old Sparky included Harry Straus (who had feigned insanity during his murder trial), Mendy Weiss, Marty Goldstein, Louis Capone, Harry Maione, Frank Abbandando, and most notorious of all, Murder Inc.'s boss, Lepke Buchalter, who made his final walk without speaking a word. Here's what happened to others:

> *Nitzberg was convicted, but his case was overturned by the court of appeals, and his indictment was thrown out because it was found faulty.

* Gurino, who confessed to three murders, was sentenced to eighty years to life in prison and died in the prison's hospital for the criminally insane.

* Parisi was luckier than most. He was tried for murder several times, and each of his trials ended in an acquittal. Since there were no corroborating witnesses, some of whom had been Parisi's accomplices, he walked out of his trials and enjoyed a long life, dying at age eighty-three on December 27, 1982.

* "Fats Brown" was tried for murder; but after the death of Reles, there were no corroborative witnesses, so he too was acquitted.

* Frankie Carbo was not prosecuted as a killer for Murder Inc. and graduated to becoming the biggest fight promoter in the country; he was known as the Czar of Boxing during the 1940s and 1950s. In 1961, he was found guilty of extorting boxing managers, trainers, promoters, and fighters. He was sentenced to twenty-five years in prison. He was released early due to ill health and died in Miami, Florida, in 1976.

* Little Farvel was convicted of narcotics trafficking, served a few years in prison, and was shot to death on Long Island in 1949.

* Blue Jaw Magoon testified against members of Murder Inc., moved to Chicago, and went into the wholesale fish business. He had known who slept with the fishes, but never said a word about it.

* Aniello Dellacroce survived his involvement with Murder Inc. and became an underboss in the Gambino Crime family and a mentor to John Gotti. He died of cancer on December 2, 1985.

* Allie Tanenbaum testified against Lepke, Workman, and Parisi. He moved to Atlanta and dropped out of sight.

*James Feraco vanished and was presumably killed in 1940 or 1941. His body was never found, and police suspected that he had been eliminated as a possible witness against Lepke, Weiss, and Capone.

*Gurrah Shapiro was sentenced to fifteen years in prison. While incarcerated, he died of a heart attack on July 9, 1947. Throughout his time in prison, he maintained that if the Commission of the National Crime Syndicate had permitted Dutch Schultz to kill Thomas Dewey, neither he nor Lepke would have met their unfortunate fates.

There was tremendous publicity about Lepke's death sentence as well as tremendous fear that he would reveal his associations with high-level politicians, judges, and business owners. But, he was an old-school mob traditionalist who did not take anyone down with him.

"Buchalter went to his death stoically, with a silence that spoke volumes. Some felt he could have pulled off the veil from politicians and other authorities who may have been in the Mob's economic sphere.

"Lepke's attorney, J. Bertram Wegman, offered a cryptic statement, open to interpretation: 'Buchalter had two keys in his hand. He chose to use the one that opened the door to eternity rather than the other one.'"

"New York Mayor Fiorello LaGuardia and prosecutor Burton Turkus also weighed in with similarly ambiguous implications. 'Some people sweated a lot of bullets in the last few days,'" LaGuardia quipped.

"Turkus called Lepke's silence 'a signal to the underworld that he was not opening up on its members.'" [3]

And so ended an era of organized murder as a business. The mob would have to operate with greater discretion and finesse. People would certainly be killed, but so would their killers. No one should be left as a witness, including the killers. There would be no evidence tying the bosses to individual murders. Those bosses who felt empowered to bask in their ability to order deaths as if they were Roman emperors were often brought down by their own hubris and eventually by the RICO Statutes.

Following the death throes of Murder Inc, prosecutors had become public heroes, who rode their celebrity to pots of gold at the end of their glittering rainbows of fame. In addition to Thomas Dewey, who won three elections as governor of New York and lost two elections for the presidency of the United States, Burton Turkus emerged as a celebrity ADA for his role in winning nine convictions of Murder Inc killers. One of his most newsworthy accomplishments was linking Abe Reles to the murder of police informant Harry Rudolph in 1933; thereafter, Reles not only agreed to testify against his Murder Inc colleagues, but also to confess to over 200 unsolved murders.

Turkus went on to being a hot commodity as a celebrated gangbuster. In 1951, he wrote a best-selling book titled *Murder Inc*. Following that, he became the host of a TV series titled *Mr. Arsenic*, the mob's sobriquet for him. Then, in 1960, his celebrity reached new heights when he was portrayed by Henry Morgan in the movie *Murder Inc.* in which Peter Falk portrayed Reles. He lived a life full of honors and was often invited to speak to legal and civic groups.

Following his death on November 22, 1982, *The New York Times* wrote: "Mr. Turkus got his first big break when Abe Reles, one of the bosses of Murder Inc., agreed to cooperate."

"'You don't have Sherlock Holmes,'" Mr. Turkus said later, "and you don't have Hollywood legerdemain. Reles was an encyclopedia. He revealed for the first time the existence of the Syndicate, the pattern or the blueprint of organized crime."

"The crowning success of Mr. Turkus's efforts was the conviction in 1941 and execution in 1944 of Louis (Lepke) Buchalter, who ruled the rackets in garment districts for nearly two decades by ordering countless underworld executions. Mr. Turkus obtained nine first-degree murder convictions and contributed to the solution of scores of other murders. Organized crime called him Mr. Arsenic.

"In 1948, Gov. Thomas E. Dewey appointed him to the State Board of Mediation, where for 10 years he served as an arbitrator and mediator in nearly a thousand management-labor disputes. . . . In a 1974 decision in which he ruled against four women who were dismissed from a Playboy club because of their supposed loss of the 'Bunny image,' Mr. Turkus wrote: 'While a freshness of youth is manifestly transitory and evanescent, it is not always easy for a Bunny to accept the inevitable—that it has finally happened to her.'" [4]

Turkus was not the only prosecutor to bathe in public admiration: his boss, District Attorney William O'Dwyer, was propelled to the summit of New York Politics. In 1946, he was elected mayor, becoming the 100th person to hold that office. He appeared on the cover of *Time* magazine. However, in 1950, the sweet smell of success had turned to the stink of rotting corruption. The once upright, uncorruptible fighter against crime was pictured as a down-in-the-dirt rascal accused of tolerating high levels of police graft. He was also vilified in the press for not having indicted Murder Inc. boss Albert Anastasia, and as an added dollop of outrage, his friendship with mob boss Frank Costello was tossed into the mix. As the flames of public outrage intensified, O'Dwyer tucked his tail between his legs and left the mayor's office, an evicted tenant. The one person not intimidated by the moral outrage expressed by ministers, pastors, reverends, and God's chosen editorialists was President Truman, who never betrayed any of his shady Missouri pals. Not giving a fig for public opinion, he risked the wrath of good government groups and self-righteous editorialists by charitably appointing O'Dwyer as ambassador to Mexico. Truman's attitude seems to have been that you can always find some good in almost all malefactors and reprobates, though not in the men of Murder Inc.

Notes

1 Robert K. Elder, *Last Words of the Executed* (Chicago: University of Chicago Press, 2010), 16.

2 https://www.atlasobscura.com/places/the-old-headquarters-of-murder-inc-brooklyn-new-york?

3 https://themobmuseum.org/blog/dead-men-walking-murder-inc-trio-electrocuted-at-sing-sing-prison-eighty-years-ago/ Christian Cipollini.

4 https://www.nytimes.com/1982/11/24/obituaries/burton-b-turkus-80-prosecutor-of-murder-inc-in-the-1940-s-dies.html

7

Little Man against the Mob

They could have been called the Pee Wees, except they were as tough as barbed wire. Meyer Lansky was a mere five feet tall, and Fiorello La Guardia was five feet two inches. Had the two ever entered a wrestling ring, their match could have started a trend of Lilliputian wrestling. Alas, the two, one a criminal genius, the other a political one, never engaged in any kind of mortal combat.

Instead, La Guardia went after bigger men, whose activities were easier to nail down than the hidden hands of Lansky, whose gambling operations were fronted by others. La Guardia aimed his gangbusting zeal at Lucky Luciano and Frank Costello, whom he considered as the two most powerful gangsters in organized crime. Luciano was reportedly in control of all the prostitution in New York, and Costello not only controlled all the slot machines in New York, but he had bought the favors of influential politicians, judges, and prosecutors. He had them in his pocket. The two gangsters were just the kinds of targets that appealed to the tough, diminutive First World War combat veteran.

La Guardia would prove to the citizens of New York that an Italian mayor could go after Italian hoodlums, thus demonstrating to xenophobic WASPs that they were wrong to consider all Italians as members of organized crime. La Guardia, known as the Little Flower, hated the negative stereotypes that emerged from tabloid stories about Italian gangsters and the Mafia. Italian immigrants, like La Guardia's parents (his mother was an Italian Jew), were casually regarded as likely members of the Mafia. Bigots often addressed Italian men as Tony or Giuseppe and referred to them as WOPS, Dagos, or Guineas. La Guardia would show the world that he would not only go after the Mafia, but that he was an exemplary American citizen who represented everything that was good about America.

Shortly after taking office, La Guardia announced on the radio that he would drive the gangsters, whom he called bums, out of New York. He began his anti-crime mission to destroy all of Costello's slot machines in 1934. With the help of dozens of cops, he raided stores, every saloon, every restaurant, every social hall, and every bowling alley that had Costello's slot machines. Cops confiscated more than 1,200 one-armed bandits, which were unloaded from trucks and piled onto a barge. There was a jumpy La Guardia waiting with a sledgehammer; he was like an impatient batter in the batter's box waiting for the first pitch. He went after the slot machines as if they might get away from him, pounding again and again, turning each machine into junk. The smashed machines were dumped into Long Island Sound. News cameras recorded the event of La Guardia's athletic prowess, and the newsreels of the event were shown in movie theaters throughout the country. The little guy was said to be gutsy and tough. He didn't seem worried that gangsters might try to send him to the bottom. After all, the rivers and bays had become standard disposal areas for the victims of mob murders. But as the mob chose not to assassinate prosecutor Dewey, they figured that assassinating La Guardia would upset all the corrupt judges, politicians, and cops on their payrolls. The Little Flower flourished.

Costello, a thoughtful pragmatist, did not waste time attempting to reinstall mechanical bandits into new Big Apple locations. Instead, he and his silent partner, Lansky, sent all the machines to Louisiana, where Costello gave Governor Huey Long a million dollars to promote the politician's good government efforts. Their relationship portended the kind of relationship that Lansky effected with Fulgencio Batista in pre-Castro Cuba and later in Las Vegas.

In La Guardia's mind, pinball machines were nefarious cousins of slot machines. He disparaged pinball as an invitation for youth to gamble the hard-earned money of their parents. He referred to the game as gambling machines. His ban remained in effect until 1976.

Lucky Luciano was a different matter: he was a crime-buster's dream target, for he could be pictured in the media as pure evil, a cruel corruptor of women. Luciano, as a pimp and panderer, was a more visceral symbol of evil than Frank Costello. Gambling was thought to be a victimless crime, but forcing women into prostitution and keeping them there by getting them addicted to drugs outraged the consciences of decent folks. The mayor ordered the chief of police to arrest Luciano on whatever charges he could find, even if he had to look under the beds in whorehouses. La Guardia assigned a hand-picked squad of sixty-three police officers to Dewey's office whose sole mission was to nail Luciano.

As soon as an arrest warrant was issued for Luciano, he took off for Hot Springs, Arkansas, where the former king of the bootleggers, Owney "the Killer" Madden, operated a resort for gangsters on the lam. It took a while to extradite Luciano, but he was eventually taken back in humiliating handcuffs to New York. Not far from his old neighborhood on the Lower East Side, he was put on trial, found guilty based on the testimony of prostitutes, some of whom had been threatened by police and prosecutors that if they didn't testify they would be indicted as accessories to a crime. Others, who were addicted to drugs, were told that if they didn't testify against Luciano they would not only be indicted, but that their drugs would be withheld, and the effects of going cold turkey would be torturous. One street hood, after making a deal with prosecutors, testified that Luciano, while sitting in his Waldorf-Astoria suite, hired him to extort money from hookers and madams.[1] The testimony against Luciano was voluminous, and he was—to no one's surprise—found guilty. What did surprise the press and other gangsters was the sentence that the judge handed down: thirty to fifty years in prison. It was a sentence far longer than others received for the same offenses, and utterly outrageous when considering that murderers often got lesser sentences. According to the *Mafia Encyclopedia*, "The underworld insisted it was a 'bad rap,' claiming Dewey framed the case with perjured testimony of pimps and whores who would say anything to avoid going to jail themselves." [2]

In fact, four prostitutes, Nancy Presser, Mildred Harris, Thelma Jordan, and Florence "Cokey Flo" Brown, all of whom had testified against Luciano, recanted their testimony. Two other prostitutes said they never heard of Luciano being involved in prostitution. Rather than Luciano, the prostitutes said they had been extorted by street thugs who had threatened them if they didn't make regular payments. Polly Adler, a famous madam, wrote in her memoirs that Luciano wasn't involved in pimping or prostitution; if he had been, she would have known about it. Joe Bonanno, boss of the Bonanno crime family, wrote in his autobiography that several of Luciano's soldiers used his name to extort madams into paying for protection. He added that Dewey built his case "not so much against Luciano as against Luciano's name." [3]

The press coverage Luciano received was so extensive that it became the inspiration for a 1937 movie titled *Marked Woman*, which starred Bette Davis as a party girl (a euphemism for prostitute) and Humphrey Bogart as a hard-hitting, Dewey-like prosecutor. Following the murder of her sister, the Davis character decides to cooperate with the prosecutor and testify against the mob boss responsible for her sister's murder. The vicious mob boss was portrayed by Eduardo Cianelli, who bore a striking resemblance to Luciano. Novelist and movie critic Graham Greene wrote: "it's been done before, of course, [. . .] but it has never been done better than in some of these scenes." Greene added that Cianelli conveyed "not only corruption but the sadness of corruption." His estimation of Davis's performance, however, was less than admiring: her acting "plugs the emotions with dreadful abandonment." [4]

La Guardia was on a tear. It wasn't only slot machines and prostitutes that were his crime-busting targets. How about artichokes? Early on the morning of December 21, 1935, La Guardia, with cops, reporters, photographers, and camera operators in tow, showed up at the Bronx Terminal Market. He leapt onto the back of a vegetable truck and in his high-pitched voice announced a ban on the display and sale of artichokes, beginning on December 26. The prices of artichokes, he said, were being controlled by a monopoly of gangsters. They had been using intimidation and violence to drive up prices and control distribution. Artichokes were a popular food in the Italian immigrant community, and its members had vociferously complained about the increasingly steep prices. Ciro Terranova, a Mafia boss known as the Artichoke King, had controlled the price and distribution of artichokes for years. His grip was ironclad, and he made sure the prices increased year after year. Again, the Little Flower could not be crushed: the artichoke ban remained in place until its price reached a normal level.

Perhaps La Guardia's most frivolous act was shutting down burlesque theaters, which offered striptease, comedians, and singers. His autocratic act struck many liberals as nothing less than puritanical censorship. The following letter appeared in *The New York Times*:

> "My three brothers (Abe, Billy and Herbert) and I were operating six theaters in Metropolitan New York, plus others throughout the country, when, on April 30, 1937, we're put out of business for corrupting the morals of the city.
>
> "La Guardia accomplished this by denying the renewal of burlesque theater licenses. We were then featuring Phil Silvers, Abbott and Costello, Red Buttons, Joey Faye, Jack Albertson, Gypsy Rose Lee and others of great talent in our burlesque extravaganzas, in competition with Ziegfeld, White, Rose and the Shuberts. We were known as the Poor Man's Ziegfeld.
>
> "Brooks Atkinson, Robert Garland, A. J. Liebling and other outstanding critics of the theater sang the praises of Minsky shows at every opportunity. They had genuine fun at Minsky's and expressed it in a variety of literary

forms. He used autocratic power to effect the closing. The burlesque industry lacked funds to fight for its constitutional rights.

"The word 'burlesque' and the name 'Minsky' were banned. Liberals of that day felt that the censorship groups were too powerful to oppose. It was a complete surrender! La Guardia had eliminated an original source in the development of today's theater. My opinion is that he did this not because of any ethical standards but to gain votes for re-election through a sensational tactic." (Morton Minsky, New York, December 15, 1981)

Though La Guardia went after genuine gangsters and innocent entrepreneurs such as the Minsky brothers, one who never appeared on La Guardia's hit list was Meyer Lansky. The diminutive gangster was smart enough not to be a target of prosecutors. He opened casinos in Saratoga and Florida, where he made deals with local officials who let him operate without hindrance. He made a lot of money for himself and for those with whom he partnered.

Though Luciano and Costello suffered at the hands of La Guardia, Lansky did what he could to help his boyhood pals. After Vito Genovese ordered a hit on Costello, Lansky and others plotted the demise of Genovese by setting him up for a drug deal. Genovese was arrested, convicted, and sent off to prison where he died. And after Dewey had successfully prosecuted Luciano and paved the way for his long prison sentence, Dewey made a deal with Lansky that ultimately led to Luciano's release. Lansky had brilliantly conceived the idea of making Luciano an essential asset to naval intelligence during World War II. Luciano agreed to use his Mafia connections to keep the docks and shipyards of New York free of Nazi saboteurs. In addition, he provided lists of people in Sicily who aided the American soldiers following their successful invasion of the island. Luciano's Sicilian associates were credited in small measure for providing American military intelligence with the names of Nazi and fascist spies and sympathizers—as long as they weren't fellow gangsters. A grateful Dewey released Luciano from prison but made sure he was deported back to Italy. Luciano thrived in Italy, becoming a major narcotics trafficker.

La Guardia had played an important role, eliminating or subduing elements of organized crime and a few harmless institutions. While burlesque remained banned in New York for decades, organized crime flourished, for wherever illegal opportunities arise for criminals to make money, they will do so. No matter how many obstacles are placed in their paths, they manage to find detours that bring them to their desired destinations.

Notes

1. Robert Weldon Whalen, *Murder, Inc., and the Moral Life: Gangsters and Gangbusters in La Guardia's New York (New York:* Fordham University Press, 2016), 114.
2. Carl Sifakis, *The Mafia Encyclopedia* (New York: Checkmark Books, 1999), 227.
3. Joseph Bonanno with Sergio Lalli, *A Man of Honor: The Autobiography of Joseph Bonanno* (New York: St. Martin's Paperback, 2003), 165.
4. John Russel Taylor, ed., *The Pleasure Dome* (New York: Oxford University Press, 1980), 166, 168, 169.

8

The Only Mob Boss Fried in Old Sparky

Louis "Lepke" Buchalter did not have the wit to avoid being the first and only mob boss to have been executed by the State of New York. If Lepke hadn't been overheard by an eager-to-testify underling when ordering the murder of Joe Rosen, a former truck driver who had refused to join a Lepke-controlled union, he may have gone on ordering murders into his old age. As the boss of Murder Inc., Lepke used the murderous means at his disposal to get rid of someone who could testify against him.

While the hitmen of Murder Inc. had itchy trigger fingers, their bosses Lepke and his partner Jacob Gurrah Shapiro were impatient to kill those who got in their way. Known as the Gorilla Boys, Lepke and Gurrah (he earned his middle name because of his frequent inarticulate angry growls) were a frightening pair who were said to order murders as easily as ordering dinner. Murder was one of their means of taking over several small businesses as well as labor unions, including ones in the garment industry, baking industry, poultry industry, and trucking. In addition to Gurrah, Lepke ran Murder Inc. with Albert "The Lord High Executioner" Anastasia, who ordered murders more impulsively than his partners. For example, when Anastasia saw Arnold Schuster on a local TV news program telling a reporter that he had spotted escaped prisoner and bank robber Willie Sutton and reported it to the police, a furious Anastasia immediately ordered a hit on Schuster.

When not murdering business owners and union members who stood in their way, they got fellow gangsters to join unions they wanted to control and then the new members voted to have their unions run by Lepke and Gurrah. During the Great Depression, law enforcement officials estimated that the Gorilla Boys were taking in twenty million dollars annually from their labor rackets. When ordering hits, Lepke established a hierarchy of command so that his name would never be associated with either the hitman or the victim. To wit: he would give the contract to either Gurrah or Anastasia, who would pass it on to one of their lieutenants, who would give it to a chosen hitman, who would not be able to testify against Murder Inc.'s bosses if he were caught.

In addition, Lepke, more than his partners, believed he was protected by politicians. However, Democratic governor Herbert Lehman was under pressure from Republicans and some newspaper publishers to hire a Republican special prosecutor to go after the mob. The governor knew he should not appoint a Democrat, since it was well known that organized crime controlled Tammany Hall, the seat of Democratic power in New York City. Four prominent Republican attorneys turned down Lehman's offer, but all recommended Thomas Dewey, who quickly agreed to take on the job. Shortly after being retained, Dewey hired sixty investigators. After going after Dutch Schultz and Lucky Luciano, Dewey set his sights on Lepke. His laser-like focus could not be interrupted or deterred by political pressure, bribes, or threats. Dewey was as determined as a guided missile and kept lining up witnesses who would testify against Lepke, who—in turn—arranged for all potential witnesses to be killed by members of Murder Inc. More than sixty bodies, shot, knifed, ice picked, garrotted, and even burnt to a crispy blackness, were found in vacant lots, along creeks and bays, in tenement basements and deserted garages in Queens and Brooklyn and upstate New York. To remain uncuffed, a paranoid Lepke went into hiding, ate himself into adiposity, and grew an undistinguished mustache. He became invisible to the law. A frustrated Dewey got New York City to offer a twenty-five-thousand-dollar reward for Lepke, dead or alive. No prospective bounty hunters were foolish enough to put their names down as potential victims of Murder Inc.

Abe "Kid Twist" Reles visited Lepke daily. He would inform his boss of potential witnesses, and Lepke ordered them killed. To make sure that Lepke remained invisible, Anastasia moved him from one location to another. Dewey's frustration resulted in angry tirades and demands that his investigators find Lepke. His investigators might have done just as well searching for Zorro or the Scarlet Pimpernel. To put pressure on the Mob, Dewey ordered that every mob-run activity in the city should be closed by the police: betting parlors, gambling dens, whorehouses, saloons, mob-owned businesses in the garment and food industries. Many low-level gangsters were arrested on charges of being vagrants. The pressure finally got to the members of the Commission of the National Crime Syndicate. Luciano and Tommy "Three Fingers Brown" Lucchese decided that Lepke must give himself up to Dewey. However, that was easier said than done. They would have to deputize a trusted turncoat to convince Lepke of the advantages of doing the right thing for his fellow mobsters. They chose Morris "Moey Dimples" Wolensky, a friend whom Lepke trusted to his later regret. Moey was instructed to dangle a carrot of an easy-to-serve prison term to Lepke. It was something he could do standing on his head. As I wrote in *Big Apple Gangsters*: "Buchalter had to believe that if he gave himself up to the FBI, he would be tried on federal charges and serve only a few years in a federal prison. By the time his sentence would be completed, Dewey would be out of office and state charges would have vanished for a lack of witnesses. Buchalter would be a free man." [1] Moey told Lepke the fix was in. So, in August 1939, Lepke said he would go forward with the plan, but he insisted that he turn himself over to none other than FBI director J. Edgar Hoover: one boss dealing with another boss. Anastasia was furious that Lepke had agreed to such a deal. He tried to convince his partner that he could continue to hide for years, well beyond the time when Dewey had left office. By then, the right people could be bribed to make Lepke a free man. However, a resigned, yet determined, Lepke said he would give himself up to Hoover.

Frank Costello, the politically well-connected prime minister of the underworld, was designated as the go-between. He called his friend, *New York Daily Mirror* columnist Walter Winchell, who agreed to bring Hoover to 28th Street and Fifth Avenue, where Lepke would meet the FBI director. On August 24, 1939, at 10 p.m., Anastasia drove Lepke to meet Hoover. He parked directly behind Hoover's car. Winchell exited from a back door, walked to Anastasia's car, and escorted Lepke to meet Hoover. The two men got into the FBI car, with Lepke seated next to Hoover. Winchell introduced the two: "'Mr. Hoover this is Lepke.' 'How do you do' said Hoover. 'Glad to meet you,' replied Lepke." [2]

Buchalter went to trial, and on January 2, 1940, he was found guilty on federal charges of drug trafficking and sentenced to fourteen years in prison. He figured he could be out in seven to ten years. It was not to be: he was turned over to the State of New York and tried for labor racketeering and extortion. Someone would have to pay for this betrayal. And sure enough, Moey met his end in a hail of gunfire.

On March 2, 1940, Lepke was found guilty on fifteen counts of extortion. As a four-time loser, he received a sentence of life in prison. He would serve fourteen years or so in Leavenworth, then the rest of his life probably in Sing Sing.

However, fate had another indignity in mind for Lepke: in September 1940, New York district attorney William O'Dwyer discussed with US attorney Harold Kennedy about having Lepke delivered to Kings County, where he would be tried for the murder of Joe Rosen. The victim had been driven out of the trucking business for refusing to join Lepke's corrupt union. Rosen opened a candy store in Brooklyn. Angry at Lepke, Rosen agreed to testify against him. As soon as Lepke heard about Rosen's threat, he ordered a hit on the rat. Unfortunately for Lepke, the order was overheard by Allie "Tick Tock" Tannenbaum, who later agreed to testify against his Murder Inc. cohorts. O'Dwyer believed that he had been dealt a winning hand and flew to Leavenworth to meet with Lepke. He offered the prisoner a deal: testify against Murder Inc. members, and O'Dwyer would drop the murder charge for ordering the death of Rosen. Lepke refused. Instead, he ordered the killing of other possible witnesses. Some men are prisoners of their habits.

On May 9, 1941, a shackled Lepke appeared in court to be arraigned for the murder of Rosen. The frozen-faced Lepke received a note from his former partner Gurrah, who had written, "I told you so." He was referring to the fact that Lepke and other members of the National Crime Commission had rejected the assassination of Dewey and instead had murdered Dutch Schultz, who was a lesser threat than Dewey. Gurrah and Anastasia, who had wanted Dewey killed, were out-voted. It was too late for regrets. Lepke was sentenced to be fried in Old Sparky in Sing Sing prison. The sentence would be delayed by a series of appeals filed by his lawyers. All the appeals, including one to the US Supreme Court, were denied and the forty-seven-year-old Lepke was slowly escorted by seven guards down the Last Mile to Old Sparky. His legs and head had been shaved. He was placed on the chair, his arms and legs firmly strapped in place to which electrodes were attached. A cap with a saltwater sponge was placed over his head. Lepke had no last words, and so quickly received a painful jolt of 2500 volts, followed by a second charge of 1500 volts. After his body cooled, he was unstrapped and taken to the prison morgue. Death had come for him on March 4, 1944. Mobsters across New York all agreed that Dewey should have been assassinated. A chill went through the underworld: if they could fry Lepke, they would get anyone. Though mob bosses would come and go, some dying of old age, some shot by those who wanted to replace them, no other mob bosses followed in the footsteps of Lepke down the long Last Mile to Old Sparky.

Having been in the same prison with Lepke, the Pulitzer Prize-winning poet Robert Lowell wrote about him in a poem titled *Memories of West Street and Lepke*. He described Lepke, whom he named Czar Lepke, as being flabby and lobotomized. He wrote: "where no agonizing reappraisal/jarred his concentration about the electric chair." [3] Lowell had been convicted for being a conscientious objector during the 1940s. In the movie *Romeo Is Bleeding*, Lepke and Lowell have a brief conversation. Lepke confesses that he is in prison because he killed someone; Lowell responds that he's in prison because he didn't kill someone. [4]

Though the tabloids focused on Lepke as the first mob boss executed in New York, there was little written about his partner Gurrah. Along with Lepke, Gurrah had been convicted in 1936 and sentenced to two years in Sing Sing Prison. Gurrah, not a fan of confinement, went on the lam for two years. He was not exactly living the life of a tourist going to the world's most exciting resorts. After two years of worry, misery, fear, and boredom, he turned himself over to FBI agents on April 14, 1938. He thought he would be able to enjoy life once he was free, but on May 5, 1944, he was convicted of extortion and conspiracy (his trademark tactics) and sentenced to fifteen years to life in prison. Locked up, he often let it be known that Dewey should have been assassinated. It became like a mantra for him, emphatically repeated following the execution of Lepke. In 1947, Gurrah died as the result of coronary thrombosis.

Murder Inc. had left hundreds of dead bodies as testimony to its mission of killing. Dewey left behind two bodies of men responsible for all those other dead bodies.

Notes

1 Jeffrey Sussman, *Big Apple Gangsters: The Rise and Decline of the Mob in New York* (Lanham, MD: Rowman and Littlefield Publishers, 2020), 71.

2 Paul R. Kavieff, *The Life and Times of Lepke Buchalter* (Fort Lee, NJ: Barricade Books, 2006), 132.

3 https://poets.org/poem/memories-west-street-and-lepke

4 https://imdb.com/title/tt0107983/faq/ Romeo Is Bleeding (1993)-FAQ-IMDb.

9

Deportations

Here today and gone tomorrow seems to have been the mantra of law enforcement about getting rid of gangsters. For years, numerous members of the Mafia were deported to Italy. That country, fighting its own organized crime organizations, was not pleased to be a dumping ground for some of America's most notorious criminals. There were paradoxes, however, playing out in the deportation playbook: though most Mafiosos fought against being deported, there were Jewish gangsters who sought escape from prosecution by deporting themselves to Israel.

Perhaps the most notorious of the Mafia deportees was Lucky Luciano. Following the 1946 commutation of his prison sentence, a reward for helping to keep the docks of New York free of Nazi saboteurs, Luciano was told he would be deported on the condition that he didn't fight the deportation order. Luciano reluctantly agreed to the deal but continued to tell colleagues and reporters that he was a US citizen and should not be deported. He also dismissed the accusation that landed him in prison of having been the pimping empresario of New York.

A deal was a deal, and on February 2, 1946, federal immigration agents escorted Luciano from his temporary home at Sing Sing prison to Ellis Island, the gateway for Italian immigrants entering the United States decades earlier. The irony was not lost on Luciano.

On February 9, Luciano's friends threw an extravagant bon voyage party for him. Though the party was not on a fancy ocean liner (it was on a freight boat), it was a joyous occasion, celebrating Luciano's freedom. Not all, however, was laughter and good cheer, for Luciano couldn't stop complaining that the government had no right to deport him. As if that were not bad enough, he added that his reputation as a businessman had been shattered by Thomas Dewey, who had accused him of being one of the country's leading gangsters, a Mafia boss. With an abundance of food and drink, the party went on for hours. The next day, Luciano watched the skyline of New York recede into a distant haze. He would never again set foot in New York. For the man who had given structure to the Mafia, a man who commanded thousands, it was a humiliating exile, though not as humiliating as Napoleon's to Saint Helena.

Luciano's sea voyage to Naples was slow and uneventful. He disembarked on February 28 and planned to make a new home for himself in Sicily. The Italian government, however, had different plans for him: Luciano was told his new home would be in Naples, and he better not leave without permission. If he broke any laws, he would find himself in prison. The uncommon organizer of the American Mafia was treated no better than a common criminal, a thief, a mugger, a pickpocket.

Though exiled from his base of power, separated from the bosses, capos, and soldiers of the five Mafia families, Luciano could not accept his tremendous loss of income. He needed to find a means for generating large sums of cash that would be invisible to law enforcement officials. He became a stealthy exporter of heroin. He had been a gangster since his youth; he knew no other way of making money.

Meyer Lansky, eager to help his boyhood pal, called for a meeting of organized crime bosses to take place in Havana, where—if only briefly—Luciano would reign supreme. Luciano would be back in the game, an absentee boss. In October 1946, Luciano secretly boarded a freighter that took him to Caracas. From there, he flew to Rio de Janeiro, where he boarded another plane that took him to Mexico City, and finally he flew aboard a private plane to Camaguey, Cuba, where he arrived on April 29. There, he would be among his cohorts, men who regarded Luciano as their leader. Lansky sent a car which drove Luciano to a well-guarded estate in Miramar. The island of Cuba wasn't as good as being back in his old stomping grounds, but it was as close as he would ever get to his favorite northern island, Manhattan. He missed Manhattan, especially its nightlife, but Havana was the second-best playground for an exiled Mafioso. Havana was alive with Mafia-run casinos and brothels. It was a city where one could find any kind of pleasure. Nothing was denied the mob in Havana.

Lansky proved to be the ultimate event planner. He had arranged for Luciano's visit with the precise planning of a military commander. He had contacted the members of the National Crime Syndicate's Commission, letting them know they would pay tribute to their boss and learn what the future would hold for them. To throw off possible law enforcement bloodhounds, mobsters were to say they were going to a tropical resort to attend a Frank Sinatra concert. Sinatra would not only entertain the gathering of mobsters, but he would deliver to Luciano a briefcase containing two million dollars. Originally, the Fischcetti brothers (Rocco and Charles), cousins of Al Capone, were to deliver the money, but to avoid being stopped and searched by police or the FBI, the brothers figured that no one would suspect Sinatra of being a bagman for the mob. Sinatra was agreeable, and though he was never permitted to be present during the discussions of mob business, he entertained the mobsters at night when no business was discussed.

One man whom Luciano was not looking forward to seeing was Vito Genovese, who—unlike Luciano—had deported himself to Italy in order to avoid prosecution for a murder in New York. Genovese had murdered fellow gangster Ferdinand Boccia, who had insisted that Genovese pay him his share of the profits from a scam they had engineered. Rather than pay Boccia, Genovese killed him. After the witnesses against Genovese had been killed or had died of natural causes, the case against him was dropped, and Genovese returned to the United States.

However, while in Italy, Genovese had been an ardent supporter of Mussolini. The gangster had given four million dollars to Mussolini's political party and had been rewarded not only with carte blanche to carry out numerous black market activities, but was also awarded the Order of Saints Maurice and Lazarus and further honored with the title Commendatore. So gratified was Genovese that, as a favor to Mussolini, he ordered the murder in New York of anti-fascist newspaper publisher Carlo Tresca, who was gunned down on the sidewalk outside of his office. The shooter was future mob boss Carmine Galante. He, too, would be gunned down. On July 12, 1979, the cigar-chomping Galante was shot multiple times while having lunch on the patio of Joe and Mary's Italian-American Restaurant in Bushwick, Brooklyn. A famous photo of the dead gangster with a cigar clenched between his teeth appeared in tabloids around the world.

Unlike Genovese, Luciano had given his services to the United States government—albeit from prison—during the Second World War, ordering the safety of New York's docks and providing lists of allied sympathizers in Sicily. Luciano had additional reasons for not liking Genovese. Going back to their early days, Genovese had complained about the Italians doing business with Jews. Frank Costello and Luciano told Genovese that he was just an immigrant. The rebuke ignited Genovese's anger, and he would look for ways to dislodge the two gangsters. Added to Luciano's dislike were comments that Genovese made about Costello having a Jewish wife and his distrust of Lansky.

During the Havana conference, Luciano and Genovese had a private meeting. Genovese told Luciano that because he was in exile in Italy, another boss should be appointed. And that boss, should—of course—be Genovese. Not only did he offer himself as boss of Luciano's family, but he wanted to be boss of all bosses. A furious Luciano said there would be no boss of bosses. The position had died with the murder of Maranzano. Luciano continued: "I turned it down in front of everybody. If I ever change my mind, I will take the title. But it won't be up to you. Right now, you work for me, and I ain't in the mood to retire. Don't you ever let me hear this again, or I'll lose my temper.[1]

Genovese hid his anger, but seethed. One day, he would attempt to be named boss of bosses. And though he said that Luciano would not be able to prevent it, he would be sorely disappointed. Luciano, Lansky, Costello, and Carlo Gambino would conspire first to undermine Genovese's authority and then set him up for a long prison term.

More important than the animosity between Genovese and Luciano was the heroin trade. As the bosses met at the Hotel Nacional de Cuba, they mapped out plans for expanding not only the mob's control of the heroin market but also the expansion of gambling in Las Vegas and the fate of Bugsy Siegel, who was treating their hotel/casino, the Flamingo, with all the flair and savvy displayed by a sociopathic thief. Though most of the mobsters, with the exception of Joe Adonis, were friends with Siegel, they approved of his ultimate demise. Before he could even be shipped off to the local morgue, he would be replaced at the casino by Gus Greenbaum and Moe Sedway.

Luciano's visit to Cuba was about to be interrupted, for the Federal Bureau of Narcotics received information that Luciano was organizing an international cartel to smuggle heroin into the United States. The Bureau's boss, Harry J. Anslinger, warned the Cuban government on February 21, 1947, that if Luciano was not expelled from the island, there would be a ban on all prescription drugs. The Cuban government quickly arranged for Luciano to be briefly jailed, then almost as quickly escorted him to a waiting freight boat. Two police officers escorted him up the gangway, made sure he didn't sneak ashore, and departed. An angry Luciano sailed to Genoa, then was driven to Naples, where he would remain in exile for the rest of his life.

Anslinger also alerted the Italian government of Luciano's plan to export heroin from Italy to Marseilles and from there to America. With that information in hand, an Italian judicial commission placed strict conditions on Luciano's movements, which did not take effect until November 1, 1954. As if he were on parole, Luciano was instructed that he must report every Sunday to a local police station and not to leave his residence at night. If he wanted to leave Naples, he would require police permission to do so. The restrictions on his movements went on for two years. Yet, with or without restrictions, Luciano was able to continue exporting large quantities of heroin. This would all blow up in the famous French Connection case, though Luciano was dead by that time. He died of a heart attack on January 26, 1962, in the Naples airport, where he had gone to meet an American movie producer who wanted to make a movie about Luciano's life. (Luciano had wanted Cary Grant to portray him in the movie.) He died without progeny, once saying, "I didn't want no son of mine to go through life as the son of Luciano, the gangster. That's one thing I still hate Dewey for, making me a gangster in the eyes of the world." [2] Though forced to live out his life in Italy, his body was brought back to New York for burial in St. John's Cemetery in Queens, New York, where numerous other Mafioso are interred.

Joe Adonis (born Giuseppe Antonio Doto), another attendee at the Havana Conference, was also deported to Italy. He had changed his name to Adonis because he believed he was the epitome of male beauty, resembling the statue of Adonis in the Uffizi Gallery in Florence, Italy. In Greek mythology, Adonis was the lover of Aphrodite and Persephone. And Joe Adonis would become the lover of many beautiful women, especially chorus girls in Broadway shows. One of his lovers, Virginia Hill, would become Bugsy Siegel's secret wife, which must have dealt a blow to Adonis's ego. It's no wonder that he came to dislike Siegel, whom many admirers said was truly movie-star handsome, much more so than the gap-toothed Adonis.

To say that Adonis was vain would be an understatement. Luciano was amused by Adonis's vanity, and after observing him taking a considerable amount of time to comb his hair with the precision of a professional hairdresser,

Luciano asked him: "Who do you think you are, Rudolph Valentino?" Adonis wheeled around and shot back: "For looks, that guy's a bum!" [3]

Adonis may have been an insecure young man when he started his criminal career as a small-time thief and pickpocket; after a few years of thieving, he met Lucky Luciano and his confidence must have grown as Luciano's loyal protégé. Soon he had grown into a major gangster, operating successful bootlegging and gambling businesses; however, just to keep his hand in, he would occasionally hold up a jewelry store or pick the pocket of some inebriated, pretentious swell who was smitten with a Follies chorus girl.

At the outset of Prohibition, he worked closely with Luciano, Lansky, Siegel, and Costello. He and Luciano controlled much of the bootlegged booze distributed to restaurants, nightclubs, and speakeasies on and around Broadway. Years later, prosecutors believed that Adonis was involved in Murder Inc., for he had a close relationship with Lepke Buchalter. However, no one was ever able to prove that Adonis ever ordered a Murder Inc. hitman to kill someone.

By the time he attended the Havana Conference in 1946, Adonis had become a powerful presence. His antipathy for Siegel had not waned, and when he had an opportunity to vote for a death sentence for his former competitor, he did so with enthusiasm: Siegel, having stolen money from the mob for the building of the Flamingo Hotel and Casino, had to be eliminated. It was agreed by all, including Siegel's boyhood pal, Lansky.

For years prior to the conference and for years afterward, Adonis was able to maintain a relatively low profile. He was adept at paying off judges, prosecutors, and politicians. Payoffs left them too nearsighted to view any crimes Adonis may have been committing. It all changed, however, when he was called to testify before the Senate Special Committee to Investigate Crime in Interstate Commerce chaired by Senator Estes Kefauver. His hair perfectly coiffed, Adonis appeared handsomely attired in a silk bespoke suit on December 12, 1950. Though he repeatedly recited his Fifth Amendment right not to incriminate himself, he became a marquee name for the Justice Department and the FBI. It could not have been worse if his name were up in lights on Broadway. Prosecutors were determined to get him. A year later, he was prosecuted for operating illegal gambling casinos in New Jersey. Following his conviction, he was sentenced to two to three years in prison. As if that were not bad enough, the Department of Justice ordered his deportation to Italy on August 6, 1953. Prosecutors claimed that Adonis was an illegal alien, but he vigorously fought against his deportation, claiming that he had been born in the United States. In fact, he had been born on November 22, 1902, in the town of Montemarano, Italy, to Michele Doto and Maria De Vito. With unchallengeable evidence against him, Adonis finally accepted that he would be deported. On January 3, 1956, he departed New York harbor on an ocean liner bound for Naples, Italy. Unlike Luciano, he was not confined to Naples and moved north to Milan, where he rented a luxurious apartment. Luciano had asked Adonis to invest in some illegal deals, but the former protégé refused. That was the beginning of the end of their relationship. It was never repaired; however, after Luciano died, Adonis showed up at the funeral with an enormous floral arrangement. Angled across it was a large banner with the words, "So Long, Pal." [4] The words were right out of a 1930s gangster movie and could have been uttered by Cagney or Bogart.

Adonis returned to his charmed life in Milan, but it was soon interrupted by Italian prosecutors. They ordered Adonis to leave the comforts of his Milan apartment and take up residence in Serra de Conti. Prosecutors had been hunting Mafioso who may have been involved in the assassination of chief magistrate and prosecutor Pietro Scaglione in Palermo. Scaglione had been assassinated after visiting the grave of his wife. Adonis was abruptly scooted out of Serra de Conti and taken to a police shack in Ancona, where he was subjected to abusive and brutal interrogations. His bruised body suffered a heart attack on November 26, 1971. Like Luciano, his body was brought back to the United States. He was buried in Madonna Cemetery in Fort Lee, New

Jersey. If one visits his grave site, one will not find a headstone for Joe Adonis; instead, there is one for Joseph Antonio Doto. Who said you can't go home again?

Not all deportees were driven out of the United States by the Justice Department; others left to escape indictment. In addition to Vito Genovese, they included Johnny Torrio, Meyer Lansky, and Doc Stacher.

Johnny Torrio, boss of the Chicago *Outfit*, who left the United States before the others, departed not only because of a failed 1925 attempt to kill him, but also because he could no longer stand Mafia violence. Prior to leaving with his wife and mother, he appointed Al Capone as the head of the Outfit in Chicago: "It's all yours, Al. Me? I'm quitting. It's Europe for me." [5] Not many men would leave behind a business that annually grossed $70,000,000 in 1925 dollars, estimated to be $1,241,304,000.00 in 2024 dollars. Though Capone honored Torrio as his boss and mentor, the money that Torrio turned over to him whetted his appetite for even larger sums. Torrio didn't mind: he had enough to last for generations. All he wanted was to enjoy Italian sunshine, the country's harvest of fresh fruits and vegetables, and the finest cuisine of the best restaurants. However, in 1928, dark political shadows threatened Torrio's ideal retirement. He believed he would become a target of Mussolini, who was cracking down on the Mafia with Fascistic brutality. He decided to return to America and settle in Brooklyn as an honored member of the National Crime Syndicate. Unfortunately, his return did not go unnoticed by law enforcement officials in the nation's capital. In 1936, he was tried for income tax evasion (the Justice Department's sure-fire way of convicting mobsters). After all his appeals failed, Torrio was sent to prison in 1939 for two years. Though he had cut off business ties with Capone in 1925, he was hit with paying for a Capone tax delinquency in 1940. A *New York Daily News* headline read: "U. S. Sells Capone Land for Taxes." [6] The property, consisting of twenty-eight acres in St. Petersburg, Florida, was jointly owned by Capone, Torrio, and two other mobsters; it was sold in 1940 to pay off tax liens. The property had been purchased for $48,000 and the liens amounted to $14,475. Throughout history, Mafia bosses and their next-in-line have been tied together by prosecutors whether they like it or not.

Though Torrio had escaped Italy to avoid being brutalized by Mussolini, Vito Genovese was determined to take his chances with the Italian dictator. It was a better bet than remaining in New York, where he would have been tried and imprisoned for murder. Soon after arriving in Italy, he began ingratiating himself with Mussolini while making money for both of them. Genovese was an opportunist par excellence.

Another self-deportee: Doc Stacher, whose original name was Gdale Oistaczer, was born in 1902 in a part of Ukraine that later fell under Polish control. When he was ten years old, he and his family immigrated to Newark, New Jersey. As an ambitious teenager driven by poverty and contempt for the law, he became a ruthless pushcart thief. His thievery came under the purview of Longy Zwillman, eventually known as the Al Capone of New Jersey. Zwillman showed the young man the foolishness of his ways: there was a lot more money to be made from illegal gambling than robbing pushcarts. He would become one of the country's premier gambling masters, eventually running the Sands and the Fremont casinos in Las Vegas. He also invested in various commercial properties and nightclubs. A nephew of his told me that Stacher once refused to seat his good friend Frank Sinatra in a Stacher-owned nightclub because the singer had not called earlier to make a reservation.

After Stacher was accused in 1952 of not paying income taxes for the years 1933 through 1941, the government perked up and began eyeing his entire criminal career. The IRS hit him with a bill for $340,000, which Stacher promptly paid. That same year, he was indicted for illegal gambling. He took off for Vegas, but after working out a deal with prosecutors, he returned to New York in 1953. He pleaded guilty to twenty charges, paid a $10,000 fine, and received a one-year suspended sentence. Stacher got off easy, and he was nearly euphoric as he returned to the world of legal gambling. Then, in 1956, disaster knocked on the door of his private world: the US Immigration and Naturalization Service (INS) revoked his citizenship for failing to disclose his criminal record in 1930, after he had become a citizen of the United States. The federal government sought to deport him to Poland, but because the country was run as a communist one, Stacher could not be deported: there was a United States law that no one could be deported to a country controlled by communists, so Stacher stayed put, a man without a country. Then in 1964, he was convicted of tax evasion and given a choice: go to prison or find another country that would offer him citizenship. As a Jew, he was entitled to become an Israeli citizen under that country's Law of Return. The Israeli law gives the right of citizenship to individuals who have at least one Jewish grandparent and/or who are married to a Jew. The law has a provision that citizenship can be denied to anyone who engages in anti-Jewish activity, presents a hazard to public health or the security of the state, or has a criminal record that could endanger public welfare. The latter, for reasons undisclosed, never came into play in the case of Stacher. In fact, he lived peacefully in Israel for the rest of his life. The only embarrassment he suffered occurred after being conned by a rabbi who was a member of the Knesset. The rabbi asked Stacher for $100,000 to ensure that full citizenship would be granted to the American gangster. The rabbi did not use the money to bribe anyone; instead, he used it to build a kosher hotel in Jerusalem. Stacher sued the rabbi and eventually got his money back, but not before being ridiculed in the press for being conned. How could a big shot American gangster be fooled by an unimposing rabbi.

Following Stacher's death by heart attack on February 28, 1977, Jack O'Brian, in his syndicated "Voice of Broadway" column, wrote that Stacher was "a genial, shrewd, witty gent who could be homicidally tough." [7]

A failed attempt at self-deportation: Meyer Lansky would attempt to follow in the footsteps of his pal, Stacher. On February 19, 1971, a subpoena was issued for Lansky to appear before a grand jury in Miami, Florida that was investigating skimming at the Flamingo Casino in Las Vegas. Lansky said he was too ill to make the journey from Israel, where he and his wife had been residing as tourists. The court issued a date for a second appearance, but Lansky remained in Israel. On March 25, he was charged with conspiring with others to skim money from the Flamingo and was liable for charges of tax evasion. Thereafter, his American passport was revoked, and he was ordered to return it to the US Embassy in Israel. Its personnel would arrange for Lansky to be flown to the United States. Two decades earlier, the Department of Justice had attempted and failed to deport Lansky; now like a fickle parent, it wanted its prodigal son at home. Lansky, who had led a quiet life in Israel, suddenly became a notorious celebrity: reporters and paparazzi, like a herd of horses and yapping dogs, raced after him as if he were a fox on the run. Lansky attempted to evade the pack. Moving from hotel to hotel he could not find peace. Finally, a friend suggested a secluded hotel in Herzliya, but he could not burrow into safety for long. His whereabouts had been discovered. Finally, he and his wife moved into an expensive house with state-of-the-art security in an exclusive neighborhood populated by ambassadors. Several newspapers wrote blisteringly mean-spirited articles about Lansky. Ma'ariv, however, agreed that if Lansky gave it an exclusive interview, its article would be fair and balanced, which it was. In places, it was almost excessively sympathetic to the poor man's flight and advocated for his right to become an Israeli citizen. The task of seeking citizenship for Lansky fell to Dr. Yosef Burg, Israel's interior minister, who privately called upon Golda Meir, asking about giving Lansky Israeli citizenship. Meir, preoccupied with more important issues of state, showed no interest in Lansky until Burg mentioned the word Mafia. Her eyebrows shot up, and she declared, "No Mafia in Israel!" [8] Robert Lacey, in his biography of Lansky, *Little Man*, writes: "[Meir] was lobbying the Nixon Administration in Washington to supply Israel with more Phantom F-14 jet fighter bombers. Israel needed these, she maintained, to counter the arrival of new Soviet weaponry on the Suez Canal, and the theory subsequently arose that Mrs. Meir's no Mafia decision amounted to a trade-off—Meyer Lansky for Phantom Jets." [9]

On March 22, 1972, the case of Meyer Lansky vs. the State of Israel was brought before the Israeli High Court of Justice. On September 11, the chief justice of the court issued the court's decision: no citizenship for the criminal Lansky. Eight days later, a cartoon appeared in the *Miami News* of Lansky carrying a suitcase in a desert; standing behind him in the sand is a stereotypical gangster wearing an ostentatious black-and-white striped suit with shoulders that would be the envy of a professional football player. In front of the two men are a pair of Arabs in native robes, one of whom says to the other, "His name is Meyer Lansky and he says he'll make use an offer we can't refuse." [10] Lansky would briefly become a version of the Flying Dutchman: no place to rest his weary head. He flew to a series of South American countries, but thanks to pressure from the US Justice Department and the revocation of his passport, Lansky's only option was to return to the United States. Teddy Lansky, Meyer's wife, was in New York, and as soon as she learned her husband would be returning to Florida, she boarded a plane to Miami. For reporters and photographers, Teddy would be the best thing, absent her husband. After deplaning, she attempted to rush through the airport to a waiting limo. However, she was surrounded by what she regarded as a pack of howling hyenas. A female reporter from WCKT-TV elbowed her way close to Teddy and proceeded to ask her a series of provocative questions. She ended her questions by calling Teddy a Godmother as if Teddy were Mrs. Vito Corleone. Rather than replying, Teddy spat on the woman's face: her way of uttering No Comment.

Though the government had brought in its best prosecutors and stacks of what it thought were definitive evidence of skimming and tax evasion by Lansky, the case was rotting like overripe fruit. The prosecutors had brought in an obese gangster from the Witness Protection Program to testify against Lansky. He was Fat Vinnie Teresa, 325 pounds of insatiable criminality. Lansky's attorney punched so many holes in Teresa's testimony that the witness proved to be an embarrassment for the prosecution. Realizing that the government's case had miserably failed, Solicitor General Robert Bork threw in the towel, and a smiling Lansky left the courtroom. Ironically, the man who wanted to nail Lansky was Attorney General John Mitchell, who was convicted of perjury, conspiracy, and obstruction of justice in the Watergate Scandal. He was sentenced to two and a half to eight years in prison, but the sentence was reduced to one to four years in prison; Mitchell served nineteen months, Lansky none. For all to see, Lansky proved to be the real Teflon Don, a man of inestimable power and resources. He was, after all, not only the man who created the Mafia, but as Carl Sifakis declared: "its real godfather." [11]

Deportation or jail was what those men faced. Either one was a means of keeping gangsters off the streets of America. For some of those who were deported, criminal enterprises in another land proved an irresistible temptation. Luciano, for example, exported heroin from Italy into the United States. Genovese, who had deported himself, operated as a criminal in Mussolini's Italy, returning to the United States after the Second World War and becoming an even more powerful criminal than he had been in the 1930s. Lansky was so cleverly secretive that the government was never able to find foolproof evidence of any criminality. Torrio, Stacher, and Adonis seemed to have lived off the money they generated as criminals in the United States, without having to resort to their criminal methods.

Most deportations were legally carried out; others were ad hoc, expedient, and wrathful. Take the case of Carlos Marcello, Mafia boss of New Orleans. Attorney General Robert Kennedy, the Mafia's foremost enemy, decided to get Marcello and rid the country of him. On April 4, 1961, Kennedy had the government grab the gangster and deposit him in the jungles of Guatemala of all places. He had been born in Tunisia.

It took Marcello two months to make his way back to the United States. He was determined to get even. He aligned himself with another Kennedy enemy: Jimmy Hoffa. Kennedy had been heading what was known as the Get Hoffa Squad in the Justice Department. Kennedy's efforts were so extreme that several of his deputies believed he was violating the constitution. When Hoffa and Marcello spoke on a bugged telephone line, they were overheard saying that if you want to kill a dog, you don't cut off its tail; you cut off its head. Killing the president would rid themselves of his attorney general, and the prosecutions of the Mafia would come to an end.

In their book *Fatal Hour: The Assassination of President Kennedy By Organized Crime*, authors Richard N. Billings and G. Robert Blakey (who was chief counsel of the House Select Committee on Assassinations and previously Special Attorney in the Organized Crime and Racketeering Section of the Criminal Division of the US Department of Justice under Attorney General Robert F. Kennedy) conclude that President Kennedy's murder was planned and carried out by Marcello and his conspirators. They claim that their book lays out convincing evidence that has been corroborated by numerous sources, including official records.

In his 1994 autobiography *Mob Lawyer*, attorney Frank Ragano writes that he relayed a message in 1963 from Teamsters Union leader Jimmy Hoffa to Marcello and Santo Trafficante, the Mafia boss of Florida, urging the two Mafia bosses to kill Kennedy. Ragano later claimed that four days before Trafficante died, the mob boss described to Ragano how he and Marcello organized the murder of President Kennedy.

Marcello was the exception to the concept that deportations were an effective means of getting rid of gangsters. Like wasps, the Mafia will attack those who attack them.

Notes

1 T. J. English, *Havana Nocturne: How the Mob Owned Cuba—and Then Lost It to the Revolution* (New York: Harper, 2008), 28.

2 Tim Newark, *Lucky Luciano: The Real and the Fake Gangster* (New York: Thomas Dunne Books, 2010), 240.

3   Olindo Romeo Chiocca, *Mobsters and Thugs: Quotes from the Underworld* (Toronto: Guernica, 2000), 59.

4   Carl Sifakis, *The Mafia Encyclopedia* (New York: Checkmark Books, 1999), 4.

5   Paul Sann, *The Lawless Decade: Bullets, Broads and Bathtub Gin* (Courier Corporation, 1957), 111.

6   https://www.newspapers.com/article/daily-news-us-sells-capone-land-for-ta/54115188/

7   10 Intriguing Facts about Mobster-Gambler Joseph "Doc" Stacher – It Really Happened! (gambling-history.com)

8   Robert Lacey, *Little Man* (New York: Little, Brown & Company, 1991), 334.

9   Lacey, *Little Man*, 334.

10 Dan Wright, *Miami News*, September 19, 1972.

11 Sifakis, *The Mafia Encyclopedia*, 205.

10

The Biggest Hit on Television

In 1950, television was new and exciting. If you didn't have a TV set, you watched one at a neighbor's house or apartment, a bar, or at an appliance store. Though there were a limited number of shows to be seen in grainy black-and-white, the US Senate offered a compelling show that turned out to be the biggest hit of the year. The show was known as the Kefauver hearings to investigate organized crime in America. It was headed by Senator Estes Kefauver, and the committee was officially named the Senate Special Committee to Investigate Crime in Interstate Commerce. Like a touring theatrical company, the Kefauver Committee held hearings in fourteen cities and presented the public with guest appearances by 600 witnesses, many of whom were top Mafioso from around the country.

By 1951, the hearings were so popular that Kefauver appeared as a guest on television programs, such as *What's My Line?* He was voted one of the ten most admired men in the world, along with Albert Einstein, Pope Pius XII, and Douglas MacArthur. As a result of his soaring popularity, Kefauver ran for the Democratic presidential nomination in 1952 and 1956. The Democratic Party couldn't afford to ignore the senator from Tennessee, so they handed him the party's vice-presidential nomination in 1956, not exactly a consolation prize. Unfortunately for the crusading senator, former general Eisenhower, who was known for leading the Crusade in Europe (the title of his 1948 memoir) that disposed of Hitler and his Nazi henchmen, had won his second term as president. Years later, his vice president, Richard Nixon, would resign as president on August 8, 1974, the only president to do so.

By March 1951, six months before the committee packed up its files and briefcases, 72 percent of Americans were familiar with the Kefauver Committee's work. Junior and senior high schools often dismissed their students early so they could watch the hearings on television. So glued to the hearings were vast numbers of people that a Brooklyn blood bank ran low and had to install a television set to attract blood donors. Thereafter, the number of viewers with needles in their arms shot up by 100 percent. *Life* magazine claimed that the hearings had spawned more conversations than any other topic.

For organized crime, the hearings were worse than an embarrassment: they led to jail terms, assassinations, and loss of business. Indeed, the hearings proved to be a pivotal threat to the mob's ability to continue doing business as usual. Among the most powerful Mafioso to appear before the committee were Willie Moretti, a New Jersey mob underboss and Frank Sinatra's godfather; Frank Costello, the prime minister of the Underworld, who had controlled as many politicians and judges as any political boss; and Joe Adonis, an illegal gambling tycoon, who primarily operated out of New Jersey, but who had points in casinos in Las Vegas and Cuba. Politicians, such as New Jersey Governor Harold G. Hoffman and former New York mayor William O'Dwyer, following their testimony, saw their ambitions for higher office wither and die. O'Dwyer, who had been appointed ambassador to Mexico by President Truman, was so evasive during his testimony that the committee initiated a perjury action against him. His reputation shattered, O'Dwyer was forced to resign his diplomatic post.

Another politician, Democratic majority leader Scott Lucas, urged Kefauver not to investigate a Chicago police scandal. Kefauver, a man on a mission, said no. Once documents about the scandal were reported in the Chicago newspapers, Lucas's career nose-dived like a Kamikaze, leading to the election of Senator Everett Dirksen, who famously enunciated his three laws of politics: "1. Get elected. 2. Get re-elected. 3. Don't get mad, get even." When asked about his principles, he responded that he was a man of "fixed and unbending principles, the first of which is to be flexible at all times." [1]

The country was absolutely fascinated by the hearings. Office workers out for lunch gathered in large groups in front of the windows of appliance stores where dozens of television sets had been stacked up and were showing the hearings. The stores piped the audio outside on multiple speakers. The hearings may have resulted in a larger television-buying season than during Christmas. One young man excitedly phoned his mother, saying, "Gee, Mom, you shoulda seen it. Gangsters and crooks everywhere. They were telling Mr. Kefauver about murders and losing millions of dollars gambling. It was just like the movies." [2]

One example of the testimony that fascinated the young man was that of Allen Smiley, former friend and partner of Bugsy Siegel: "He refused to explain why, after Siegel's untimely death, a Houston man had asked him to come down to Texas, and why Smiley had shuttled back & forth between Houston and the Beverly Club, the gambling casino near New Orleans controlled by New York's Frank Costello. Smiley's reward for these questionable services was 'a small piece of property.' What kind of property? 'Well, it may have had a few oil wells on it,' said Al, and departed with curled lip." [3]

The committee members, though accused of political grandstanding, actually uncovered significant crimes. In 1950, the committee members were astonished at the amount of illegal gambling it had discovered in Florida. The committee had traced organized crime's political connections to Florida governor Fuller Warren, a Democrat, who accused Kefauver of being a crazed Caesar. The governor flung his accusations like mud pies, but nothing stuck to the senator. Instead, Warren's illicit gambling activities resulted in his political downfall.

The Committee moved to Chicago, where it heard testimony from local gangsters who paid off politicians. The police, in particular, were said to be bribed and not only to look the other way, but to be part of various gambling enterprises. Chicago papers reported that one-fifth of the city's police captains would have to be fired. Among those law enforcement officials who were questioned was Dan Gilbert, chief investigator for the state attorney in Illinois. Known as the richest cop in the state, he claimed that all his wealth came from his astute stock market picks and his even more astute betting on sporting events. He was not the only senior law enforcement official who was revealed to have accumulated significant wealth on a small salary: the chief of detectives in New Orleans managed to stuff his safe deposit box with $150,000, though his monthly salary was a piddling $186.

When Chicago Outfit member Jake "Greasy Thumb" Guzik appeared before the committee, he recited his Fifth Amendment right not to incriminate himself as if it was his mantra. Carl Sifakis writes, "Guzik appeared without a lawyer and said he'd learned all about the Fifth by watching television." [4] Apparently he wasn't listening very closely, for when he declared his right not to incriminate himself, he said he did not want his responses to discriminate against him. And, of course, his responses were not all discriminatory.

After the committee set up shop in New York City, interest peaked. New York was home to the largest number of Mafia families, and the cast of witnesses would be worth every second devoted to watching the hearings. One witness who had absolute star appeal was Frank Costello. The committee identified Costello as the leading figure in the nation's gambling syndicates, a boss of bosses. He appeared in a well-tailored, bespoke silk suit and looked the part of a corporate CEO. However, unlike a polished CEO, he spoke in a gruff, gravelly voice that may have inspired Marlon Brando's portrayal of Vito Corleone in *The Godfather*. When asked what he had done for America, he said he had paid his taxes. That was it. His lawyer had objected to his client being seen on camera, so the committee decided to just show his hands. While Costello muttered often unintelligible answers to questions, his hands demonstrated his nervousness by repeatedly clenching and twisting. His hands looked as if they might suddenly go berserk and start wrestling, one with the other. Costello was not only queried about his control of numerous gambling enterprises but how he managed to control the selection of judges to various courts in New York. As the questions grew more probing, Costello's hands clenched more quickly and looked like they might leap from the witness table and strangle a few of the senators. Frustrated and angry by the grilling he received, Costello refused to answer any further questions, twice left the hearing room, and was cited for contempt, resulting in a jail sentence. Costello's cousin, Willie Moretti, who was underboss of the Genovese crime family in New Jersey, provided some comic relief. Because he was Frank Sinatra's godfather, he was one step removed from celebrity status and was seen as a high-profile witness. However, suffering from syphilis, his thoughts erupted in uncensored comments that made the Mafia very nervous. When a senator asked if he was a member of the Mafia, he said no. Why? Because he didn't have a membership card. And how could you be a member of anything without a membership card? The Mafia is not known for its sense of humor, and none of the five family members were guffawing. It's a serious organization, not like Shriners who wear funny hats and drive tiny cars during Shriner circuses. Prior to departing the hearing, Moretti complained that that only reason he was accused of being a Mafioso was because he earned a high interest rate on money he loaned. Of course, you don't have to be a member of the Mafia if you're a loan shark. However, you would probably have to pay them a percentage of your earnings just to stay in business. Moretti was well liked by the soldiers, capos, and bosses, but they all knew that at some point he might be pulled in by the cops and blab about scams and murders. Better to shut him up. On October 4, 1951, at 11:28 in the morning in Joe's Elbow Room restaurant in Cliffside, New Jersey, Moretti was shot and killed. Out of respect, the shooters did not shoot him in the back of his head. Here's to you, Willie: they shot him in his face and forehead. A photo of the crime scene appears in the first *Godfather* movie.

In addition to Costello, Moretti, and other Mafia bosses, the committee interrogated many who were Mafia associates. When it came to Mafia associate Virginia Hill, the former girlfriend of criminal mastermind Bugsy Siegel, the committee, reporters, and TV viewers were in for a treat. She arrived like a movie star, an elegant mink stole draped over her shoulder, and a wide-brimmed hat giving a look of glamour and mystery. Once seated and questioned, she denied having any knowledge of Siegel's criminal activities and had nothing to say about Adonis and the Fischetti brothers, all of whom had been her lovers. She claimed that all of her money came from betting and as gifts from Siegel. As the questioning grew more intense, her patience and frustration became apparent. Her responses were sharp and often sarcastic. She lived up to the mob's opinion of her as being a tough broad who did not suffer disrespect with coolness and poise. Some of the questions she was asked were about Joe Epstein, a major Chicago bookie for the Outfit and protector of Hill.

The following exchange occurred between Hill and Senator Charles Tobey of New Hampshire:

> Senator Tobey: "But why would Joe Epstein give you all that money, Miss Hill?
> Virginia Hill: "You really want to know?"
> Senator Tobey: "Yes, I really want to know."
> Virginia Hill: "Then I'll tell you why. Because I'm the best cocksucker in town."

Senator Kefauver, in response to raucous laughter, pounded his gavel and shouted, "Order. I demand order!" [5] Hill was dismissed and strode out of the hearing ready to do battle with anyone who got in her way. Say hello to

New York City reporter Marjorie Farnsworth, who asked Hill a provocative question. Hill responded by slugging Farnsworth with a hard right cross to the reporter's jaw. Then turning to the scrum of reporters and photographers, she yelled, "You goddamn bastards. I hope an atom bomb falls on all of you." [6] She was escorted to a waiting car and driven off.

The committee's hearings did more than provide entertainment for millions of television viewers; they were an irritant to J. Edgar Hoover, head of the FBI, who for years had denied the existence of organized crime. The unguent he applied to that irritant was an announcement that the FBI would go after members of organized crime. Very few mobsters believed him.

Indeed, Frank Costello may have guffawed, for he was allegedly blackmailing Hoover about his gay, clandestine relationship with Clyde Tolson, while also providing Hoover with inside information on fixed horse races. Costello's FBI spies may have alerted him to a letter Hoover wrote to Tolson and found in the institution's files: "Words are mere man-given symbols for thoughts and feelings, and they are grossly insufficient to express the thoughts in my mind and the feelings in my heart that I have for you. I hope I will always have you beside me." [7]

Following the end of the committee's run, *Time* magazine published the following: "'The evidence demonstrates quite clearly that organized crime today is not limited to any single community of any single state, but occurs all over the country.' Big Crime's big men know each other, deal with each other, meet frequently, 'and on occasion do each other's dirty work when a competitor must be eliminated, an informer silenced, or a victim persuaded.' What the committee found most shocking was 'the extent of official corruption and connivance in facilitating and promoting organized crime.' In every big city, top mobsters remain 'immune from prosecution and punishment.' The committee found cops bribed, political leaders bought or pressured, sheriffs indifferent or even encouraging, well-meaning officials made helpless by others who worked hand-in-glove with crime. 'At the local level, this committee received evidence of corruption of law-enforcement officers and connivance with criminal gangs in practically every city in which it held hearings.'" [8]

The committee's work did not result in any important legislation. Kefauver had proposed the creation of a federal crime commission, but (surprise, surprise) it was opposed by Hoover and the Department of Justice. However, as a result of the committee's work, its second chairman, Herbert O'Connor, sponsored legislation to control the distribution of illegal drugs, which was achieved by increasing the budget of the Narcotics Bureau.

The real star of the hearings was television. It was seen as a hot new medium for generating significant publicity for politicians and investigations. From Joe McCarthy to Senator McClellan to the Watergate Hearings and many other events, television was the exciting medium that informed and occasionally misled a fascinated and often gullible public.

Notes

1 www.azquotes.com/author/3997-Everett_Dirksen.com
2 http://www.time.com/time/magazine/article/0%2C9171%2C805815%2C00.html
3 http://www.time.com/time/magazine/article/0%2C9171%2C805815%2C00.html
4 Carl Sifakis, *The Mafia Encyclopedia* (New York: Checkmark Books, 1999), 194.
5 Jeffrey Sussman, *Sin City Gangsters: The Rise and Decline of the Mob in Las Vegas* (Lanham, MD: Rowman and Littlefield, 2022), 14–15.
6 Sifakis, *The Mafia Encyclopedia*, 195
7 https://slate.com/culture/2011/11/clint-eastwoods-j-edgar-hoover-were-j-edgar-hoover-and-clyde-tolson.html
8 http://www.time.com/time/magazine/article/0%2C9171%2C805815%2C00.html

11

Another Committee Hearing

The Kefauver hearings generated so much publicity that it fueled political careers. So why not another hearing, perfect for television, and one that would shoot other ambitious politicians into national prominence? The new committee was officially named the United States Senate Select Committee on Improper Activities in Labor and Management, not exactly a name suitable for newspaper headlines; and for TV newscasters, it was a mouthful. So, for the sake of brevity, the media referred to it as the McClellan Committee, named for its chairman, Democratic Arkansas senator John L. McClellan. The committee was born on January 30, 1957, and breathed its last on March 31, 1960.

Among the rising stars on the Committee, other than McClellan, were Democratic senators John F. Kennedy (who would go on to be president), Sam J. Irvin (who would gain international fame for leading a senate committee's investigation of the Watergate scandal that led to the resignation of President Richard Nixon in 1974), and Frank Church (who in 1975 chaired the senate's Church Committee, officially known as the Senate Select Committee to Study Governmental Operations with Respect to Intelligence Activities). The rising star of the Republicans was Arizona Senator Barry Goldwater, who would run for president in 1964 and lose in a landslide to Lyndon Johnson. The shooting star about to flame out was Republican Wisconsin Senator Joseph McCarthy, whose name had already become notorious for his anti-communist witch hunts that often prosecuted people not only for being communists but also for associating with them. The committee's chief counsel was Robert F. Kennedy, who would serve as attorney general in his brother's administration, then serve as senator from New York, and finally be assassinated while running for president in 1968.

The committee hearings did not feature as many colorful gangsters as the Kefauver committee, but it was just as disruptive to the mob. Of the 1,526 witnesses, 343 expressed their patriotic reliance on the Fifth Amendment. Watching tough guys repeat themselves over and over again is less than exhilarating. One would have expected them to curse out the interrogators, at least for the benefit of the television cameras. The dullness of repeatedly hearing that nobody wanted to incriminate himself can put an audience to sleep.

What finally caught the committee's attention was the battle between Dave Beck, president of the Teamsters Union, and Jimmy Hoffa, a tough fireplug of a man who wanted the presidency for himself. And why not? Being number two is no fun, especially if you think you're smarter and tougher than your boss. Hoffa had enlisted the help of New York mobster Johnny Dio.

(Here I have to admit a personal interest, for my father was threatened by Dio. My father owned two garment factories, and Dio wanted one of his fake paper-thin Teamsters' locals to represent my father's workers, who had voted against joining the union. The union was called a paper union because it existed only on paper. Unable to unionize my father's workers, Dio insisted that my father retain his trucking company. If the trucking company wasn't retained, someone else could be found to run my father's company, probably before his body was fished out of the East River. With no protection from corrupt cops who had less than an ardent desire to round up Mafioso, my father reluctantly retained Dio's trucking company.)

The committee became an enthralled audience when listening to audio tapes of Dio and Hoffa conspiring to take over the taxi cab industry of New York City. They planned to unionize 30,000 taxi drivers by force, if necessary, and extort millions of dollars. The drivers would become members of a paper union.

However, before they could put their plan into action, Hoffa and Dio conspired to unseat Beck by creating fifteen paper unions, and those unions would cast their votes for Hoffa to be the union's international president. Once he was boss, Hoffa would be free to participate in whatever scams and schemes the Mafia wanted to execute. And as a man who owed his career to mob favors, Hoffa was their perfect stooge. Senator McClellan accused Hoffa not only of attempting to take over the Teamsters by using support from Dio's paper unions but also of attempting to take over the economy of the entire country. He could do so, the committee claimed, by setting up a secretive private government. One element of Hoffa's plan, according to the committee, involved giving a $400,000 loan to the International Longshoremen's Association, thus allowing Hoffa to control the indebted union. Accusations were one thing; proving it in court was something else.

Beck knew that in addition to Hoffa being in the committee's crosshairs, he was also a target. Like a wild animal sensing that hunters were closing in on him, Beck took off for parts unknown. He remained in self-exile for a month. Dio was no slouch either, and he quickly tore up the charters of several paper unions. Poof!

What paper locals you talkin' about?

The remaining paper locals suffered mysterious losses of their records.

Someone must have brokin' into the offices and cleaned out the desks.

Who did it?

You got me.

Without the records, a frustrated Chief Counsel Robert Kennedy berated witnesses, often browbeating and insulting them. The thirty-one-year-old chief counsel was all piss and vinegar. He wanted total victory, complete surrender of the enemy, and the establishment of crime-free unions. His performance was riveting television. His anger became so intense, he looked like he might throw ashtrays at smart-alecky witnesses. Kennedy's interrogations of Beck and Hoffa were a TV producer's dream come true. Kennedy's behavior was said by many to be over the top; he was cuttingly vicious, so much so that civil libertarians, who were no friends of organized crime, accused Kennedy of attempting to violate the rights of witnesses. Self-righteous editorialists nearly wept that Kennedy was engendering sympathy for unsympathetic characters by badgering them and letting his anger rule his professional responsibilities. Nevertheless, he continued to browbeat witnesses. So easy to anger was Kennedy that he became a target for some of the more aggressive witnesses, especially Jimmy Hoffa, who was like a kid poking a hornet's nest with a stick. In response, Kennedy's anger would fire up beyond a boiling point, and he would have to be cooled down by McClellan, who—in one instance—grabbed Kennedy's sleeve to prevent him from rushing forward to attack Hoffa. Kennedy then resorted to insulting Hoffa, who grinned as if dealing with a temperamental child. Sometimes Hoffa would mutter a remark, and Kennedy would demand to know what Hoffa had said. Hoffa would merely smile. For a politician, Kennedy was proving to be especially impolitic. His father, Joseph P. Kennedy Sr., upon watching his son's behavior on television, flew to Washington to confront him. Nothing must be done to endanger the political prospects of older brother John F. Kennedy, who was planning on running for president of the United States. The future president, unlike Robert, proved to be a picture-perfect candidate, a man of charm, good cheer, and ingratiating wit.

Meanwhile, TV viewers remained engaged, if not transfixed, by the battle between Hoffa and Kennedy. If Hollywood had wanted to cast a tough guy to run a union, it could not have done better than pick Jimmy Hoffa. He seemed like the corrupt union boss in the movie, *On The Waterfront*. Hoffa was not only made for the union, he was made for television. Not trusting the committee's intentions, Hoffa tried to bribe an aide to one of the committee's members: a standard practice of many mobsters facing the possible loss of freedom. The bribe was reported, and Hoffa was arrested. He denied that he had tried to bribe anyone on the committee and was subsequently acquitted. Beck faced his own self-made problems: less than a week after he returned from exile, he admitted to the committee that he had taken an interest-free loan of $300,000 from the union. Not only had Beck not repaid the loan, but he and several of his cohorts were recipients of additional loans amounting to $900,000. The committee did what Hoffa had been trying to do; it got rid of Beck, indicting him for tax evasion on May 2, 1957. Then in 1959, he was prosecuted for racketeering and embezzlement. He was sentenced to three years in prison, which he entered in 1962. After serving thirty months of his sentence, he was paroled. A year after President Ford pardoned former President Nixon, Ford signed a pardon for Beck. Following the pardon in 1975, Beck lived in a basement apartment in a house he had built for his sister in the 1940s. He received an annual Teamsters pension of $50,000 and invested much of it in parking lots. By the time he died in 1993 at age ninety-nine, he left an estate worth millions of dollars.

Dio was in and out of prison throughout the 1950s and 1960s. By 1957, he was serving time for bribery and conspiracy. A court arranged for his parole so that he could testify before the committee. For two hours, sitting beside his lawyer, he recited the Fifth Amendment 140 times. One response from a committee member caused reporters to erupt in laughter: Dio was asked how he pronounced his surname, Dioguardi. Dio covered his microphone and whispered to his lawyer. A committee member then asked if he "needs to consult your attorney on that?" [1] Dio left the hearing an extremely angry man and attempted to flee before photographers could snap his picture. Unfortunately for Dio, International News photographer Jim Mahan captured an image of the snarling Mafioso with a cigarette dangling from his curled angry lips as he pushed photographer Stanley Tetric out of his way. Dio then raged at the photographers: "You sons of bitches. I got a family!" [2]

Dio not only didn't take kindly to being photographed; he didn't like being the subject of investigative newspaper columns. A target of his fury was nationally syndicated labor-relations columnist Victor Riesel. On April 5, 1956, at 3 a.m., Riesel, who the following week was to testify before a grand jury about mob infiltration of labor unions, had just left Lindy's restaurant, following a late-night radio program on which he had been the guest host. Riesel did not see a slim man in a blue and white jacket suddenly rush out of an alley of shadows by a nearby theater. The man, without saying a word, threw a vial of sulfuric acid on Riesel's face; Riesel, suffering from fire-like burns, shouted: "My gosh! My gosh!" [3] The acid burned his eyes, and his forehead and cheeks felt as if they were on fire. His secretary managed to drag him into Lindy's, where several people poured water over his face and eyes. But fearing they might inflict additional damage to his eyes, they ceased pouring water: a well-meaning mistake. Later, at St. Clare's hospital, doctors tried to save his sight. It was too late: he was blind and scarred.

When the event became known, there was an immediate outcry to arrest the man who had thrown the acid as well as the person who might have ordered the attack. The *Daily Mirror* newspaper, which published and syndicated Riesel's column, offered a $10,000 reward leading to the arrest and conviction of the attacker. That was followed by the Newspaper Guild of New York, the New York Press Photographers Association, the Overseas Press Club, and the New York Newspapers Association adding an additional $5,000 to the reward. The amount soon rose to $41,000.

The FBI, after interviewing several Mafioso, was able to identify Abraham Telvi, an associate of the Lucchese crime family, as the attacker. Following the attack, Telvi was angry: acid had splashed onto one side of his face and ruined his jacket. In addition to the $500 he was paid for the attack, he demanded

$50,000. Dio initially agreed to pay Telvi but told him it would take two weeks to get the money. On July 28, 1956, Telvi was shot to death, and his body was dumped on a street on the Lower East Side. On August 29, Dio was arrested for conspiracy to attack Riesel. He pleaded not guilty, posted a $100,000 bond, and was released. The FBI had been able to identify Dio because Gandolfo Maranti, who had been hired by Dio to get someone to attack Riesel, confessed his part in the crime. After being hired by Dio, Maranti contacted Dominick Bando to assist in hiring a hitman. Telvi was the fool who agreed to carry out the attack. At trial, Maranti and Bando were found guilty; a judge sentenced Maranti to eight to sixteen years, while Bando was given a sentence of two to five years, plus an additional five years for contempt of court.

Dio's lawyer, using a series of motions, was able to delay his client's trial for five months. By the time a trial commenced, Maranti recanted his testimony implicating Dio and claimed he had no idea who had ordered the attack on Riesel. Without that testimony, there were no charges against Dio. The government, thereafter, gave up trying to nail Dio for the attack. Robert Kennedy, fearful that his own children might become victims of an acid attack, arranged for them to wait in their principal's office every day after school. A car picked them up and drove them home. When President Eisenhower was informed of the acid attack on Riesel, he was appalled and said something must be done to rid labor unions of racketeers.

As the McClellan committee concluded its investigations of Mafia infiltration of labor unions, it received plaudits from editorialists and political leaders for performing a valuable public service. The committee then decided to extend its investigation into the activities of several mobsters, and so it was granted a one-year extension. Through the spring and summer of 1959, the committee subpoenaed several high-level mobsters to testify before the committee. The marquee names were Anthony "Tony Ducks" Corallo, Anthony "Tony Pro" Provenzano, Joey Glimco, and Carlos Marcello.

*Anthony "Tony Ducks" Corallo was boss of the Lucchese crime family and controlled much of the trucking in New York's garment center and the city's construction unions, including painters and textile workers. He was Dio's partner in setting up paper unions. He received the sobriquet Tony Ducks from his former boss Tommy "Three Fingers Brown" Lucchese, who said that Tony ducks his convictions again and again. On August 15, 1959, Ducks appeared before the committee which wanted information about his alleged theft of $70,000 from one of the Teamster locals. Addressing the committee, he recited his Fifth Amendment right 120 times, much to the frustration of investigators. However, over the next few decades, he was unable to duck convictions and was repeatedly jailed. Then on November 19, 1986, Ducks and other Mafia bosses were found guilty during the famous Mafia Commission Trial. On January 13, 1987, he was sentenced to 100 years in prison, so much for ducking.

*Anthony "Tony Pro" Provenzano, whom the FBI suspected of ordering the murder of Jimmy Hoffa, was president of Local 560 of the International Brotherhood of Teamsters in Union City, New Jersey. He appeared before the committee and when asked about his position as a Teamster official, his relationship with Jimmy Hoffa, and his role in the Genovese crime family, he recited his Fifth Amendment right forty-four times. (Not even a close second to Ducks). Provenzano, like Ducks, was not able to continually duck prison. While in prison, he and Hoffa became enemies because Hoffa denied Provenzano a Teamster pension. Following his release from prison on December 23, 1971, Hoffa wanted to regain his presidency of the union. However, his replacement as union president, Frank Fitzsimmons, was far more pliable to Mafia demands than Hoffa had been. The Mafia, therefore, preferred Fitz to Hoffa. Hoffa appealed to his old allies in the Mafia to support his taking over the union again. They refused. An investigator later said that Hoffa was pissing against the wind. Yet, Hoffa would not give up. He called Provenzano and told him he would run again for president and dump his old Mafia pals.

Provenzano replied that if Hoffa didn't accept Fitz as the president, he would come to Hoffa's home and yank out his guts and kidnap his grandchildren. ⁴

It wasn't Hoffa who turned the tables on Provenzano; it was the law. On June 14, 1978, Provenzano was convicted of the murder of Teamster official Anthony Castellitto, and sentenced to life in prison. As if that were not sufficient, he was sentenced on July 10, 1979, on RICO charges and sentenced to twenty years in prison. He died in prison on December 12, 1988, aged seventy-one.

*Joey Glimco (a name that one DJ said sounds like the name of a glam rocker) had the dubious billing of being known as Chicago's top labor racketeer in the 1950s. He oversaw all of the Chicago Outfit's labor racketeering. He could not have done so without conspiring with Jimmy Hoffa, who was glad to do favors for Glimco in return for his help in maintaining control of the Teamsters. Hoffa never interfered with or objected to Glimco using the Teamsters as his cash cow. According to an article in *Time* magazine, "The Chicago Crime Commission estimated his rake-in from all sources—union salaries, business profits, kickbacks, extortion payoffs—at $70,000 a month." ⁵

The committee couldn't wait to get its hands on Glimco's personal financial records as well as those of Teamster Local 777, which he controlled. At first, Glimco claimed he didn't have any records, then said he would let the committee look at the records only in his presence. As one might have expected, when Glimco finally turned over the records, there were large gaps; missing was any information that might have led to indictments. When seated as a witness in front of the committee, he continued the Mafia tradition of reciting his Fifth Amendment right against self-incrimination; he did so eighty times. His very presence and attitude seemed to have annoyed McClellan and Kennedy. The following exchange took place:

> **Kennedy:** And you defraud the union by charging the construction of your own home to the union, just like Mr. Dave Beck?

Glimco: I respectfully decline to answer because I honestly believe my answer might intend to incriminate me.

Kennedy: I would agree with you.

McClellan: I believe it would.

Kennedy: You haven't got the guts to answer, have you, Mr. Glimco?

Glimco: I respectfully decline to answer because I honestly believe my answer might intend to incriminate me.

McClellan: Morally, you are kind of yellow inside, are you not?

Glimco: I respectfully decline to answer because I honestly believe my answer might intend to incriminate me. [6]

Glimco's testimony before the committee was an inspiration for further investigations, which began in the fall of 1961. Federal investigators concluded thereafter that Glimco owed $144,000 in back taxes, following which a grand jury indicted him on seventeen counts of income tax evasion. On December 17, 1964, Glimco pleaded not guilty. After years of delay, he finally went on trial and a federal district court found him liable for $94,465 in back taxes, fines, and penalties. He directed his attorney to appeal, and the case went to the US Supreme Court. The court rejected his appeal on December 9, 1968. Then, without a legal leg to stand on, Glimco refused to pay the government, so in February 1970, the government sued to seize his home and automobile. Glimco, seeing that all exits from this ongoing turmoil were closed, finally gave up and agreed to pay. In May 1973, he paid the government more than $200,000, which included interest, fines, and penalties. The amount of money he made from 1961 to 1973, based upon his previously reported earnings, was significantly greater than $200,000.

*Carlos Marcello, Mafia boss of Louisiana, may have been the most consequential Mafioso in American history for his alleged complicity in the murder of President Kennedy. But several years before that horribly fateful day, Carlos Marcello appeared before the committee on March 24, 1959. He faced his two most determined enemies: Robert F. Kennedy and Senator John F. Kennedy. Like his Mafia brethren, he refused to answer questions, citing his Fifth Amendment right not to incriminate himself. Whatever antipathy he had developed toward the government after he had been interrogated by the Kefauver Committee in 1951 was magnified as a result of being aggressively questioned by the relentless Kennedy brothers. The committee branded Marcello "one of the worst criminals in the country." [7]

By 1961, Marcello's hatred of the Kennedy's was a fire out of control, for on April 4, 1961, Attorney General Robert Kennedy had the US Justice Department arrest Marcello at a New Orleans government immigration office. Once in custody, he was flown to Guatemala and dumped like a pile of garbage. It took Marcello two months to get back to New Orleans, where he expressed his undying hatred for Robert Kennedy. As if pouring oil on Marcello's fiery hatred, the government again tried to deport him. However, Marcello's lawyer, Jack Wasserman, beat back the government's efforts. In a telephone conversation bugged by the FBI between Marcello and Jimmy Hoffa (whose hatred of Kennedy matched Marcello's), the two discussed killing their nemesis, but finally agreed that if you want to kill a dog, you don't cut off its tail; you cut off its head. Marcello and Hoffa were not the only ones who wanted to be rid of the attorney general. Because Kennedy had gone after the Mafia as an avenging angel, prosecuting hundreds of members of organized crime, the Mafia would have cheered his demise. Kennedy's prosecutions not only led to convictions but destroyed illegal businesses or significantly curtailed profits. How could the Mafia let one man threaten their power and empires that produced billions of dollars?

In its 1978 investigation of the assassination of John F. Kennedy, the House Select Committee on Assassinations issued a report that found that "Marcello had the motive, means, and opportunity to have President John F. Kennedy assassinated, though it was unable to establish direct evidence of Marcello's complicity." [8]

In *Fatal Hour: The Assassination of President Kennedy By Organized Crime*, a book written by G. Robert Blakely (chief counsel of the House Select Committee on Assassinations) and Richard N. Billings, the authors write that President Kennedy's murder was planned and carried out by Marcello and his conspirators. They affirm that their conclusion is based on official records and numerous sources. Independent investigator and author John H. Davis presented credible evidence in his book *Mafia Kingfish* that Marcello was the force behind the conspiracy to murder President Kennedy. And Frank Ragano, who was an attorney for Florida mob boss Santo Trafficante, wrote that Jimmy Hoffa had urged Marcello and Trafficante to kill the president.

Following the assassination of his brother, Robert Kennedy suspected that his relentless pursuit of the Mafia, first as chief counsel for the McClellan Committee and then as attorney general, may have resulted in the murder of his brother. But four years earlier, Kennedy was still his brother's devoted acolyte and resigned from the committee to manage John's presidential campaign. Whatever goals he pursued, Robert was indefatigable. The Mafia was also indefatigable. It remained as opportunistic as ever and adapted to the climate of investigations. Bosses and capos used the same means they always had to achieve their goal: bribery, sweetheart deals, threats, and murder. Gangsters kept right on roaring down their roads of golden opportunities, avoiding government roadblocks and speed bumps, thriving all the way to offshore banks.

Notes

1 https://www.youtube.com/watch?v=3aIUB_BmzzU "Johnny Dio Takes the Fifth Amendment."

2 *Life Magazine*, "Strong Arm Dio Doing What Comes Naturally," August 19, 1957, 36.

3 A. H. Raskin, "Thug Hurls Acid on Labor Writer," *New York Times*, April 16, 1956, 1.

4   https://www.nytimes.com/1975/08/05/archives/threat-to-hoffa-in-74-is-reportd.html

5   https://content.time.com/time/subscriber/article/0,3333,009,825,881,00.html

6   Richard D. Mahoney, *Sons & Brothers: The Days of Jack and Bobby Kennedy* (New York: Arcade Publishing, 1999), 30.

7   http://www.onewal.com/kef/kef3b.html

8   "I.C. The Committee Believes, on the Basis of the Evidence Available to It, That President John F. Kennedy Was Probably Assassinated as a Result of a Conspiracy. The Committee Was Unable to Identify the Other Gunmen or the Extent of the Conspiracy," Report of the Select Committee on Assassinations of the US House of Representatives (Washington, D.C.: United States Government Printing Office, 1979), 149, 171.

12

Unseating the Lord High Executioner

Albert Anastasia (the Lord High Executioner, the Mad Hatter, the One-Man Army, the Earthquake) enjoyed killing. The more people he killed or had killed, the happier he was. If his appetite for murder was not satiated, he didn't become morose; he simply found someone deserving of death. One example of his spontaneous impulse to kill occurred in 1952. There was a young man: a naïve amateur sleuth named Arnold Schuster, who when not sleuthing made his living as a clothing salesman, not working for his cousin Lincoln Schuster of Simon and Schuster publishers. One day, Schuster was on his way home when he spotted a man whom he thought was Willie "the Actor" Sutton, a notorious bank robber and clever prison escapee. He followed Sutton to a garage, where the bank robber was working on a car engine. After a few minutes, Sutton began charging the car's battery. Schuster hurried off to a public phone and called the police. He told them that he believed he had found Willie Sutton, wanted for bank robbery and for having escaped from prison. Officers quickly arrived on the scene. Sutton didn't deny his identity and did not put up a struggle. Though a career criminal, he was not a violent man. And though he would often flash a pistol at stunned and frightened bank tellers and customers, the pistols were never loaded. Sutton was arrested, and Schuster was celebrated as a citizen hero, profiled in nearly all of New York City's newspapers and interviewed on local TV news programs. He received a thousand-dollar reward. When asked if he was scared of being assaulted or killed by a Sutton friend, he said no, though he admitted to receiving threatening phone calls. Upon watching a TV news interview of Schuster, Anastasia flew into a rage. "I can't stand squealers! Hit that guy!" [1] Anastasia yelled to one of his associates. On March 8, 1952, a carefree Schuster was walking home after speaking with four of his friends, whom he agreed to meet after he changed out of his business suit. As he approached his home, a man wearing a dark hat with the brim pulled down over his forehead came toward him. From a raincoat pocket, the man pulled out a .38 caliber pistol and rapidly fired four shots. Two bullets penetrated Schuster's groin, then a single bullet smashed into one eye and another bullet into the other eye: a Mafia message that he should not have spoken about what he saw after spotting Sutton. The gunman quickly ran off, but not before a few witnesses saw him and were subsequently able to give cops a description of the fleeing gunman. Neighbors stood around stunned; an elderly woman wept; there lay the once affable neighbor Arnold Schuster sprawled and bleeding on a sidewalk.

From eyewitness testimony and information surreptitiously obtained from informants, the FBI identified Frederick J. "The Angel" Tenuto as the probable killer. Tenuto was already on the FBI's Ten Most Wanted List. He had a reputation as a gun-crazy killer who enjoyed nothing more than being a feared hitman. Coincidentally, he had served time with Sutton in the Philadelphia County Prison, from which both men had escaped on February 10, 1947. Sutton had been something of a mentor to Tenuto, but was never able to convince his student that the best crimes do not involve violence. Nevertheless, Tenuto was an attentive student as Sutton instructed him and ten other convicts about how to plan and carry out a successful prison escape. Sutton and his band of convicts spent fourteen months digging a tunnel that spanned ninety-seven feet from inside the prison to freedom beyond the prison's walls. The tunnel was wide enough for each man to crawl through comfortably, and they even illuminated their journey with electric lights they had installed. As successful as the escape was, freedom was ephemeral. Tenuto was soon captured and locked up, but escaped again after stabbing a guard who refused to turn over a set of cell block keys.

Anastasia, who liked criminals who were as violent as he was, provided Tenuto with protection and a place to hide following the hit on Schuster. And since Tenuto had admired Sutton and regarded him as a friend, he had been happy to carry out Anastasia's order. However, as heat from law enforcement increased, Tenuto was sent out of town to be hidden by other Mafioso. It didn't matter, for the police and FBI continued putting a great deal of pressure on the Mafia, shutting down illegal gambling dens, arresting bookmakers, and loan sharks. Tenuto was an obstacle to smooth-running operations. For that reason alone, he had to be eliminated. In addition, Anastasia was worried that if Tenuto was arrested and interrogated, he might flip and implicate the Lord High Executioner. Anastasia, therefore, arranged for Tenuto to come to his office, ostensibly to discuss tactics for a successful escape and provide the killer with some money. However, according to an FBI file, Anastasia had Tenuto killed. And Joe Valachi, a Mafia soldier who was flipped by the Justice Department, told investigators that "To cover himself, Anastasia had Schuster's killer Frederick Tenuto, murdered. At the time, Tenuto was being sought by the FBI for breaking out of prison. His body has never been found." [2] After informants told the FBI that Tenuto was dead, the agency finally removed his name from its Ten Most Wanted list in 1964.

By Mafia standards, it was acceptable that Anastasia had Tenuto killed. What was not acceptable was the murder of Arnold Schuster. Anastasia had violated a cardinal Mafia rule: We don't kill civilians unless they pose a threat to our operations. Lansky, Luciano, Costello, and Genovese had always known that Anastasia was kill crazy, but he had served many useful purposes, such as being co-head (along with Lepke Buchalter) of Murder Inc. He was also extremely loyal to Luciano and had promised in the early 1930s that he would kill anyone who tried to get in Luciano's way. Investigators had speculated whether it was Anastasia's position as boss of Murder Inc. that made him love killing, or was it his love of killing that made him an efficient boss of Murder Inc.?

Regardless, Anastasia had violated a rule succinctly stated by Bugsy Siegel: when Del Webb, a nervous builder of the Flamingo Hotel and Casino, asked Siegel if the mob would kill him as a result of cost overruns, Siegel replied, "Don't worry. We only kill each other." [3] By his intemperate order to have Schuster hit, Anastasia had convinced the mob bosses that he was unhinged, capable of committing acts that would endanger their own lives and operations. Anastasia had more than earned the sobriquet, the Mad Hatter.

Added to his murderous impulses was also a constant fever of paranoia. In some cases, his paranoia was justified; in others, it was difficult to understand. In 1955, Anastasia was facing trial for tax evasion and had no desire to spend years in prison. He was determined to eliminate any witnesses whom the prosecutors might call to the stand, even witnesses who would testify they knew nothing of Anastasia's criminal activities. One such person, not a criminal and not a member of the Mafia, was a plumber who had worked on Anastasia's twenty-five-room, 6,529-square-foot mansion in Fort Lee, New Jersey. How could he be considered a danger to Anastasia remains a mystery. The plumber, Charles Ferri, had been paid more than $8,700 for the work he had performed, and he knew nothing about Anastasia's criminal activities. However, when Anastasia learned that Ferri was to be called as a witness, he not only had Ferri killed but also had the man's wife killed. The bodies of the two were never found, but investigators were sure they had been murdered after examining the blood-spattered Ferri home in Miami. It was more reasonable for Anastasia to assume that some angry gangsters might testify against him, so he had two of them killed. They were the Macri brothers, Vincent and Benedicto. Vincent was shot and folded into a car trunk in the Bronx, while Benedicto's dead body was dumped in the Passaic River. According to Carl Sifakis, "At Anastasia's trial [without any witnesses to testify against him], the crime boss suddenly entered a guilty plea and was sentenced to one year in prison. It was unlikely the government would have accepted what amounted to a plea bargain had it still had a full arsenal of witnesses against him." [4]

The mob approved of Anastasia's skill in ridding himself of possible unfriendly witnesses, but it was his impulsive murderous behavior that continued to worry them. Any boss who went around ordering the murders of people who did not threaten the Mafia would bring unnecessary heat on the gangsters. A clock was ticking, and only a final excuse was needed to pull some triggers that would unseat the Lord High Executioner. It was what Vito Genovese was maneuvering to accomplish. But he would need the approval of Costello, Luciano, and most of all, Lansky.

Genovese also wanted to eliminate Costello, boss of the Luciano crime family, so he could assume the role of boss for himself. Costello had been appointed boss after Luciano was deported by Governor Dewey, and Genovese had run off to Italy to avoid being indicted and tried for murder. After Genovese succeeded in having witnesses killed, he returned to the United States knowing that there was no corroborative evidence against him for a murder trial. Back in the United States, Genovese had a burning ambition to take over the Luciano family, but Anastasia remained an obstacle. The Mad Hatter had always been loyal to Luciano, having told him back in the 1930s that he would do anything, kill anybody to help Luciano be the boss of bosses. Luciano, Costello, and Lansky worried about Anastasia's behavior, but the Mad Hatter was nevertheless a powerful deterrent to a mob war. Genovese would need a powerful excuse for killing Anastasia, an excuse that all the bosses would accept. Fate would comply with his wishes. But first, he would tempt fate by having his subordinate, Vincent "the Chin" Gigante, kill Costello.

On the evening of May 2, 1957, as Costello was coming home to his Central Park West apartment, a three-hundred-pound Gigante (who had turned into a fat man to disguise himself) approached Costello in the lobby of his apartment building. As Gigante pointed a gun at Costello, he called out, "This is for you Frank." Costello quickly turned his head to see who had spoken to him just as Gigante fired a single shot that grazed Costello's head. The lumbering fat man then quickly waddled out of the building and got into a waiting car. Gigante went into hiding, where he would lose the layers of fat that had disguised his muscular boxer's body. Though Costello was not killed, he decided that he valued his life more than being boss of the Luciano family and so he retired. He also refused to testify against Gigante.

Anastasia now wanted to take revenge on the man who had ordered the shooting of his cohort, even if that meant going to war against Genovese. Joseph Bonanno, boss of his own eponymously named crime family, was concerned that the hot-tempered and impulsive Anastasia would trigger a Mafia war. He decided to intervene before any more shots were fired. He persuaded Anastasia to wait until the commission members could be assembled and decide on a remedy. Anastasia said he was willing to wait, but not for too long.

Genovese knew that Anastasia might send some hitmen to end his life at any time. But then Anastasia made a fatal mistake: he told Lansky, who controlled the biggest casinos in Cuba, that he wanted a greater share of the casino profits than Lansky was giving him. Lansky said no. It was impossible. He was already distributing money to various gangsters who had points in his casinos. Anastasia, not one to accept refusal, said he didn't care: he would build his own casino to compete with Lansky's. Anastasia had foolishly just issued a contract on his own life. Lansky wasted no time in letting Luciano and Costello know what Anastasia intended. They were furious. But rather than give Genovese the contract to hit Anastasia, which might be perceived as a preemptive attack that could trigger open warfare, they gave the contract to Joe Profaci, the olive oil king of America, who was boss of his own eponymously named crime family. Profaci, in turn, subcontracted the hit to the three wild Gallo brothers: Crazy Joey, Kid Blast, and Larry. The brothers brought in a fourth hitter, Carmine "the Snake" Persico. (There may have been a fifth member, but his name is unknown).

On October 25, 1957 at 10:20 a.m., Anastasia entered the barbershop of the Park Sheraton Hotel on Seventh Avenue between 55th and 56 Streets. His bodyguard had parked Anastasia's car in an underground garage and then went for a walk. (He would later maintain that he had never left his home in New Jersey on that day.) As Anastasia took his usual seat in chair number four, barber Joseph Bocchino greeted him with his customary warmth, asked after his health, told him he looked well, and then placed a hot towel over his face. Anastasia took particular pleasure in a professional shave. As Bocchino stropped his straight razor, two masked gunmen rushed into the shop; their faces were covered just below their eyes with bandanas. They pulled out guns, aimed at Anastasia's head, and fired ten shots, hitting Anastasia in his head, right hip, and left hand. Like a raging wounded lion, Anastasia sprang from his chair to attack his attackers. In his furious confusion, he rushed at his attackers in the mirror image of them opposite his chair. His attackers fired a few more bullets into him until he collapsed onto the floor. Blood pooled around his fallen body as his killers and their backups fled the scene, racing into a nearby subway station, lost in a crowd of commuters. A proud Joey Gallo later bragged to his gang, "You can just call the five of us the barbershop quintet." [5]

The unseating of the Lord High Executioner opened the door for Genovese to take over the Luciano family without having to worry that Anastasia might seek revenge for the attempted assassination of his friend and fellow boss, Frank Costello.

Genovese was too pleased with himself to realize that a plot against him was brewing. Costello, Lansky, Luciano, and Carlo Gambino, all of whom disliked and distrusted Genovese, would soon engage in a plot to set him up. And they would do so without firing a single shot. A clever act of betrayal was less likely to cause a war than an assassination. The bosses figured they could smoothly operate without a power grab by a man who wanted to be boss of bosses.

Genovese hadn't learned from the fate of Salvatore Maranzano, who had also wanted to be a boss of bosses.

Notes

1   Carl Sifakis, *Mafia Encyclopedia* (New York: Checkmark Books, 1999), 355.
2   https://web.archive.org/web/20110707163240/http://www.arnoldschuster.com/valachi_hearings.htm
3   Dean Jennings, *We Only Kill Each Other* (New York: Pocket Books, 1967 and 1992), 17.
4   Sifakis, *The Mafia Encyclopedia*, 11.
5   Nicolas Gage, *New York Magazine*, July 10, 1972, 44.

13

The Apalachin Disaster

After the embarrassing raid on the Apalachin Conference in 1957 by New York State Police, Mafioso had as much desire to attend large conferences as a herd of cows desire to enter a slaughterhouse. Mafioso meeting in Apalachin had no idea they had been set up by the most powerful mobsters in America.

On November 14, 1957, more than one hundred members of the Mafia attended a conference at the estate of Joseph "the Barber" Barbara at 625 McFall Road in Apalachin, New York. The meeting was to be held at the behest of Vito Genovese, ostensibly to discuss gambling, narcotics, labor relations, loan sharking, and bookmaking, but really to formalize his position as a boss of bosses. As the recent self-declared head of the Luciano crime family, Genovese believed he was not only at the top of the Mafia pyramid but also at the top of his game as a brilliant strategist: he had avoided being tried for murder, had profited in Italy during the reign of Mussolini, and forced Costello to abdicate his position as boss. If pride precedes a fall, then Genovese was on his way to being a perfect example of a fallen leader. He had no foreknowledge that his crown would soon rust and be a mockery of his power.

Missing from the conference of the most powerful one hundred mob bosses were Frank Costello, Meyer Lansky, Doc Stacher, Lucky Luciano, Moe Dalitz, Longy Zwillman, and Carlos Marcello, all of whom had shared interests that could be threatened if Genovese became the supreme boss. In addition to their shared interests, Lansky, Stacher, Luciano, Zwillman, Dalitz, and Marcello were all aligned with Costello and were determined to get even for the failed hit on him. Though all those in attendance were Italian, the four non-Italians, the Jewish Stacher, Dalitz, Zwillman, and Lansky had so many joint operations with the other conferees that their presence would not have been odd. In fact, it struck some of those in attendance as indeed odd that some of the most powerful men in organized crime were absent. The Italian and Jewish gangsters had been partners in crime since the beginning of Prohibition, and their partnerships continued. If the absence of powerful mob bosses portended something worrisome, no one seemed to sense it: an unheeded warning.

It was understood by all that Luciano, who was living in exile in Italy, could not have attended. What they didn't know was that Luciano had warned several gangsters from western states not to attend. Nevertheless, he had an ally at the conference who acted as eyes and ears for the missing mobsters. He was crafty Carlo Gambino, who knew of the planned raid but attended the conference not only as a spy but also so that Genovese would not grow suspicious about Gambino's loyalty. Some skeptics have asked why the absentee gangsters and Gambino would risk having the state police raid the conference and garner information about the Mafia. John Davis in his book *Mafia Dynasty*, writes: "It was worth the risk to ensure the undermining of Genovese. Almost anything was worth the risk if it would diminish Genovese's power and curb his ambitions." [1]

When one of the attendees named Bartollo Guccia had gone outside Barbara's house to check on the delivery of provisions for the mob's feast, he noticed a roadblock at the end of the driveway. In addition to the roadblock, there were more than a dozen state police milling around as if preparing for an attack. Guccia rushed inside and alerted everyone. It was like shouting fire in a crowded theater. Panic ensued, and what followed was low comedy. Dozens of men in their fifties and sixties came tumbling out of windows like clowns at a circus. However, they weren't wearing clown costumes, but fine, bespoke Italian silk suits. Picking themselves up, they scattered, running like victims of the Keystone Cops through the nearby woods. Some were cursing, others merely huffing and puffing. Many were not exemplars of physical fitness. Their thin-soled, custom-made loafers had not been made for dashing over rough ground. Burrs, sticker bushes, and thorns scratched and tore at them; a gauntlet for exasperated runners. Only a few of them avoided the clutches of the law, but they all cursed Genovese for their humiliations. The state cops were like cowboys rounding up cows from a stampede. The escapees were finally corralled into Barbara's home, where they were required to give up their wallets, containing drivers' licenses and more than $300,000 in cash. Was the money to be given to Genovese as tribute for a new boss? Humiliation was piled on humiliation. This was no way to treat men of respect. In a tapped telephone conversation, Sam "Momo" Giancana had the following exchange with Stefano Magaddino, boss of the Buffalo crime family: Magaddino: "It never would've happened in your place." Giancana: "You're fuckin' right it wouldn't. This is the safest territory in the world for a big meet . . . . We got three towns out of Chicago with the police in our pocket. We got this territory locked up tight." [2]

Among those rounded up were the most prominent Mafia bosses, such as Santo Trafficante, Carlo Gambino, Carmine Galante, Joseph Profaci, Vito Genovese, Jerry Catena, Joseph Bonanno, and fifty-one lesser-known bosses. When questioned, each of them said they were visiting Barbara because he had been sick and they came to cheer him up. However, when checking the records of those who were netted, their stories had as much substance as a rainbow. And was their sick friend in need of $300,000? He didn't live like a man in financial need.

Police discovered that "Of 58 [detainees], 50 had arrest records, 35 had convictions, and 23 had served prison sentences. Eighteen had been involved in murder investigations, 15 [were] netted for narcotic violations, 30 for gambling, and 23 for illegal use of firearms." [3] Twenty of the attendees were charged with obstruction of justice for lying about the purpose of the conference. In January 1959, they were found guilty, sentenced to prison terms of three to five years, and each was fined $10,000. However, all the convictions were later overturned on appeal.

Not only was the raid and arrest a tremendous embarrassment for Genovese, but also for the FBI, which had either downplayed the existence of the Mafia or pretended it did not exist. After reams of publicity about the raid, FBI director J. Edgar Hoover announced to reporters that he had created the Top Hoodlum Program, and his agents would begin arresting top hoodlums throughout the country. Fearful of FBI penetration of the Mafia, the bosses closed their membership books. It was as if they had attempted to build a Great Wall of China around their operations. It wasn't until 1976 that the Mafia began accepting new members known as made men.

One person who was not embarrassed by the raid was state trooper Edgar D. Croswell, who had been aware since 1956 that Barbara associated with Mafioso. During that year, he had pulled over Carmine Galante, who had been driving without a license and had a long rap sheet. From that date onward, Croswell took an interest in Barbara and those who visited him. Shortly after guests arrived at Barbara's estate for the Mafia conference, Croswell drove by and was impressed by the vast parking lot of shiny new Cadillacs and Lincoln Continentals parked around Barbara's house; he ran the license plates and discovered what he had anticipated: the cars were registered to known criminals. A convention of criminals! He called for backup, and a posse of state troopers arrived, some armed with shotguns. Of course, no one in the media knew that Lansky and his cohorts had alerted Croswell that the Mafia was to have a summit meeting.

Lansky, as crafty as a fox, chose to have Genovese humiliated in the eyes of all Mafia bosses and then set him up for a long prison term. It was a more effective means of getting rid of Genovese than having him whacked. Humiliation and imprisonment would cause Genovese more suffering than a bullet fired into the back of his brain. Besides, an assassination could lead to a mob war and that would only serve to have a negative effect on business.

Following Genovese's humiliation at Apalachin, Lansky, Costello, Gambino, Stacher, and from a distance, Luciano, put in place their plan to have Genovese arrested as a drug dealer. It would be the final blow, a symbolic coup de grâce, to Genovese's career as boss. The lynchpin of their plan was an imprisoned drug dealer named Nelson Cantellops.

In the book *Meyer Lansky: Mogul of the Mob*, the authors write: "The bait was set by one of Meyer's couriers, Nelson Cantellops. Meyer had been angry with Nelson after he got himself mixed up in running drugs at the same time he was working for Meyer. When Nelson was caught, Meyer refused to help him, and he went to Sing Sing on a narcotics charge. Then, using his brother, Jacob, Meyer passed the message to Nelson that he would forgive him if he would take on a little job. Cantellops was promised a pension for life. So our friend Nelson Cantellops, despite the danger he would be in, asked for an interview with the Narcotics Bureau of New York and told an agent, George Gaffney, that he would provide information about how Genovese and his partners were smuggling narcotics from Europe into the United States." [4] In addition to a lifetime pension, Cantellops was given $100,000 following his testimony in court against Genovese. If his testimony led to a conviction, he was promised a reduced sentence. Altogether, it was an irresistible deal. Together, Lansky, Costello, and Luciano contributed $50,000, and Gambino put in the additional $50,000. Almost as an afterthought, Costello contributed an additional $25,000 to ensure that Gigante, who had tried to kill him on orders from Genovese, would also be convicted and imprisoned. On July 7, 1958, Genovese and twenty-four others were arrested for drug dealing. On April 17, 1959, following testimony by Cantellops, Genovese and his cohorts were all convicted. Genovese was sentenced to fifteen years in prison. The conviction was appealed, and the appeals failed. On February 11, 1960, Genovese began serving his sentence in the Atlanta Federal Penitentiary in Georgia.

Organized crime detective Ralph Salerno told me that it is "unbelievable that an insulated Mafia boss would get involved in such a drug deal. He would have isolated himself through the layers of low-level Mafioso and associates." [5]

To note that Genovese was furious would be an understatement. He raged against his enemies, real and imagined. He would settle scores. He ordered the murder of Anthony Carfano for not attending the Apalachin conference. Genovese believed that Carfano had not attended because he knew in advance of the police raid. On September 25, 1959, bullet-riddled bodies of Carfano and his mistress were found in Carfano's Cadillac on a street in Jackson Heights, New York. From his prison cell in 1962, Genovese ordered the murder of Anthony Strollo. Genovese believed that Strollo had been a conspirator in the plot to set him up for the alleged drug buy. On April 8, Strollo left his home and was never seen again. FBI officials speculated that he was buried in a Mafia burial ground or that his body had been dismembered and compacted at an auto graveyard. Genovese was not only determined to kill those who had betrayed him at Apalachin and set him up for the drug conviction; he also arranged to have Ernest Rupolo murdered for testifying against him during a 1944 murder trial. Rupolo's body was a tabloid picture of a traditional Mafia hit: his decomposing corpse was found in Jamaica Bay, his hands had been tied together, and his legs were sealed in cement.

Even knowing that Genovese had ordered the murder of men whom he thought had betrayed him, prison inmate Joseph Valachi was stunned when Genovese grabbed his head and firmly implanted a kiss of death on his lips. He was a crazy man, Valachi later told detectives. Valachi, who had survived Mafia wars, was not about to let himself be taken without a fight: he would kill the hitman before his own life could be snuffed out. Why had Genovese ordered the death of Valachi? Because Genovese suspected that Valachi had made a deal to testify against him in exchange for a reduced sentence. When Valachi heard through the prison grapevine that Genovese offered $100,000 to anyone who would kill him, he knew that his life in the prison yard could quickly end with a shiv in his guts. The prison yard could be a jungle where an insulting word or a dirty look or bumping into someone and not apologizing could result in a quick death. One had to be continuously on guard; one needed allies just to survive. And never let yourself be surrounded by an enemy's allies. Valachi entered the prison yard not knowing if he would make it back to his cell alive. A $100,000 bounty was irresistible; Valachi had killed for a lot less. On June 22, 1962, Valachi spotted an inmate he thought was Joseph DiPalermo, the inmate whom Valachi suspected would try to kill him. An unarmed Valachi looked around for a weapon (he should have been carrying a shiv) and saw a pipe lying on the ground next to some construction work. He picked up the pipe and held it against his thigh. He approached his target with the stealth of a leopard, then quickly sprang into action. Again and again, the pipe smashed into the cranium of the man Valachi had assumed was DiPalermo. He had killed the wrong man! "Shit," he muttered. Murdering another inmate in prison, and you just made yourself eligible for the death penalty. Valachi needed to save himself, to find a way out. He became a government witness and the first man to break the code of omerta in a public setting. His testimony would electrify the media and introduce the term Cosa Nostra into the lexicon. His testimony was like an earthquake that shook the foundations of organized crime and caused its members to attempt to be so low profile as to be nearly invisible.

Valachi's boss, Genovese, could not catch a break. That damn Valachi had made himself untouchable and revealed secrets that no man of respect would ever have spoken. Genovese had been humiliated at Apalachin, then set up in a drug deal, and finally held up to ridicule for not succeeding in having Valachi murdered. Genovese was like a character out of a Greek tragedy, his anger consuming the organs of his body. His health began to deteriorate, and he was sent to the United States Medical Center for Federal Prisoners in Springfield, Missouri. In 1969, on Saint Valentine's Day (a milestone in Mafia history from forty years earlier), Genovese died of a heart attack. He, like many other Mafioso, is buried in Saint John Cemetery in Middle Village, Queens, New York.

Notes

1   John H. Davis, *Mafia Dynasty* (New York: HarperCollins Publishers, 1993), 83.
2   Carl Sifakis, *The Mafia Encyclopedia* (New York: Checkmark Books, 1999), 20.
3   Sifakis, *The Mafia Encyclopedia*, 19.
4   Dennis Eisenberg, Uri Dan, and Eli Landau, *Meyer Lansky: Mogul of the Mob* (New York: Paddington Press, 1979), 248.
5   Interview with the author in 1990.

14

The Canary Sang

Joe Valachi was the first Mafioso to take a sledgehammer to Omerta. His shattering testimony to a senate investigations committee transfixed senators, spectators, reporters, celebrities, and TV audiences. His riveting performance inspired a scene in *Godfather II*, but his testimony was combustible to the Mafia, where it ignited contempt and fury. So much so that the Mafia put a $100,000 contract on Valachi's life. To the mob, Valachi was a Judas who had to be crucified as an example to other possible turncoats.

Who was this notorious betrayer against the codes of Omerta? Joseph Valachi was a low-level gangster in the Genovese crime family, who never gained greater status than being a soldier. He was born in 1904 to Italian immigrants and grew up in the Italian section of East Harlem. His father was a sadistic alcoholic whose only gift to his son was a shot of Scotch on Christmas morning. Angry, deprived of parental affection, and bitingly poor, a young Valachi embarked on a career of crime. He became a getaway driver for a gang of smash-and-grab thieves known as the Minutemen, because they could carry off a theft in one minute or less. Having learned that police took five minutes to respond to one of their robberies, the Minutemen perfected a technique of smashing a store window, usually with a brick, then clearing it out of valuable merchandise, such as furs or jewelry, before the police arrived. Valachi then drove like a speed demon, never causing an accident or mowing down pedestrians, while making a clean getaway. His star status as a consummate getaway driver became known among professional criminals, and he was soon in demand by other gangs. However, the police slammed on the brakes of Valachi's criminal career in 1921. He was arrested that year, did little time, and was arrested again in 1923. He plea-bargained, pled guilty, and was sentenced to eighteen months in Sing Sing prison. He was an obedient prisoner, never arguing with guards and never fighting with other prisoners. As a reward, he was released after serving half of his sentence. In prison, Valachi learned of scams that were more sophisticated than his smash-and-grab thefts. He became a dealer in forged gas stamps with a partner named Frank Luciano. With the money he earned, Valachi invested $15,000 in opening a restaurant in 1946. He and partner Luciano named the restaurant the Lido, and it became a popular hangout for mobsters. It was located in the Castle Hill section of the Bronx, where it also attracted off-duty cops. Valachi and his partner were each taking in $2,500 a week from the restaurant. However, Valachi soon discovered that Luciano's share of profits exceeded his own: Luciano was feeding his gambling habit with embezzled funds. Is there anything worse than a thief stealing from another thief? Valachi didn't think so and pounced on Luciano, nearly beating him to death. This was a no-no in Mafia law.

Members of the Mafia are not supposed to beat up one another. In fact, there is a stringent hands-off policy. If a member has a complaint against another member, he must submit his complaint to his boss for mediation. Without such a policy, there would be chaos, and the structure of the Mafia would shatter and fall apart. The five Mafia families in New York and a sixth in New Jersey need to cooperate with one another not only to keep the cash flowing but also to keep the cops from descending on them. If one member killed another, that would instigate an investigation that might shut down some profitable operations. Price fixing, respected territorial borders, and peace among family members are all necessary for the smooth running of illegal operations. Valachi's violent reaction to Luciano's embezzlement had to be addressed, mediated, and peacefully settled.

Valachi was called to a meeting. No Mafioso wants to be called because he may leave the meeting in a coffin. Valachi had no choice but to go, so he nervously went to Duke's restaurant in New Jersey. He knew he had to arrive unarmed, for packing a gun could be misinterpreted. He was escorted to the meeting by Anthony Strollo (aka Tony Bender), a capo, then underboss of the Genovese crime family. (Years later, Genovese would accuse Bender of betrayal and arrange for his death. The same accusation, but not the same outcome, awaited Valachi years later.) Valachi was interrogated by another underboss, Albert Anastasia, a man whose anger could cause the toughest Mafioso to quake, if not wet himself. Anastasia, who had a soft spot for men of violence, decided that Valachi's actions were justified. However, there would have to be a settlement: Valachi was awarded sole ownership of the restaurant but had to pay Luciano a small amount of money.

"Afterwards Joe went upstairs to a private room and met up with Genovese, whom he had last seen almost ten years before. Their meeting was cordial, and Genovese even offered to help Joe out of his temporary financial predicament. Unknown to Joe, this was all part of a scheme Genovese was putting in place to regain the loyalty of the soldiers of his old Family. He had a long-term plan to regain control—which he would achieve ten years down the road." [1]

Valachi moved on from assault to murder. In 1952, Lucky Luciano, while in exile in Italy, where he oversaw an international narcotics operation, heard that Mafia soldier Eugenio Gianinni was speaking with federal US narcotics investigators. Such talk could lead to a disaster: a furious Luciano ordered Genovese to have Gianinni killed. Genovese, in turn, gave the murder contract to Anthony Strollo, who passed it to Valachi. As is the custom in the Mafia, murder contracts are handed down through numerous levels to shield the top men from being incriminated. Valachi then gave the contract to his nephew, Fiore Siano, and to a pair of ambitious Harlem gangsters named Joe and Pat Pagano, both of whom hoped that killing Gianinni would be their ticket to becoming made men.

While all three men organized the hit, it was Siano who pulled a deadly trigger, firing bullets that crashed into Gianinni's cranium. Siano was proud of himself, for now he was on his way to becoming a made man. He earned his button in 1954, one of the first new members since the Mafia had closed its membership books twenty-five years earlier.

"Joe Valachi sponsored his nephew, along with the Pagano brothers . . . young men in waiting, who were made into the crime family now referred to as the Genovese or West Side Mob. He joined a crew of hard-nosed guys, under Tony Bender." [2]

Genovese was always ready to carry out murders for his respected boss Luciano. And after he became boss, Genovese issued murder contracts as casually as an exterminator ordering an employee to kill rodents. Steven Franse should have been the last person Genovese ordered killed: he was no rat and had been devoted to Genovese, who trusted him as a loyal soldier. In fact, Genovese trusted him so much that when he fled to Italy in 1937 to avoid being tried for murder in the States, he made Franse caretaker of his various businesses. Franse was honored by the responsibility, carried out his duties efficiently, and regularly sent money to his boss. Franse and Genovese operated several nightclubs in Greenwich Village on East 4th Street as well as a gay nightclub named Club 181 on Second Avenue and 12th Street. Genovese and Franse were not the only partners in the nightclubs: Genovese's wife Anna and John Boggiano were also partners with the two men. In addition to caretaking Genovese's businesses, Franse was tasked with helping Anna, making sure that she was protected at all times. However, Anna was not happy in her marriage, and in 1952, she filed for divorce. Mafia wives were supposed to be obedient; filing for divorce was a blow to a mobster's dignity and a potential threat that might reveal criminal activity. A furious Genovese was not about to agree to a quiet out-of-court settlement. So, the case went to court. And there Anna erupted with narratives about Genovese's businesses, legal and illegal. For any other Mafia wife, such testimony would have resulted in a few lethal head shots. However, Genovese decided the fault lay with Franse. Perhaps Franse had seduced her, though Anna was reportedly having an affair with a woman. Genovese even heard tales of Anna participating in lesbian orgies. It didn't matter; Franse had to go. Again, the reliable Anthony Strollo was given a murder contract: kill Franse! As in the past, Strollo gave the contract to Valachi, telling him that the reason for the hit was that Franse had become a government informer. A thoughtful uncle as ever, Valachi passed the contract to his ambitious nephew Siano. He and Pasquale Pagano set up Franse for the killing. They invited Franse to Valachi's restaurant, where the two killers were lying in wait. On June 18, 1953, while Franse was sitting at a table sipping a brandy, Siano stealthily came up behind him and strangled him.

"Siano [went on to have] a somewhat checkered career in the mob, being arrested numerous times, for burglary and robbery with a gun, and received an eight year stretch in 1954 for violation of the Federal Narcotics Laws. He went down for being, as assistant district attorney Fred Nathan claimed: 'the principal dealer in cocaine along the Eastern seaboard.' Fiore disappeared from Patsy's Pizzeria on 1st Avenue, between 117th and 118th Streets early in 1964. The first pizzeria to open in New York in 1933, it was a preferred mob hangout for the wise guys uptown." [3]

Valachi, for all his good deeds, remained a low-level soldier; he was respected for carrying out hits, but he was not a great earner. And money is the lifeblood of the Mafia. Or as the character Irene (played by Kathleen Turner) says in the movie *Prizzi's Honor*: "The Jews in this business are bad enough, sweetheart, but them Sicilians! They'd rather eat their children than part with money and they are very fond of children." [4]

For a gangster eager to score huge profits, dealing narcotics could be the answer. But Valachi's "actions were drawing the wrong kind of attention. Joe's problems originated . . . from the attention he was receiving from the Federal Bureau of Narcotics. Under their hard-driving boss, Commissioner Harry J. Anslinger, the FBN was feared and despised by the mob. It continually harassed them, often using undercover operatives to infiltrate and gather evidence. It also established a major network of informants that gave Cosa Nostra a constant case of diarrhea. The FBN was the first government agency to recognize the existence of organized crime and no other law enforcement agency had done more to dislocate it. At the end of the day, when all was said and done, Joe was basically a bum. Until [Valachi's senate testimony, the mob] had been so secretive about their existence they made the order of Masons appear to be a bunch of blabbermouths." [5]

After Valachi decided to save himself and cooperate with the Department of Justice, attorney William G. Hundley became his protector and ersatz pal, he said, "We'd put dark glasses and wigs on him and take him to the Roma restaurant. He was a hell of a guy." [6]

"When Hoodlum Joe Valachi appeared before Arkansas Senator John McClellan's Permanent Investigations Subcommittee last week, he rasped out a 31-hour rhapsody of names, crimes and Cosa Nostra syndicate secrets. Valachi's song held nothing new for U.S. lawmen: he had been holding private recitals for them for more than a year. But his testimony might provide some ideas for show biz scriptwriters. Last week he found U.S. Senators treating him with patronizing respect. John McClellan addressed him warmly as 'Joe,' inquired if he wasn't tired from testifying, quickly adjourned the hearings until this week when the mug from the Mafia said he was indeed weary. In fact, Valachi's act was introduced—with some pride—by none other than Bobby Kennedy, Attorney General of the U.S. Boasted Bobby: 'For the first time an insider, a knowledgeable member of the racketeering hierarchy, has broken the underworld's code of silence.'"

"Thinking of Themselves. No one seemed certain just what Valachi's appearance before the committee might gain. Bobby spoke about new wiretap laws and extending immunity from prosecution for racketeers who cooperate with the Justice Department. McClellan said vaguely that he had in mind some kind of law to 'prohibit membership in such a criminal and secret organization as Cosa Nostra.' And Joe Valachi thought organized crime should probably be outlawed—largely because 'the bosses been thinking only of themselves for years.

"But if Valachi's testimony does nothing else, it has already produced a shocking commentary on the underworld jungle in the U.S. prison system." [7]

The Valachi hearing was a magnet for Washington's social elite. There were Ethel Kennedy and Alice Roosevelt Longworth seated like royalty and riveted by Valachi's testimony while having their photos snapped. Ms. Longworth, without the use of a lorgnette, sniffed to reporters that she wanted to "get the smell of it." [8]

"Even Caroline Kennedy's White House kindergarten teacher was there. The Valachi hearings were plainly the place to go in Washington last week. But they were still a pretty shabby show, with hoodlum Joseph Valachi, 60, being fawned over merely because he had turned squealer.

"Valachi seemed to enjoy it thoroughly. Bronzed from a District of Columbia jail sun lamp and sucking a juice-filled plastic lemon to soothe his sore throat, he mumbled a litany of remembered violence on the sidewalks of New York in the '30s. He described the bloody revolution among rival Neapolitan and Sicilian Cosa Nostra families in the New York-New Jersey area that took 60-odd lives with stiletto and chopper, involved intricate double and triple crosses and led to the 'Got Dat, Senators?' With professional nonchalance, Valachi detailed hits (murders) he had a hand in, punctuated his scrambled syntax ('There was this fella named which he died a long time ago') with a solicitous 'got dat clear, Senators?' They sometimes had not. Cried South Dakota Republican Karl Mundt at one murky point: 'You're getting me all confused. It sounds like a Chinese chess game.' To others it sounded more like a fairy tale. Police and gangsters alike scoffed at Valachi's melodramatic recital of his initiation into the mob.

"'This knife and gun business is nonsense—strictly amateur-night material,' said one. Added a cop: 'Valachi must be talking off the top of his head. We know that some of these things can only be hearsay because by his own testimony he was only small potatoes in the mob. He just wouldn't have been privy to what was happening.' Even worse than the stale underworld gossip being mouthed by Valachi was the fact that he got mixed up on names and places." [9]

What the article missed is that Valachi was the first Mafioso to reveal the existence of the secret criminal society and its name, La Cosa Nostra (i.e., our thing). He also provided the senators with an insider's history of the Mafia. Though his testimony led to no immediate arrests of Mafia members, it did cause many bosses to keep their doors locked and shades drawn. When out and about, they sported sunglasses like movie stars pretending to be incognito.

Senators were mighty pleased with themselves after Valachi completed his testimony. At first, they were all in agreement that he should publish his memoirs; then they decided it would be a bad thing. Publishers, as you might have guessed, were salivating to publish what would be a sure bestseller. That was not what the Mafia bosses wanted. The publication of Valachi's memoir would have been another blow to the Mafia's secrecy. The bosses were pleased that the senators ultimately denied Valachi the right to publish, but their pleasure turned to disappointment when it was announced that Peter Maas would be writing a book to be titled *The Valachi Papers*. It would be based on Valachi's memoir and interviews with him. And as if that were not bad enough, a movie based on the book and starring Charles Bronson was about to be filmed. La Cosa Nostra would become an expression known throughout the world.

The rat must be killed, said Buffalo mob boss Stefano Magaddino. To let him live would be an invitation to other mobsters to make deals with the government. So the Mafia placed a $100,000 bounty on Valachi. For his protection and as a reward for his testimony, Valachi "was housed in a two-room, air-cooled suite at La Tuna [prison]. His large cell, isolated from the general prison population and built specifically for him, had couches and a kitchenette." [10]

The Mafia never had to pay the $100,000 bounty, for Valachi died on April 3, 1971. It really didn't matter: there was no more that Valachi could testify to, and even what he did know was low-level information. Yes, La Cosa Nostra was real, but so what? What would be far more devastating than Valachi's testimony would be laws that permit prosecutors to conduct court-ordered wiretaps of Mafioso and the establishment of the Witness Protection Program to protect informants. A far-reaching result was the passage of the Racketeer Influenced and Corrupt Organizations Act (RICO) that permits prosecutors to indict and try mob bosses for crimes in which they didn't directly participate.

According to Carl Sifakis, "At the end of the 1966, a survey of the New York Police Department shows that in the three years since Valachi talked more members of the syndicate in the New York-New Jersey-Connecticut metropolitan area had been jailed than in the previous 30 years." [11]

Following his death, Valachi garnered more than the usual obituary: a woman named Marie K. Jackson of Niagara Falls, New York, claimed his body, which was buried four days after his death at the Gate of Heaven Cemetery in Lewiston, New York. Reporters, of course, immediately wanted to know what the relationship between Jackson and Valachi was. She was not his wife, but was she his mistress? When Valachi's last will and testament became public, it revealed that Jackson was Valachi's executor and beneficiary. And when she died, she was buried beside him.

The following story appeared in a local newspaper:

"Mystery Lady Claims Joe Valachi's Body and Has Him Buried in Lewiston"
"Who was Marie K. Jackson? She was a mysterious woman from Niagara Falls who had a secret Love affair with a Mafia hit man for decades. Historians don't know much, but she did consent to a rare interview with the Buffalo News in 1995. The report indicated she was a quiet, law-abiding divorcee who worked as a saleswoman in a Niagara Falls Clothing store. 'We were introduced at the home of a mutual friend in Niagara Falls,' she recalled of her

first meeting with Valachi, who was married. Although their relationship went on for many years, including the time of Valachi's much publicized testimony before the U.S. Senate, Miss Jackson was not publicly linked to Valachi until he died. She claimed his body from a federal prison in 1971 and had him secretly buried in an unmarked grave in Gate of Heaven Cemetery in Lewiston. It was later learned that Valachi's will listed her as his executor and beneficiary. When the best-selling book, *The Valachi Papers*, was published it was Jackson who 'made a lot of money' from the royalties. Valachi reportedly didn't make a penny. Jackson died in 1999 and is buried next to Valachi." [12]

Notes

1 The Dying of the Light: The Joseph Valachi Story by Thomas L. Jones. https://web.archive.org/web/20030906071209/http://www.crimelibrary.com/gangsters_outlaws/mobbosses/valachi/times_8.html

2 Hit in Harlem: The Life and Times of Eugenio Giannini By Thom L. Jones for Gangsters Inc. https://gangstersinc.org/2008/09/25/-in-harlem-the-life-and-times-of-eugenio-giannini/

3 Hit in Harlem: The Life and Times of Eugenio Giannini. https://gangstersinc.org/2008/09/25/-in-harlem-the-life-and-times-of-eugenio-giannini/

4 https://www.slantmagazine.com/film/summer-of-85-prizzis-honor/

5 https://web.archive.org/web/20030906071209/http://www.crimelibrary.com/gangsters_outlaws/mob_bosses/valachi/times_8.html

6 http://www.time.com/time/magazine/article/0%2C9171%2C875227%2C00.html

7 http://www.time.com/time/magazine/article/0%2C9171%2C875227%2C00.html

8 http://www.time.com/time/magazine/article/0%2C9171%2C873080%2C00.html

9 http://www.time.com/time/magazine/article/0%2C9171%2C873080%2C00.html

10 https://themobmuseum.org/blog/joseph-valachis-autobiography-reveals-mafias-inner-workings/

11 Carl Sifakis, *The Mafia Encyclopedia* (New York: Checkmark Books, 1999), 372.

12 https://historiclewiston.org/wp-content/uploads/2023/01/Valachi-Buried-in-Lewiston.pdf

15

Robert F. Kennedy, Mafia Nemesis

After President Kennedy appointed his 35-year-old brother Robert as attorney general in 1960, RFK went after the mob with the tenacity of a pit bull. Though his father, Joseph Kennedy Sr., had argued that Bobby should not go after the mob, Bobby refused to listen. What's wrong with you? The senior Kennedy had business dealings with the mob, especially during Prohibition and during his time in Hollywood, and the mob in Illinois had been instrumental in helping John get elected president. The Chicago mobsters believed that the Kennedys were in debt to them. It didn't matter to RFK. He had gone after the mob when counsel to the McClellan Committee, and his commitment never wavered. Shortly after taking office as attorney general, he made a list of more than 1,100 leading mobsters and hired dozens of lawyer/investigators to bring in indictments. When RFK came into office, there were only seventeen lawyers under his command; in short order, the number had risen to sixty, and their marching orders were to get indictments against the mob.

One of RFK's biggest obstacles was J. Edgar Hoover, who resented the youthful prosecutor. In addition, Hoover preferred going after bank robbers and kidnappers because those cases didn't take long to investigate and prosecute. Gun battles in which FBI agents shot down notorious bank robbers were always good for positive headlines. To add to his glory, Hoover also went after communists and could rely on senators and newspaper columnists to praise his efforts. Long drawn-out court cases against the Mafia did not afford the same quick opportunities.

As Evan Thomas writes: "In New York, Kennedy asked for the FBI's files on organized crime and got mostly newspaper clips. The New York office had four hundred agents out looking for communists and ten devoted to the mob. Kennedy was scornful. By 1961, the American Communist Party had only a few hundred members, Kennedy knew, and most of them were undercover FBI agents."[1]

Unlike Hoover, the Bureau of Narcotics was prepared to help RFK. He met with two agents, Angelo Zurlo and Joseph Amato, who agreed to help. Kennedy also worked closely with the IRS. Its commissioner, Mortimer Caplin, agreed to hire 180 agents whose jobs would be to examine the books of major racketeers. Perhaps, the IRS would be able to nail mobsters for either failing to file tax returns or not paying all the taxes they owed.

RFK began Operation Big Squeeze, which wound up arresting 128 illegal gambling operators, bookmakers, and loan sharks in twenty-two cities. RFK also worked with Congress to get anti-racketeering bills passed. The most notable was the Federal Interstate Wire Act, which was passed and signed into law on September 13, 1961, prohibiting the transmission of information about bets across state lines. Several gambling wires almost immediately went out of business.

In 1961, RFK sent one of his investigators to Newport, Kentucky, where a man named George Ratterman was running for sheriff. Ratterman ran on a platform of getting rid of corruption. His opponents drugged him, dumped him in bed with a stripper known as April Showers, and photographed the couple. However, with the help of RFK's people, Ratterman won the election in what was known as Sin City, and crime decreased. Up until then, Newport had been a center for national gambling interests, where bookmakers representing interests from all over the country operated. RFK was able to use Newport to demonstrate the Mafia's gambling interests extended across all state borders.

Ultimately, RFK got Hoover to be cooperative, if for no other reason than the attorney general had the support of the most powerful man in the world, his brother, the president.

"RFK: *I said, 'This is what we're going to concentrate on; this is what we're going to do.' He agreed to do it.... There was a unit in the Department of Justice which wasn't very active or very effective in organized crime. We reorganized that, with the understanding that these other people would become actively involved in it—the other agencies. And that's what happened. I met with all the investigative representatives of these other agencies. They brought them in from all over the country, and I discussed our program with them and what we wanted done.'*

"Some officials in Treasury and the IRS remained opposed to the idea for about the first six months of the Kennedy administration. Treasury was afraid they would collect less delinquent tax money and embarrass the agency when it reported to Congress, RFK told [*New York Times* columnist, Anthony] Lewis.

"'*As it turned out they've collected more money making these investigations than they would have otherwise. So not only has it paid off in convictions and in intelligence information, but it's paid off financially. And they've done a helluva good job at the Treasury Department. The FBI was reluctant to get into it. In the first place, they never shared information with any other investigative agency; and I said if we were going to all work together, they had to give the information to the other investigative agencies.'*

"It only worked, he said, because of his special relationship as brother of President Kennedy.

"'*If they could have gone over my head to the president, I couldn't have gotten the Treasury Department to do it. I couldn't have gotten them to reverse their position, because a lot of them in the hierarchy were opposed to it. They hated the idea. And of course J. Edgar Hoover didn't want to get in.*'

"RFK said he understood Hoover's uneasiness about RFK's role because of 'the idea that I was coming in and making changes of the things that had existed for a long period of time.' So he had a special phone installed in his office to reach Hoover directly and arranged for JFK to meet with Hoover for lunch every two or three months.

"In his conversations, Hoover, RFK said, 'had some good ideas about reorganizing some of the departments' such [as] the CIA.

"'He talks a hellava lot—J. Edgar Hoover—but I think that the president always felt they were worthwhile. . . . The relationship we had was not difficult. I mean, it wasn't an impossible relationship.'

"President Kennedy, in his second term, surely would have replaced Hoover with someone else, although he might have extended Hoover's 1965 scheduled retirement date for a time, RFK said. Hoover, Bobby said, 'didn't like me much' because of the major changes he and JFK made in the FBI to tackle organized crime and civil rights in the early 1960s.

"'For the first time since he had been director of the FBI, he had to take instructions or orders from the attorney general of the United States—and couldn't go over his head. . . . Therefore, he couldn't like it. Why would he like it? He hadn't made any changes himself for 20 years.'"[2]

From 1961 to 1964, RFK was able to get the FBI to wiretap the phones of nearly 800 members of organized crime. The FBI was able to do so by what is known as "black bag jobs," defined as illegally breaking into homes and surreptitiously installing listening devices. Because the taps were illegal, information from the taps could not be used in court; however, the information gave the FBI agents a road to travel on, leading to several fruitful destinations that could be investigated without illegal taps. However, some of those investigations, which revealed evidence of criminal activities, proved embarrassing to the FBI and the Justice Department. In particular, a carload of wiretapped documentary evidence against Las Vegas casino owners involved in skimming money from their casinos was thrown out of court. The casino owners sued the Justice Department, claiming that their privacy had been illegally invaded. They won.

Sam (Momo, short for Mooner, meaning crazy) Giancana, head of the Chicago Outfit, was another prime target for wiretapping: though RFK had bugged Giancana and gathered a full criminal dossier on the mob boss, he couldn't use the material to prosecute him. RFK had to be cautious for another reason: he knew that the president and Giancana were sharing a lover named Judith Campbell Exner. She had been introduced to the president by Frank Sinatra. It was all reported to Hoover, who informed RFK about the liaisons. If such information had become public, it not only would have precluded JFK from running for a second term, but it might have caused Republicans to impeach him. A frustrated RFK felt shackled.

Giancana, nevertheless, believed that RFK was capable of using other tactics to get him. So he prevailed upon his good friend Frank Sinatra to persuade RFK not to investigate or prosecute him, and not to get other agencies, such as the IRS, to indict him. RFK refused to lay off of Giancana, much to Sinatra's chagrin; the Rat Pack singer had foolishly bragged to Giancana that his friendship with the Kennedys would ensure that they would take a hands-off approach to the gangster. Evan Thomas writes: "Giancana personified evil to RFK, who as ever saw his job in personal and moral terms. The mobster 'was violent, crazy, unstable as an animal. He'd kill people for kicks. He wasn't like Mafia leaders in New York,' said William Hundley, Kennedy's chief of the organized crime section. Kennedy was determined to behead the Mafia's leadership. He was not about to lighten up on Giancana to please Frank Sinatra." [3] He would find ways of getting at the gangster.

Giancana was infuriated by the failure of Sinatra's promise and put out a contract on the life of the singer. When Sinatra heard about it, he was terrified. Fortunately for him, Giancana's mistress, Phyllis McGuire, convinced her gangster lover not to kill the singer; she enjoyed making love to Sinatra's music.

Giancana held another ace in his hand for keeping Kennedy at bay: he had made a deal with the CIA in 1960 to assassinate Fidel Castro. Though the Kennedys were not party to that deal, they were to later ones, and Giancana could reveal that information. Such a revelation would be a political bombshell. Giancana skillfully played his winning hand. He evaded being a prisoner of war in RFK's war on crime and war against Castro. His pillow talk with Judith Campbell Exner was an earful of her pillow talk with the president. It kept Giancana delighted. He believed he had JFK and RFK by their short hairs.

Unable to accept defeat, RFK settled on a way of attempting to drive Giancana nuts: he ordered that FBI agents follow Giancana wherever he went: into restaurants, on golf courses, outside his home, to his private clubs, arriving and leaving airports. Giancana was under the closest possible physical surveillance that the FBI could provide. They were as close to him as his own shadow. It made the gangster furious. He went to court and much to the consternation of the FBI and RFK, a judge agreed to an injunction. The agents were required to maintain a respectful distance from Giancana. But even more than the round-the-clock surveillance that infuriated Giancana was FBI agent William Roemer Jr., an agent for thirty years and the most highly decorated agent in the history of the FBI.

"'[Giancana] was a runty, bald and big-nosed gentleman who talked in street-bully accents. But in the eyes of Phyllis [McGuire] and dozens of other women, he seemed to have a special charm,' Roemer writes. He likens Giancana's appeal to that of Henry Kissinger who often bragged that 'power is the great aphrodisiac.'

"'In the summer of 1961, Giancana and McGuire shared a Phoenix motel room that was bugged by the FBI. Phyllis appeared to be the aggressor in the affair' Roemer writes. That peccadillo inspired the agents to obtain a subpoena for McGuire that would order her to testify before a Justice Department Strike Force investigation of the mob.

"The agents plotted to serve the subpoena to McGuire as she returned to Chicago with Giancana. Roemer drew the assignment of distracting Giancana at the airport. When confronted, the mob chief offered the usual 'I don't know nothin' about nothin',' and then, in colorful thug language, suggested that the agents leave him alone.

"When they didn't, Giancana grew more and more agitated and, at one point, hinted that he might be prepared to add a couple more notches to his gun-for-hire reputation if the G-men didn't take a hike.

"Roemer, who, like the mob chief, was not accustomed to taking lip from anyone, was only encouraged to push closer to the bone. He noticed that Giancana was carrying his girlfriend's purse.

"There followed from Giancana several sputtering references to a 'Butch' and his 'machine gun' and the damage they might inflict if so directed. There were also expletive-studded statements made regarding J. Edgar Hoover, Bobby Kennedy (then-U.S. Attorney General over the FBI) and then-President John F. Kennedy.

"Roemer was to spend many years contemplating the mobster's angry claim that 'I know all about the Kennedys, and Phyllis knows more about the Kennedys and one of these days we're going to tell all.' (He decided years later that this was a reference to the reputed extramarital affairs of the brothers).

"Giancana's diatribes continued to the point that Roemer lost his cool and summoned closer about 100 bystanders inside the O'Hare Airport terminal.

"'Come over here! I want you to see something! Take a look at this piece of slime! This is Sam Giancana! He is the boss of the underworld here in Chicago! Take a good look at this garbage! The big boss! Giancana!'

"Roemer's superior at the scene then intervened, but not before Giancana vowed, 'Roemer, you lit a fire tonight that will never go out!'

"The two would tangle many times over the years, but in the end, Giancana would step down from the mob leadership, weary of his opposition from within and outside the mob. In 1975, he was shot to death by a gang killer in the basement of his Oak Park home." [4]

In addition to initiating investigations and bringing indictments, RFK proved to be an effective media performer. Through speeches that were covered by reporters and articles that appeared in magazines and newspapers, RFK pounded home information about the extent of Mafia involvement in day-to-day activities of private citizens and corporate America. There was a secret enemy in America eating at the fabric of the country. The allusion to rats was intentional. RFK spoke of a secretive government comprising organized criminals from all over the United States that had an annual income of billions of dollars, which was parasitical and earned its money from human suffering and moral corrosion.

To fight that secretive government, he created a coordinated network of twenty-six federal law enforcement agencies, which targeted organized crime. Some of the gangsters, in addition to Giancana, who felt the heat of pursuit on their necks, were Carlos Marcello, the Louisiana Mafia boss, and Joey Aiuppa, who became boss of the Chicago Outfit. RFK was relentless and ruthless: he dumped Marcello into the jungles of Guatemala and skillfully managed to convict Aiuppa for violating the Migratory Bird Treaty Act of 1918. In addition to getting Congress to pass the Federal Wire Act, he got it to pass the Travel Act and the Interstate Transportation Paraphernalia Act. RFK was unstoppable. The Mafia hated him; and why not? During RFK's term as attorney general, his office increased the number of convictions against organized crime members by 800 percent! By 1962, the Justice Department had indicted more than 350 top mobsters. It was a harrowing time for mobsters. Hundreds of them stood on the brink of being arrested. The daughter of one mobster said to me: "My dad was spitting mad. He called Bobby a rich, spoiled punk." It was an opinion shared by Hoffa: "He wasn't a good attorney general—in all probability, a worse senator. I would hate to think what would happen if he became president of the United States. He'd probably have a fascist government." [5]

Hoffa's hatred of RFK matched the attorney general's hatred of Hoffa. They were like a pair of poisonous vipers, each intent on being the superior predator. In fact, RFK was so obsessed with Hoffa and pursued him with such vengeance that many Justice Department lawyers believed Kennedy was not only acting out of intense personal animosity for Hoffa, but that he was also stretching the law to get his man. RFK's "Get Hoffa" squad was perceived by Hoffa and his entourage as a band of lawless fanatics. To those who supported RFK's quest to nail Hoffa, the "Get Hoffa" squad were members of a posse representing good against evil. Hoffa referred to his battle with Kennedy as a blood feud.

On July 7, 1961, following Hoffa's reelection as president of the Teamsters, RFK told reporters that nothing had changed at the Department of Justice, that a small group of Teamsters, who had supported Hoffa, made no difference to the government's intention to free the Teamster union of its corrupt officials. In a show of bravado, a Teamster official told a reporter that RFK had been bodily removed from Hoffa's office. When asked about it, Hoffa said that RFK had been ejected.

The tough head of the union was finally nailed on March 4, 1964, convicted of attempting to bribe a juror during an earlier trial for conspiracy. He was sentenced to eight years in prison and fined $10,000. Following the conviction of Hoffa, Kennedy phoned his three prosecutors and praised them for their skill as litigators. They weren't finished with Hoffa, who was out on bail during an appeal of his conviction. On July 26, 1964, Hoffa was convicted in a second trial on one count of conspiracy and three counts of wire and mail fraud. He was sentenced to an additional five years in prison. On March 7, 1967, after his several appeals had been rejected, Hoffa began serving a thirteen-year prison sentence in the Lewisburg Federal Penitentiary in Pennsylvania. There, his job was stuffing mattresses. He was an ideal prisoner, never violated rules, and never disobeyed an order given by a guard.

Though RFK had gotten his man, he lost the most important man in his life when his brother, the president, was assassinated. He said to an associate, "There was so much bitterness. I thought they would get one of us. I thought it would be me." [6] For Hoffa, the assassination of the president came as a gift: Hoffa jumped onto a chair at a party and shouted, "Have you heard the good news! They killed the son of a bitch. This means Bobby is out as attorney general. Lyndon will get rid of him." [7]

Since President Johnson and RFK intensely disliked one another, the attorney general knew that the president would, out of spite, not support his anti-organized crime agenda. In addition, without his brother to back him up against Hoover, RFK knew that the head of the FBI would no longer be cooperative. The year after RFK resigned, Johnson gave Hoover a lifetime appointment as director of the FBI. Kennedy was not surprised. Camelot was dead and gone. RFK was no longer a player in the administration. And as expected, the impetus to investigate organized crime members cooled, and so the number of prosecutions decreased. However, after Hoover died in 1972, prosecutions heated up again.

The legacy of Robert Kennedy as attorney general is extraordinary. There was never anyone like him before 1961, and there has never been anyone quite like him since he resigned as attorney general. Though organized crime breathed a sigh of relief in 1964, RFK had set in motion laws and statutes that would haunt organized crime for decades.

According to historian Becky Little, RFK "in his stint as attorney general, . . . had been responsible for the indictment of 687 members of organized crime, and his office's conviction rate was 90 percent. By the time he left as A.G., his office had indicted 687 organized crime figures. Its conviction rate reached nearly 90 percent. His targets included New Orleans crime boss Carlos Marcello, Chicago Outfit second-in-command Sam Giancana, Joseph Bonanno's crime family in New York, Raymond Patriarca's Mafia family in Rhode Island and the

DeCavalcante crime group of New Jersey. He orchestrated the largest and most successful attack on organized crime that the country had ever witnessed."

"His stewardship led to future legal strategies and methods—such as RICO, the Racketeer Influenced and Corrupt Organizations Act, passed by Congress in 1970—that FBI and Justice employed to severely damage La Cosa Nostra from the 1970s to the present day. A half century is a long time."[8]

"Had his brother lived, it is almost certain that Bobby Kennedy would have persisted against organized crime. Had RFK himself not been killed in 1968, and won the presidency, he would have known how to proceed and likely would have made even more progress." [9]

Nevertheless, organized crime adapted as usual and continued its focus on a wide array of illegal activities, such as extortion, stock fraud, lending money at exorbitant rates, prostitution, illegal gambling, and so forth. And its means of enforcement remained the same: beatings, murder, and the threat of violence.

Notes

1. Evan Thomas, *Robert Kennedy: His Life* (New York: Simon and Schuster, 2000), 115.
2. https://www.history.com/news/robert-kennedy-started-war-on-mafia-gangs
3. Thomas, *Robert Kennedy: His Life*, 162.
4. https://www.chicagotribune.com/1989/11/26/an-eye-on-the-mob/
5. https://www.grunge.com/588255/the-truth-about-jimmy-hoffa-and-robert-kennedys-feud/
6. https://themobmuseum.org/blog/robert-f-kennedys-crusade-mob
7. https://themobmuseum.org/blog/robert-f-kennedys-crusade-mob
8. https://www.history.com/news/robert-kennedy-started-war-on-mafia-gangs
9. https://themobmuseum.org/blog/robert-f-kennedys-crusade-mob

16

The Gallo Wars

Before RFK could take the helm at the Justice Department, he encountered a gangster more brazen than most of those whom he had interrogated. He was Crazy Joey Gallo, a gangster who modeled himself on a psychopathic movie gangster named Tommy Udo, played by Richard Widmark in the movie *Kiss of Death*.

Gallo had been summoned to Kennedy's office in 1959 and swaggered in, a cool tough dude. In the style of Udo, Gallo wore a black shirt, white tie, and shaded his eyes behind dark aviator sunglasses. A cigarette hung from one corner of his smirking lips. All that was missing was a photographer. Gallo looked down, peered over the tops of his sunglasses at the rug in RFK's office, and purred: "Hey, this would be a great spot for a crap game."[1] He grinned at his host and swaggered out of the office.

This was the same man who told a courtroom judge, "The cops say I've been picked up 15, maybe 17 times. That's junk. It was 150 times. I been worked over for nothing until my hat sits on my head like it belongs on a midget." [2]

Gallo and his brothers, Larry and Albert "Kid Blast," were like old west outlaws who turned their Brooklyn neighborhood into a war zone. After the Gallos started a war with the Profaci crime family, you didn't have to watch a movie of the Gunfight at the OK Corral. Though it was not Dodge City or Tombstone, Brooklyn had it all in 1961: shots rang out day and night. Police sirens wailed from neighborhood to neighborhood. Bloody bodies were scattered around the streets of Brooklyn. Ambulances, serving as delivery vans, carried corpses to morgues. Brooklyn had become a Mafia war zone, and no one was safe: not Mafiosos, not civilians. Cops were helpless to prevent bloodshed. And though RFK was determined to lock up as many gangsters as possible, he hoped that they would kill each other and leave civilians alone. Those sentiments were later reiterated by D. A. Charles Hynes. But it didn't work out that way. On a quiet Sunday morning at 10:05 a.m., shortly after the Wanna Bagel shop opened, its innocent counterman, Matteo Speranza, was shot and killed. Earlier, at 9 a.m., James Malpiso was taken to Coney Island Hospital. He had been shot in the chest. He refused to give police any information; nothing about the shooter, nothing about the person who had driven him to the hospital. On the previous Friday, a bullet penetrated the back of the head of Vincent Fusaro as he was hanging Christmas lights on the facade of his Brooklyn home. Hit men were firing off guns as if it were the Fourth of July. A week earlier, Rosario Nastari, seventy-nine, a Colombo associate, and Gaetano Amato, seventy-eight, a soldier in the Genovese crime family, were killed in separate incidents. Fortunately for some, unfortunately for others, the gun-toting gangsters had an accuracy rate of about 20 percent. They were not steely-eyed lawmen like the Earp brothers who attempted to tame Tombstone. Instead, they were the gangs that couldn't shoot straight. John Miller, a TV news reporter, noted that the Colombo Family had a history of tripping over themselves—probably with loaded guns in their hands.

The fuse for the bloody mob war was lit in 1959, and the bomb went off in 1960. It began as a dispute between Joseph Profaci, head of a powerful crime family, and the Gallo brothers.

Joseph Profaci, who presided over his eponymous crime family for thirty years, could have been a millionaire without turning to crime. He was the olive oil and tomato paste king of New York. But for many gangsters, legitimate businesses are boring, serving only as fronts for their illegal activities and means of laundering money. When it came to his Borgata, Profaci was as tightfisted with money as Scrooge; however, when it came to family and friends, he was as generous as Don Vito Corleone. (Many members of Profaci's biological family were also members of his crime family.)

His intense rapaciousness to own or control businesses, whether legitimate or not, had always been rocket propelled. He wanted everything he could lay his hands on, whether nailed down or not. In 1930, the year the Castellammarese war started, Profaci gained control of the loan sharking and prostitution rackets in Brooklyn. He benefited from the outcome of that war without getting blood on his hands. He didn't have to pull any triggers; there were plenty of itchy fingers in his Borgata who did as they were ordered. The Castellammarese war was in many ways a precursor to the wars with the Gallos. It was during the Gallo wars that Profaci proved to be as elusive as a phantom. The Gallos had wanted to kidnap Profaci, but he was as hard to pinch as a wet lemon pit.

The Gallos were acting in the tradition of all Mafioso: kidnap a prime target, hold him for ransom; and if the ransom isn't paid, then kill the kidnap victim. And make sure that some part of the dead man's body or a symbol of it is returned to his family. To avoid this happening again, future victims know that if they don't pay up, bodies will keep piling up. The Gallos, like all students of the Mafia, knew that kidnapping is ineffectual without the threat of murder. They also knew the history of the Castellammarese War, which has served as a historical lesson for all ambitious gangsters who want to become family bosses.

Profaci set his soldiers grumbling after he demanded a monthly tribute of $25 from each of them. Tactful soldiers, not wanting to die, never complained directly to Profaci. Instead, they complained among themselves, ever fearful of doing so within earshot of their boss. Though $25 from each soldier does not appear to be much, it amounted to $50,000 a year when forked over by hundreds of men. Profaci's lust for money, no matter how much he received in tribute, was never satiated. In the late 1950s, Profaci demanded a large tribute from capo Frank "Frankie Shots" Abbatemarco, who controlled a highly lucrative policy racket in Brooklyn that generated more than $2.5 million annually and as much as $7,000 a day. Abbatemarco claimed he couldn't pay what Profaci demanded because he was in debt, had enormous expenses, mortgages on several homes, and had made generous pledges to several Catholic charities. It didn't matter to Profaci. Pay me what I'm entitled to . . . or else. Or else was about to happen. Profaci offered Joey, Larry, and Kid Blast the opportunity to wipe away their debt to him (for they too had refused to pay tribute) if they killed Frankie Shots. As a further inducement, Profaci offered the brothers all of Frankie Shots' policy business after they carried out the hit. On November 4, 1959, Shots walked out of his cousin's bar in Park Slope, Brooklyn, and was shot eight times in his head and body by Joseph "Joe Jelly" Gioielli, a member of the Gallo gang. Fearful of retribution from the son of Shots, Profaci demanded that the Gallos hand over the dead man's son, Anthony. The Gallos refused, and so Profaci refused to hand over the father's policy game. Profaci probably never had any intention of handing it over, and the Gallos provided him with an excuse for not doing so. It was too much for the Gallos. They were frustrated and angered at being unrewarded. They had wanted to move up; now they were left as minor league gangsters. Yes, they were the bosses of their neighborhood, centered at 51 President Street in the Red Hook section of Brooklyn. But it was small potatoes. They couldn't stop dreaming of being big time, and the money that Frankie Shots collected would have been more than enough to bankroll them into being important players. Their anger ignited a fire to go to war. They knew how Luciano had become a boss of the biggest Mafia family in the east by starting the Castellammarese War. They would start their own war. If they could kidnap Profaci and be given the policy racket of Shots as ransom, they could become the new (big) Shots. They formed an alliance with the Garfield Boys, whose leader was Carmine Persico. Just in case their kidnapping venture failed, they were ready for a true gun battle. One way or another, there would be some kind of war followed by either a negotiated peace or a violent destruction.

Kidnapping, however, was the preferred course of action. Ransom might be paid in dollars, in the takeover of another mobster's territory, a takeover of his business, or a combination of all three. Kidnapping would cost less than bullets and bombs and bring less heat on them than a massacre.

Nevertheless, the Gallos were armed to their teeth, for you could never tell when a gun battle would erupt. It was best to be prepared as they later would be when they made their President Street headquarters a fortress. But, on February 27, 1961, the Gallos did not fire a shot; instead, they kidnapped four of Profaci's top men: underboss Joseph Magliocco (Profaci's second cousin and brother-in-law), Frank Profaci (Joe Profaci's brother), capo Salvatore Musacchia, and soldier John Scimone. Profaci, who seemed to have a cat burglar's ability to elude capture, was driven incognito to an airport, where he boarded a plane to Florida. He may have breathed a sigh of relief, but he was also profoundly pissed off. He was determined to kill those Gallo rats, but first he would have to negotiate the release of his top executives. The Gallos, meanwhile, locked each of their hostages in hotel rooms in different parts of the city. Each was guarded by a well-armed thug and advised not to try to escape. The Gallos were contacted by Profaci consigliere Charles "the Sidge" LoCicero, who had been appointed negotiator by his boss. The Gallos demanded, at the very least, a significant piece of the policy racket. LoCicero said that no deal could be made until the hostages were released. Joey angrily responded that he would kill one of the hostages just to show how serious he was. In addition, he wanted a good faith payment of $100,000, which would prove that Profaci was negotiating honestly. Joey's brothers and Joe Jelly thought that such a demand was unrealistic. Joey was letting his anger cloud his judgment: Larry and Kid Blast told Joey to go to California and relax; they would take care of the negotiations and get them all a good deal. LoCicero convinced the two remaining Gallo brothers and Joe Jelly to release the hostages. He said that Profaci would then make a deal that the Gallos would appreciate. Once the hostages had been safely returned to their homes, Profaci was free to exact his revenge. He and his top men pretended that they would give the Gallos exactly what they had wanted. It would be a win-win arrangement for everyone. As part of the ersatz goodwill that emanated from the Profaci family, some of his men invited Joe Jelly on a deep-sea fishing excursion. Jelly arrived at the dock and boarded a high-powered cabin cruiser, outfitted with the latest fishing gear and food for a terrific lunch. He was never seen again. However, several days later, a bundle of his clothes tied with a rope was flung to the front door of 51 President Street. Wrapped in the clothing was a large rotting, putrid fish. (It became the basis for announcing the death of Luca Brasi in *The Godfather*.)

Days before that happened, Larry Gallo had gotten a call from one of Profaci's men. To celebrate their détente and the sharing of the profits from the Shots policy racket, Larry was invited to the Sahara Lounge for a toast to the future. Once there, Gallo was greeted by a Profaci soldier, who handed Larry a hundred-dollar bill. He said it was symbolic of all the hundred-dollar bills that would flow to the Gallos. He suggested that Larry order a drink while he went to the men's room to take a leak. As Larry sat on a bar stool, sipping his drink and contemplating a profitable future, two hands emerged out of the darkness behind him. In each hand was a rope that was quickly slung around Larry's neck. Two men were pulling the rope back and forth like lumberjacks cutting down a tree. The rope quickly tightened, and Larry lost consciousness, tumbling onto the floor. The killers continued tightening the rope, preventing a last breath of air from saving their victim.

"Hey, what's going on?" shouted a cop, entering the bar. The killers turned to see the uniform. The cop shouted for his partner, who quickly ran in. One of the killers pulled out a revolver and shot the cop's partner in the face. The two hit men then ran out the back door. The uninjured cop called for backup and an ambulance. His partner was rushed to a hospital, and doctors worked feverishly to save his life. They succeeded.

Lying on the floor, Larry Gallo coughed, gagged, and groaned awake. A purple rope burn encircled his neck. There is a photo of him on the back seat of a car, sitting beside his brother Joey. Larry looks to be deep in meditative anger, while Joey, a cigarette dangling from his lips, looks to be consumed with rage. You can see the need for revenge in his smoldering eyes.

It did not take long for the Gallos to identify the two hit men who had attempted to kill Larry. They were Salvatore "Sally" D'Ambrosio and Carmine Persico, an erstwhile ally of the Gallos. For Persico's betrayal, he became known as Carmine "the Snake." He, as well as the Profacis, was on the Gallo hit list. The first Gallo War was on. Underboss Joe Magliocco (aka Joe Evil Eye) directed soldiers in the Profaci family to kill as many members of the Gallo gang as they could track down. Each side succeeded in ambushing members of the other side. The bodies of nine murdered men were found in different Brooklyn neighborhoods. Three others disappeared. Their bodies were never found.

Meanwhile, Joey had been attempting to extort the owner of a check cashing business. He had attempted to force the owner into making him a partner. The man refused, and after several threats against his life, he contacted the police. Joey and the businessman sat in a booth in a restaurant, and undercover cops sat nearby. They heard Joey's threats, and his arrest was forthcoming. Found guilty at trial, Joey was sentenced to seven to fourteen years in prison. He would serve ten.

Profaci and Magliocco were relieved, but the Gallo gang was still on the warpath. Profaci had been diagnosed with liver cancer, and on June 6, 1962, he succumbed, never having seen the end of his war with the Gallos. Magliocco quickly elevated himself from underboss to boss. The Commission members, however, were not impressed; they thought that Magliocco was too weak to be a boss. To impress them, Magliocco ordered the death of the remaining Gallo brothers. He knew that commission members regarded the Gallos as a possible future threat to their own positions and would be happy to see them eliminated. However, the commission had no faith in Magliocco and ordered his retirement. Joe Colombo won commission approval, and he renamed the Profaci family after himself.

The Gallo gang still continued to shoot their enemies and plant bombs, many of which were duds, under the cars of Profaci soldiers. One bomb, however, exploded, nearly killing the hated Carmine Persico. His enforcer, Hugh McIntosh, was shot in the groin. On May 19, 1963, a team of Gallo hit men finally succeeded in ambushing Persico, shooting him multiple times. However, they took off before they could finish him off; Persico was rushed to a hospital and survived. The Gallos cursed Persico's luck.

The Gallo gang continued conducting wild drive-by shootings; on the streets of Brooklyn, the pop pop pop of guns caused civilians to flatten themselves on sidewalks or huddle behind parked cars. Police sirens wailed too late for cops to catch any of the shooters. One cop told a reporter that Brooklyn had become the new Dodge City. After each attempted attack against the Profacis, the Gallos would retreat to 51 President Street. In Mafia terms, they had gone to the mattresses, protecting themselves against retaliation. They had turned their President Street headquarters into an armored dormitory. To protect themselves against hand grenades and Molotov cocktails, the gang put heavy metal mesh screens on the outside of the building's windows. Anything thrown against the windows would bounce off and land in the street.

While Joey was serving time in prison, angry Mafia bosses declared that the shootings and bombings had to end. It was bad for business. The cops were making life miserable for soldiers. The politicians were complaining to the bosses that the mayhem had to end. The bosses were pissed that fewer dollars were flowing up to them in tribute. So, in 1963, Raymond L. S. Patriarca, boss of his eponymously named crime family based in Providence, Rhode Island, was chosen to be the Henry Kissinger of the mob. He was charged with negotiating a peace treaty between the two warring gangs. He was a man with little patience for those who disagreed with him and would order murders as easily as ordering dinner. In fact, he allegedly ordered the murder of his brother for not noticing an FBI listening device in his office. Very few, if any, other mobsters chose to disagree with him. He seemed the perfect choice for ending the Profaci/Gallo war. The perfect choice, indeed, to everyone except Joey Gallo. Upon his release from prison, he announced that he was not party to the peace agreement because he had been in prison and not consulted. In addition, his brother Larry had died of cancer while Joey was in prison, which meant that only one Gallo brother had to face the will of the commission. Joey was prepared to restart the war. One can only imagine the bosses cursing at the renegade who had the balls to defy them.

Joey was welcomed back by Joe Colombo, who offered the ex-convict a thousand dollars for a welcoming home party. Joey scorned the offer; he figured he was owed $100,000 for his time in prison. Colombo, in effect, had told him to get lost. Joey now had another reason for going to war.

Though Colombo's position as boss had the blessing of Carlo Gambino, head of the most powerful Mafia family, he was skating on melting ice. Colombo loved bathing in media floodlights more than most politicians running for office. With the skills of a master PR manipulator, he created and publicized the Italian American Civil Rights League. This was a definite no-no in Mafia land. Each Mafioso was supposed to maintain a low profile, remain unnoticed by the media and law enforcement. Colombo, however, courted the media like a movie star attempting to win plaudits for his role in a new movie. He appeared on TV talk shows, regularly gave interviews, and held demonstrations to protest prejudice against Italians. He persuaded President Nixon's attorney general John Mitchell never to use the word "Mafia." He even succeeded in convincing the producers of *The Godfather* never to use the words "Mafia" and "Cosa Nostra" in the movie. His public persona, TV talk show appearances, and well-covered press conferences made him a magnet for celebrities, each eager to join his anti-defamation league. Frank Sinatra, for example, jumped on board as did numerous other Italian-American celebrities.

Colombo's relentless crusade, however, had foolishly antagonized his friend and former mentor, Carlo Gambino. Without realizing it, Colombo had set a fire under Gambino by holding a League rally that comprised 50,000 protesters. That was bad enough; now Colombo was planning another rally, perhaps an even bigger one.

Gambino had enough; Colombo was not acting like a Mafia boss, but rather like a Broadway impresario. Something had to be done to put an end to Colombo's shenanigans. The foxiest of Mafia bosses, Gambino decided on a plan to get rid of two irritants: Colombo and Gallo. Gambino knew that while Joey was in prison, he had recruited a number of black gangsters to be members of his gang. Joey had mentored them on how to run a successful drug business. Following his release from prison, he had paraded through Gambino territory with several well-armed black gangsters. It was a tough guy's show of bravado; his way of putting a thumb in the eye of Gambino: I'm so big, so tough that you have to recognize my power. However, Gambino did not perceive Joey as a man of power: he saw a punk with the arrogance and tempestuousness to attempt to disrupt the smooth-running operations of the Mafia. Gambino met with a Black hitman, eager to gain favor. His name was Jerome A. Johnson.

On June 28, 1971, Colombo held his second massive rally in Columbus Circle in Manhattan. Shortly after he was introduced to the crowd of cheering supporters, Colombo prepared to address his supporters. Johnson, pretending to be a reporter, strode over to Colombo and shot him three times, each bullet driving deep into Colombo's brain. Within a minute, Colombo's bodyguards shot and killed Johnson. Colombo didn't die; instead, he was left paralyzed and succumbed seven years later on May 22, 1978. The Colombo family agreed that Johnson had been hired by Joey. Gambino could not have asked for a better outcome, for Joey's days were now numbered.

The Colombo family, minus its eponymous boss, needed a new boss. Top members of the family called for a conference, during which they decided to name Salvatore "Charlie Lemons" Mineo as their acting boss. Mineo, perhaps not wishing to be a target and in poor health, declined the offer. He said that the family needed a younger man as boss. Their next choice was consigliere Joseph "Joey Yack" Yacovelli. Following Yacovelli's acceptance, the family decided that Joey had to be eliminated. Yacovelli said the time to get rid of Joey should come at a later date. He didn't want to create the impression that another mob war was taking place; it would only serve to stir up a hornet's nest of police activity. The police already suspected that the Colombos would want to take revenge on Joey; their suspicions led them to provide Joey with round-the-clock protection. Officers followed Gallo wherever he went. The police did not want another headline-grabbing murder to make them look incompetent. And they also worried that if Joey was killed, it would ignite another mob war. And mob wars invariably caused problems in the often tidy relations between the mob and the cops. From the mayor to the police commissioner to borough presidents, the city's powers did not want any more mob wars. By 1972, they all relaxed. Politicians, police officials, and district attorneys figured that the time for killing Joey had passed. They were wrong: a contract on his life had been issued.

In prison, Joey had attempted to turn himself into an intellectual. He voraciously read books on philosophy and history. He even took up painting, producing numerous watercolors, some of which hung in the warden's office. He was a new man, a reformed but charming rogue, someone that people in the arts would want as a friend. In fact, he became a favorite of such celebrity New Yorkers as Jerry Orbach, Don Rickles, David Steinberg, and others. Orbach's wife, Marta, took a particular interest in Joey, and the two began working on his memoir. Joey believed that his life story would be a perfect subject for a movie and looked forward to selling it for big bucks to a Hollywood studio. He told his new-found pals that he read ten books a week; his list of esteemed authors, he said, included Sartre, Camus, Machiavelli, Hemingway, Dos Passos, and more. He often hung out at the 8th Street Bookstore in Greenwich Village, where he could be seen thumbing through books on philosophy. When not musing about his favorite authors, he was allegedly writing poetry. Going into Elaine's, the Upper East Side celebrity hangout, he was greeted by a host of A-list actors, writers, movie directors, and producers. He was the offbeat, au courant reformed bad guy. Everybody, it seemed, wanted to be his friend. A reformed gangster still radiated danger and that radiation was a magnet that drew people close to him. Later, several of them were glad they had not been close on the night Joey was shot.

But before that happened, they all felt safe as if they had befriended someone who only played the part of a gangster in a movie. Several celebrities joined Joey on the night of April 7, 1972, to celebrate his birthday. The party was held at the famed Copacabana Nightclub, which had been owned by Frank Costello. Accompanying Joey were not only Jerry and Marta Orbach but also the comedian David Steinberg, who had been the best man at Joey's wedding. Steinberg was accompanied by his date. They were joined by celebrity gossip columnist Earl Wilson, who would be provided with great copy the next day. The non-celebrities at Joey's table were his wife of three weeks Sina Essary and her daughter Lisa, Joey's sister Carmella, and Joey's bodyguard Pete "The Greek" Diapoulas. On stage, Don Rickles wittily insulted Joey with comments that caused him and the audience to roar with laughter. The Copa closed at 4:00 a.m., and Joey invited his entourage to join him for breakfast in Chinatown. Steinberg, the Orbachs, Wilson, and Rickles made their excuses, so Joey, Sina, Lisa, Carmella, and Pete all got into Joey's Cadillac and drove to Chinatown. Not finding a restaurant that was open, Joey drove to Little Italy. There, on Mulberry Street, the lights of Umberto's Clam House sparkled in the night. The restaurant was owned by Genovese capo Matty "the Horse" Ianiello. Joey parked his car, and everyone went into the restaurant. The Gallo party sat at one of the restaurant's butcher block tables. Joey and Pete had taken seats that faced a wall, their backs to the door. It was an unusually incautious arrangement for a gangster and his bodyguard; gangsters and their protectors invariably choose seats at the back of restaurants that face the door. Every gangster assumes that he may be a target for a mob hit, and he wants to get off the first shots, not offer his back as a target. Upon entering the restaurant, Joey and Pete had noticed a lone man at the bar, but the man's presence didn't arouse their suspicions. There was no one else in the restaurant. The man at the bar, nursing a drink, was Joseph Luparelli, a gangster wannabe who regularly attempted to ingratiate himself with gangsters by being a gofer. Luparelli immediately recognized Joey and had heard that the Colombos had issued a contract on his life. Luparelli quickly swallowed the remainder of his drink and strode out of the Clam House and to a nearby Colombo social club. There, he found four gangsters engaged in a card game. He quickly approached the four card players, then blurted out that the crazy one was in Umberto's with his family. One of the players got up and went to a wall phone from which he called Yacovelli, who allegedly gave the men an order to whack Joey. The five men left the club, got into cars, and drove to Umberto's. All but Luparelli exited the cars. With revolvers in their hands, they rushed into the restaurant and fired multiple rounds at the Gallo party. Bullets exploding from .32 and .38 revolvers were deafening. The women screamed and dove onto the floor as Joey quickly turned over a table to shield them. He cursed and frantically fired back at his attackers. The attackers fired more than twenty shots, three of which hit Joey: one in his elbow, one in his ass, and one in his back. The attackers, having unloaded their guns, ran out of the restaurant. A bleeding Joey staggered after them, firing his pistol. He made it onto the sidewalk, where he collapsed. A bullet had severed one of his arteries. Not yet unconscious, he fired one more shot at the attackers' cars as they screeched away. Pete had also run out onto the street, firing his pistol at the attackers' cars. He, too, had been shot in his ass, though his wound was not fatal. Police cars and an ambulance, sirens screaming, raced to Umberto's. Gallo was placed on a stretcher and taken to Beekman-Downtown Hospital, where he was pronounced dead in the ER room at 5:30 a.m. He had died from a loss of blood.

Meanwhile, the hit men and Luparelli drove to Yacovelli's east side apartment, received further orders, and drove to a safe house in Nyack, New York. After five paranoid-filled days, during which Luparelli dreaded being killed to silence him, he sneaked out of the house and drove to Newark Airport, where he boarded a plane to Los Angeles. He stayed with relatives but was unable to shake off his fears of being killed. He contacted the FBI and was soon taken into the Witness Protection Program. However, he never testified because prosecutors did not believe his story would be sufficient for a conviction. No one was ever indicted for the murder of Joey Gallo.

Burning for revenge, Albert Gallo sent a hit man from Las Vegas to the Neapolitan Noodle restaurant in Manhattan, where Yacovelli, Alphonse Persico, and Gennaro Langella were dining. The hit man had not been supplied with photos of his targets and so could not identify them. Instead, he shot four innocent diners, two of whom died from their wounds. This was too much for Yacovelli; he feared that he might be next on Albert's hit list. He fled from New York. It was not only too much for Yacovelli, it was too much for the Mafia commission. The new boss of the Colombos, Joseph "Joey" Brancatto, and the bosses of the other Mafia families negotiated a truce. It resulted in Albert Gallo becoming a member of the Genovese family and ceasing any attempts to avenge the murder of his brother. The recovered Pete Diapoulas told a reporter at *The New York Times* that "Gang wars are always used to clean house and settle grudges. If you kill someone during peacetime, you may have to answer to the bosses, but in wartime nobody asks questions. There's a lot of money in organized crime, but in the long run, unless you're Carlo Gambino, there's no future in it." [3]

Notes

1 https://time.com/archive/6877562/crime-death-of-a-maverick-mafioso/

2 https://time.com/archive/6877562/crime-death-of-a-maverick-mafioso/

3 https://www.nytimes.com/1975/07/07/archives/key-mafia-figure-tells-of-wars-and-gallocolombo-peace-talks-a-key.html

17

The Colombos Go to War Again

Carmine Persico seemed to be able to see around corners. He could see who was about to come gunning for him and who had the power to supplant his enemies. And like most gangsters, he was an opportunist; he was a man who could change his loyalty as easily as some could change a shirt. It's not surprising that he was first loyal to Profaci, then to the Gallo gang, and then again to Profaci, all the while upping the ante on his ability to survive and conquer. In addition, he had a kind of blasé toughness that permitted him to survive multiple attempts on his life as if dealing with pesky mosquitoes. For example, in May of 1963, when the Gallo crew was seeking revenge on Persico for his betrayal, they located his car and sprayed it with a barrage of bullets. Persico didn't duck fast enough, and bullets creased his head and invaded one of his arms and a hand. Yet, he was able to spit out a bullet that ripped into his mouth. As soon as his attackers sped off, Persico drove himself to a hospital. Lying on a hospital bed, he refused to give cops information about his attackers. Though he switched his loyalty from one family to another and back again, he remained forever loyal to the code of omerta.

Out of the hospital, Persico continued to manage one of the most profitable crews in the Profaci family. It conducted all the standard Mafia activities: murder for hire, hijackings, extortion, burglaries, loan sharking, labor relations, stock frauds, etc. The crew was so dependent on Persico's leadership that when he was sent to prison in 1972 on a hijacking conviction, their profits significantly decreased. Nevertheless, he still held the reins while in prison and directed his crew to commit a variety of crimes. He did so for eight years. Upon his release, he continued his old ways, but his business plans were temporarily interrupted when he was arrested for extortion and usury; at the conclusion of his trial, Persico sported a Cheshire grin that lit up his face: all the prosecution witnesses had failed to identify him.

The grinning capo was now in a position to move up to being boss of the family. A vacuum had been created after Albert Gallo had failed to rid the world of his brother's murderers, including reigning Colombo boss Yacovelli; not wanting to end his days being whacked by a vengeful Gallo, Yacovelli prudently departed New York. In Yacovelli's absence, Persico became boss of the family. Almost as an act of modesty or one of fidelity, he did not change the name of the family to Persico. He didn't need his name on the door, just the power and the money that are the trappings of being a boss.

Becoming a boss is not announced via a press release to the media, but the FBI soon became aware of Persico's ascension to the throne, and they were intent on removing his crown and circumscribing his kingdom to a jail cell. They would be the ones to put out a press release along with a mug shot. It was not long before he and his leadership team were indicted. It happened on October 14, 1984, and the charge was racketeering. The indictment led to what the feds and the media named the Colombo Trial. Persico, however, decided not only to avoid trial but also a long prison sentence that he figured would be the outcome of a trial. He went into hiding. From Lepke on, bosses on the lam have never stayed hidden for long. A defier of history, Persico would attempt to establish a new precedent. Eight days after the indictment was published, the FBI placed Persico on its celebrated Ten Most Wanted list. The FBI doubted that Persico would be an exception to the rule: the FBI always gets its man.

The Mafia values blood relations and genealogy. However, their trust in relatives and other Mafioso has often been a cruel disappointment for them. Persico, a Mafioso loyal to family, chose to hide in the home of his wife's cousin, Fred DeChristopher. The two kept a low profile in Fred's home on Long Island. What Persico did not know was that Fred, as a Mafia associate, had made a deal with the FBI to protect himself by providing information about mobsters. His relationship with the FBI had been ongoing for two years. Learning of Persico's hideout and to protect Fred's role as an informant, the FBI pretended it was engaged in a massive manhunt for Persico. When an FBI agent phoned the home and asked to speak to Mr. Persico, Fred handed the phone to his cousin. The caller informed Persico that the house was surrounded. Persico, with his hands up, surrendered to the FBI. He was accompanied by several other guests of the house.

The New York Times reported that "Carmine Persico, described by Federal authorities as the boss of the Colombo organized-crime family, was arrested on Long Island yesterday as a fugitive charged with racketeering. Mr. Persico, who is 51 years old and lives in Brooklyn, was listed by the Federal Bureau of Investigation as one of its 10 most wanted fugitives. The F.B.I. said he and three other men had been arrested at a private house at 3020 Wilson Avenue in Wantagh, L.I., owned by a cousin of Mr. Persico.

"One of the arrested men was identified as Dominic Montemarano, 46, of Brooklyn, described as a 'capo' or captain, in the Colombo group. The two others, identified as Joseph Russo and Fredrick DeChristopher, were arrested on suspicion of harboring fugitives. Mr. Persico and Mr. Montemarano had been sought by authorities since October, when they disappeared and failed to answer charges in a Federal indictment against them and nine others.

"At 4:30 P.M., after more than 20 Federal agents and police officers had surrounded the home, Mr. Persico and the other three men answered a telephoned order to come out, said Lee F. Laster, assistant director in charge of the F.B.I. office in New York.

"Mr. Laster said Mr. Persico was a cousin of Mr. DeChristopher's wife, Katherine. The DeChristophers own the house.

"Mr. Persico and Mr. Montemarano will be arraigned this morning in Federal District Court in Manhattan, according to Bruce A. Baird and Aaron R. Marcu, the prosecutors in charge of the case. The 51-count indictment charged the defendants with operating the Colombo group through 'a pattern of racketeering activity' that included extortion, theft, loan sharking, gambling, bribery, and drug trafficking.

"On Oct. 24, the indictment was announced in Manhattan by Attorney General William French Smith, who said a grand jury had 'indicted the entire leadership of the Colombo family.' He said the Colombo group 'strongly influences both the construction and restaurant industries in this city.' The F.B.I. conducted a three-year investigation, called 'Star Quest,' that led to the indictment. The investigation used extensive undercover operations, including a yacht. All 11 defendants were named in a racketeering charge, which carries up to 20 years in prison, and most of them were also named in several related charges.

"Nine of the 11 were arraigned on the charges and pleaded not guilty. Besides Mr. Persico, the indictment named two others as top leaders of the group. They are Gennaro Langella, 45, and Thomas DiBella, 78, both of Staten Island. Mr. Langella was described as the underboss and Mr. DiBella as the group's advisor.

"Three captains, besides Mr. Montemarano, were also identified in the indictment. They were John J. DeRoss, 47, of Brooklyn; Anthony Scarpatti, 51, of Brooklyn, and Frank Melli, 42, of Staten Island.

"Two men identified as Colombo members were Dominic Cataldo, 48, of Valley Stream, L.I., and Ralph Scopo, 55, of Queens. Two men identified as associates of the group were Frank Falanga, 64, and Vito Pitta, 57, both of Brooklyn." [1]

In 1979, Persico was released from federal prison, but in 1981, he was convicted of conspiracy and racketeering and sentenced to five years in prison. As bad as that was, worse was to come: on February 25, 1985, Persico and nine Mafia bosses, including Langella, were indicted for narcotics trafficking, loansharking, gambling, labor racketeering, and extortion against construction companies. They had been netted in the famous Mafia Commission Trial (which is the subject of a later chapter), which targeted all the New York families. Persico, prior to his trial, made one of the most tactically foolish decisions of his life: he decided to act as his own defense counsel. ("He who will be his own Counsellour, shall be sure to have a Fool for his Client," wrote William De Britaine in 1682.) Persico's tactic backfired when he cross-examined prosecution witnesses and admitted to participating in previous crimes. He was sentenced to 100 years in prison. Though Persico had failed to convince the jury of his innocence, Judge John F. Keenan addressed the defendant, telling him, "You are a tragedy. You are one of the most intelligent people I have ever seen in my life. You did a very good job [defending yourself]." [2]

The Colombos were shattered by the trial. Persico at fifty-three years was the youngest of the bosses, and he would spend the rest of his life in prison.

In 1988, the imprisoned Persico named Victor Orena as acting boss. Persico gave Orena the power to induct new members and order murders. That power would be the impetus for another Colombo war.

Three years into his reign, Orena had come to believe Persico had been away too long from the family's day-to-day business operations; the imprisoned boss did not have his hand on the pulse of the family's operations. The result was that the family had failed to partake in numerous profitable deals that were scooped up by the other families.

Not only did Orena believe that Pesico wasn't focused on family business, he was startled to learn that Persico wanted to be the subject of a made-for-TV movie. That was not the kind of publicity that would benefit the family. In fact, it might be an additional impetus for the FBI to zero in on family operations. Orena was furious. Didn't Persico realize that prosecutors had used Joe Bonanno's autobiography (*A Man of Honor*) as source of information for the Commission Trial? Orena was now determined to give up his position as acting boss and become the permanent boss. Orena asked the Commission to declare him boss; however, the Commission refused to do so.

Not willing to accept that refusal, Orena attempted to overrule the Commission through an act of democracy. He assigned his consigliere, Carmine Sessa, to poll the family's capos to see if they would support him as their permanent boss. Rather than polling the capos, Sessa informed Persico of what Orena had proposed. That ignited a fuse that would lead to the next family war; it began with Persico ordering a hit on Orena.

The first bullets were fired on June 21, 1991. As Orena drove to his home in Cedarhurst on Long Island, he spotted gunmen on the road near his home. One of them prematurely opened fire, causing Orena to floor the gas pedal of his Mercedes and speed to safety. He knew who had ordered the hit, and he was determined to take them out. He sent two of his nephews on a murder mission. No one outside the family knows what the nephews did. However, the FBI calculated that twelve people, including innocent bystanders, were shot and killed. In addition, eighteen others, a combination of family members and associates, disappeared. Prosecutors went after the warring factions, indicting eighty members and associates from both sides.

The first person to be killed was Henry Smurra, a Colombo soldier who was shot in the head while sitting in his red Lincoln Continental outside a Dunkin' Donuts shop. Another Colombo confederate was Vincent Fusaro, who was shot in the head while hanging Christmas decorations on his house in Brooklyn. Shortly thereafter, a 79-year-old bookie was shot while playing cards at a social club; his 47-year-old girlfriend suffered a superficial chest wound. And the killings continued with the murder of 62-year-old Colombo captain Nicholas (Nicky Black) Grancio, who was whacked while sitting in his Toyota Land Cruiser.

One of the most notorious of Persico loyalists, who performed many hits, was Gregory Scarpa, known as the Grim Reaper. He was considered a killing machine. The FBI believed that Scarpa may have killed from 80 to 120 people. And the FBI should know, for Scarpa was an FBI informant. Scarpa once bragged that he loved the smell of gunpowder. And he so enjoyed killing that he was accused of saying he wanted to dig up one of his victims and kill him again.

Orena believed that Scarpa headed the five-man hit team that had waited to kill him near his home. Orena put together his own hit team and sent them on a mission into Brooklyn. On November 18, 1991, Scarpa escorted his daughter, who was carrying her infant son, to her BMW. He told her to follow his car. He got into his Mercedes and his daughter dutifully followed in her BMW. Within a few feet, a white van pulled into the road and blocked the two cars. Gunmen quickly exited the van and began firing at the two cars. A torrent of bullets sprayed the two cars. Scarpa and his daughter floored their cars, drove over lawns and sidewalks, turned over garbage cans and lawn ornaments, and sped away. The death-defying Grim Reaper was determined to kill Orena and all of his cohorts.

At a later time, while gunning for two men, Scarpa was shot in his left eye. He rapidly drove himself home and, once there, he poured scotch into the bleeding socket. He had been under house arrest at the time and was required to wear an electronic monitor on one ankle. When its alarm sounded in an FBI office, an agent called Scarpa's home. Scarpa, still bleeding from his wounded eye, calmly told the agent that he had merely left the house to pick up a prescription.

Neither a wounded eye nor an ambush that could have resulted in the deaths of his daughter, grandchild, and himself prevented Scarpa from going after Orena. However, for all his vengefully ignited anger, he failed to track and nail Orena. What prevented his mission had nothing to do with either law enforcement or the Mafia: he had been diagnosed with AIDS in 1986 after receiving a tainted blood transfusion from a member of his crew. He died of the virus on June 4, 1994. But he had left his mark on the bloody war in Brooklyn.

About the war, Charles Hynes, the Brooklyn district attorney, said, "I have no problem letting these folks blow each other away. It's good for us ultimately. The problem is most of them don't get annual firing practice, so when they begin to miss, they end up killing innocent people." After an innocent man was killed at a Brooklyn bagel store, Hynes issued forty-one grand jury subpoenas to Colombo associates, capos, and soldiers. It certainly interrupted the war, for as Hynes added in a television interview, "when they are under subpoena they can't shoot. They all hide." [3]

The bloody street battles continued until 1992 when Orena was convicted of racketeering and murder. Scarpa never got his revenge. But he must have been pleased that Orena was given three life sentences, plus—for good measure—an additional eighty-five years. He wasn't the only one: fifty-eight soldiers and associates, all members of the Persico faction and sixteen from Orena's faction, all went to prison. That left seventy-five made members of the Colombo family to continue.

During the war, the other New York Mafia families turned their backs on the Colombos. They refused to allow any member of the family a seat on the Commission. The members of the Commission considered a proposal to divide what was left of the Colombos among themselves. Then Joseph Massino, the boss of the Bonanno family (no stranger to internecine warfare), suggested that since the war had ended without further killings, the Colombos should be allowed to rejoin the Commission. A vote was taken, and the Colombos were seated with the other families.

The aftermath of the war was a succession of arrests, indictments, and trials that resulted in a progression of bosses becoming permanent prison inmates. One who was emblematic of the trials and tribulations of the bosses was Andrew "Andy Mush" Russo. Unlike his predecessors, he served two non-consecutive terms as boss, both of which concluded with his arrest. On

January 11, 2011, he was charged with murder, narcotics trafficking, and labor racketeering. Then, on September 14, 2021, the Colombo family and boss Russo were indicted for infiltrating and taking control of a Queens-based labor union and its affiliated health care benefit program. In addition, they were charged with fraud regarding workplace safety certifications.

According to a report in the *New York Daily News*, "Colombo family kingpin Andrew "Mush" Russo, the mob veteran busted for racketeering last year before myriad health woes led to his release on a $10 million bond, died Monday night, his attorney confirmed to the Daily News."

"The 87-year-old Russo, a cousin of the late and legendary boss Carmine Persico, was arrested in a huge federal sweep last September over the crime family's attempt to violently seize control of a local labor union, according to court documents. He was turned loose a month later and died in the company of his family without facing trial in the pending case, attorney Jeffrey Lichtman said Wednesday. The veteran gangster, caught on a wiretap before his 2011 guilty plea to federal charges, offered a glimpse of his management style: 'I don't hesitate, I've never hesitated' to use violence against mob colleagues who stepped out of line.

"Russo, who lived in Glen Head, L.I., was convicted alongside his relative Persico in a 1986 mob trial on racketeering charges, and was reportedly bumped up to acting boss after his release from prison eight years later. In late 2020, Russo assembled the family's top hierarchy for a mob sitdown at the legendary Brennan and Carr restaurant in Brooklyn as federal agents surreptitiously watched, the *Daily News* previously reported.

"Russo was long involved in the Colombo family hierarchy, serving as an acting underboss in the mid-1970s before his 1994 promotion by the imprisoned Persico. According to authorities, he became the official head of the family in 2010 after his parole on a prior arrest ended. He then continued to head the Colombos from behind bars after his conviction on a separate charge one year later.

"Russo, freed in June 2013, stayed on in the top spot until his arrest in last year's massive racketeering sweep that initially left him behind bars with 13 other Colombo leaders and associates.

"The mob boss was also a schoolboy pal of *The Godfather* actor James Caan, who was subpoenaed to appear at Russo's 1985 Manhattan Federal Court trial.

"'We grew up together,' Caan told reporters at the time. 'I've never heard anything about this. He's got eight grandchildren. This is unreal.'" 4

Russo, Persico, and the Gallo brothers inspired numerous newspaper and magazine stories, as well as books and movies. The bosses and their warrior capos and soldiers were some of the most colorful mobsters in the history of the Mafia.

Though the Persico faction ultimately declared itself victors of the bloody war, the family was weakened by the elimination of so many of its members and loss of business opportunities. Nevertheless, until the day he died, Persico continued to issue orders from his prison cell.

Even within prison, he continued to have a gravitational pull, and one of the people he drew into his orbit was the massive Ponzi schemer, Bernie Madoff. Shortly after Madoff arrived to begin serving his 150-year sentence, he walked into the prison's television room to watch a report about himself on *60 Minutes*. An inmate was watching another program, but that didn't prevent Madoff from changing the channel to a local CBS station. The inmate who had been watching TV leapt to his feet and angrily shouted at Madoff to turn the TV back to the earlier program. Madoff refused, and the two men challengingly exchanged harsh words. A brief struggle ensued that was broken up by a guard, but not before Madoff's opponent slapped him. Though a remote-control device was not involved, the struggle was referred to by several inmates as a fight for the remote.

This was too much for Persico; he would not tolerate having some low-level inmate slap the man whom Persico admired for his brilliance in pulling off the largest Ponzi scheme in American history. Persico ordered a few of his prison pals to call on the slapper. The man was warned, as only a Mafia victim can be warned, never to interfere with Madoff's choice of programming. The slapper, silently sullen and subdued, skulked off.

Madoff was pleased by Persico's protective behavior, and a friendship quickly developed between him and the mob boss. While Persico remained a powerful boss of a Mafia family, Madoff had once been the nonexecutive chairman of the Nasdaq Stock Market. To several observers, the friendship between the two old imprisoned criminals seemed inevitable. Their prior positions, one said, gave them a lot in common. Their common interests included Madoff explaining to Persico the mechanics of a great Ponzi scheme, and Persico briefing his new friend on prison etiquette while guiding him through the vagaries of prison culture. Persico even gave Madoff a pair of shower slippers. When a reporter interviewed Madoff and asked what he thought of Persico, Madoff replied that his friend was a very sweet man. Madoff, who was not visited by his family, watched in envy and admiration as Persico met with his grandchildren. He was an affectionate grandpa.

"The former Wall Street money manager, who once hobnobbed with the deep-pocketed elite, has assembled an unusual fellowship in jail. 'He doesn't really fit into the prison life, which is very segregated by race and sexual orientation, among other things,' [journalist, Steve] Fishman said. Madoff 'moves from group to group. He has social relationships with some of the gay prisoners, the child molesters, the mob guys. It doesn't matter to him.'" [5]

Their friendship ended when Persico at age eighty-five on March 7, 2019, died at the Duke University Medical Center in Durham, North Carolina. His death was expected, for his health had been deteriorating for years. One of his attorneys had written, "'Mr. Persico is legally blind in his right eye, and has diminished vision in his left eye. He also has limited use of his left and right arms and a deformity of his left wrist that . . . severely impacts his upper mobility,' his lawyer, Anthony DiPietro, wrote in March 2016." [6]

"Persico sued the prison warden and a doctor there in December, alleging 'deliberate indifference' to his deteriorating medical condition and calling for his compassionate release. He had serious infections in his legs, and was trying to block doctors from amputating his leg above the knee. [Benson] Weintraub said he suspected Persico died of the leg infections, which he said 'spread as a result of deliberately indifferent treatment.'" [7]

Madoff died on April 14, 2021, in the Federal Medical Center in Butner, North Carolina, a facility for federal prisoners with special health requirements. His death was caused by hypertension, atherosclerosis, and kidney disease. He was eighty-two years old.

Notes

1. https://www.nytimes.com/1985/02/16/nyregionreputed-leader-of-colombo-crime-group-is-arrested-as-a-fugitive-on/-li.html?scp=15&sq="carmine+persico"&st=nyt

2. https://www.nytimes.com/1986/11/18/nyregion/persico-his-son-and-6-others-get-long-terms-as-colombo-gangsters.html?scp=5&sq="carmine+persico"&st=nyt

3. www.youtube.com/watch?v=gfYXZuZ7qB4

4. https://archive.ph/20220420200531/https://www.nydailynews.com/new-york/nyc-crime/ny-mob-boss-death-colombo-andrew-mush-russo-20220420-ux4bwytflzh2pdtavbqmtcbohe-story.html

5. https://nypost.com/2017/05/20/bernie-madoffs-closest-prison-pal-is-a-crime-family-boss?iframe=true&theme_preview=true

6. https://www.nydailynews.com/2019/03/08/carmine-persico-storied-new-york-mobster-and-longtime-colombo-family-boss-dead-at-85/

7. https://www.nydailynews.com/2019/03/08/carmine-persico-storied-new-york-mobster-and-longtime-colombo-family-boss-dead-at-85/

18

The Banana Wars

The Banana Wars, named after the Bananno crime family, were wars between different factions of the family. One boss of the family after another was brought to ruin either by a prison sentence or a bullet. The self-destructive, intra-family war nearly wrecked what had been one of the most cohesive and tradition-bound Mafia families. What follows is the story of its decline.

As its name indicates, the Bonanno crime family was founded by a man named Bonanno, Joseph Bonanno to be precise. He turned out to be the last of the original Mafia Commission members. He died at age ninety-seven. At the founding of the Commission in 1931, he was its youngest member, age twenty-three. By the time of his death, he had outlived all of the original members. He had become an institution. He had also written an autobiography (*A Man of Honor*) that revealed the existence of the Commission, and that revelation led to the devastating Commission Trial.

Though each of the Mafia bosses was extremely ambitious, greedy, and cutthroat, Bonanno was perhaps the most dynastic in his ambitions. Like Maranzano before him, Bonanno had dreams of becoming boss of bosses. And like Maranzano, Bonanno wanted the members of his family to come from his hometown of Castellammare del Golfo, Sicily. (The name of the city, by the way, translated into English is Sea Fortress on the Gulf, deriving its name from the medieval fortress in the harbor.) Crazy Joey Gallo's mother and Salvatore Maranzano were also born in Castellammare del Golfo.

In addition to his illegal businesses, Bonanno had a number of legitimate businesses, including garment manufacturing companies, commercial laundries, funeral homes, a cheese distribution company, and a trucking company. All provided legitimate sources of income, thus blocking the IRS from indicting him for tax evasion. One of his funeral homes was not entirely legit; it was used to dispose of murdered bodies: many of the home's coffins were like double-decker bunk beds. First to be dropped inside was a murder victim, snuggly placed on the lower deck; above him on the upper deck was placed the prettified body of an innocent civilian. Because two bodies made the double-decker coffins exceedingly heavy, well-muscled pallbearers were required to carry the coffins to the hearse and from the hearse to the grave site. The funeral director referred to his pallbearers as his strong-arm men.

Bonanno's business interests extended beyond the city of New York: "During his 33 year reign [as boss], Bonanno used his considerable ill-gotten gains to extend his empire, . . . acquiring major interests in Arizona, California, Canada, Cuba, and Haiti." [1]

In 1957, Bonanno was one of the gangsters who attended the infamous Apalachin Conference, where he was arrested after being caught while attempting to flee through the woods. Though there was a trial of the arrested attendees, Bonanno was fortunate to have had a heart attack and was not included in the roll call of the indicted.

By 1963, Bonanno's plans seemed to have been an echo of Maranzano's to become the boss of bosses. His path to ascension was almost clear: Luciano had been exiled to Italy; Costello was having problems with the Justice Department; Albert Anastasia had been assassinated in 1957. However, there was an obstacle that Bonanno had not originally foreseen. In 1962, following the marriage of Carlo Gambino's son and Thomas Lucchese's daughter, Gambino and Lucchese became the two most powerful bosses on the Commission. They were like a pair of sentries who could block Bonanno's path to crowning himself boss of bosses.

Bonanno would have to take radical action to remove the obstacles to his ambition. He decided to bring in Joseph Magliocco (aka, Joe Evil Eye) into his plot. Magliocco, boss of the Profaci family, was pissed because he had been denied a seat on the Mafia Commission. Its members thought he was too weak. Magliocco accepted a contract from Bonanno to murder Gambino, Lucchese, Stefano "The Undertaker" Magaddino, boss of the Buffalo crime family, and Frank "One Eye" DeSimone of the Los Angeles crime family. Why DeSimone was put on the hit list is difficult to understand. He posed no threat to Bonanno; his sphere of influence was the southwest, though he interacted with the eastern mobsters. He was a graduate of the University of Southern California Law School and became a licensed lawyer in 1933. It wasn't until he attended the Apalachin Conference and was arrested that he was publicly outed as a Mafioso. He was eventually disbarred. After he learned of Bonanno's contract on his life, he became understandably paranoid and refused to go out at night. He stayed locked in his house with his mother and only left to take care of business.

Magliocco, who was assigned the task of killing the bosses, may not have been the best ally for Bonanno. His first mistake was subcontracting the hit to Joe Colombo, who had a good reason for not carrying out the hit. He wanted to be boss of the Profaci family! Ever opportunistic, Colombo cleared a path to his greater power by revealing the murder plot to its targets. Gambino and Lucchese thereafter realized that Magliocco would never have planned such a murderous coup. The targeted bosses called Magliocco to appear before the Commission. A shaken Magliocco readily admitted the origin of the planned coup. He was fortunate not to be killed. Instead, he was forced into an ignominious retirement, had to pay a $50,000 fine, and subsequently died of a heart attack. For revealing the plot, Colombo was rewarded by being recognized by the Commission as the new head of the Profaci family.

Colombo, no shrinking violet, immediately named the family after himself. Bonanno, meanwhile, had no intention of honoring a summons to appear before the Commission. He knew that such an appearance would result in a death sentence. He therefore arranged to convince the world that he had been kidnapped, a story that the media bought into. *The New York Times* reported that Bonanno had been kidnapped by men working for the Commission and taken to a hideout in the Catskill Mountains. There, according to the report, Bonanno convinced his captors not to kill him because it would start a national Mafia war. After he agreed to retire, he was released. Tabloid newspapers, still reporting about Bonanno's disappearance, ran the headline, "Yes, we have no Bananas." The soldiers in his family were not amused; according to an FBI wiretap, they cursed him, referring to him as a son of a bitch, for deserting them.

In his book *Honor Thy Father*, Gay Talese writes, "the FBI recorded a conversation in which De Cavalcante [boss of the eponymous named New Jersey Mafia family] was asked by one of De Cavalcante's men, Joseph La Selva, to explain the Bonanno mystery."

> "So what happened?" La Selva asked.
> "He [Bonanno] pulled that off himself," De Cavalcante said.
> "That figures," said La Selva.
> "Well, who the hell is he kidding?" De Cavalcante asked. And then answered the question, "He kidded the government."
> "Yeah," La Selva agreed.
> "It was his own men," De Cavalcante said. "We figure it was his kid and Vito [possibly meaning Vito De Filippo, his captain with gambling concessions in Haiti]."

"It was to La Selva that De Cavalcante also confided that Joseph Bonanno in 1963 had been the mastermind behind Joseph Magliocco's scheme to dispose of the two commission dons, Carlo Gambino and Thomas Lucchese, and that when the plot failed, the commission was convinced that Joseph Bonanno arranged for the murder of Magliocco." [2] De Cavalcante went on to claim that

Magliocco had not died of a heart attack, but that Bonanno had poisoned him so that he could not reveal Bonanno's plan to take over the commission by killing its most powerful members.

Meanwhile, Bonanno was portrayed in the media as elusive as Bigfoot. *Life* magazine reported that he was in Haiti, a guest of President Francois Duvalier, who had given him casino concessions.

Bonanno remained incognito for two years. During that time, Gaspar DeGregorio, a capo in the family, declared himself the boss and sought Commission approval. The Commission agreed and quickly voted to name him boss of the Bonanno family. The move infuriated Bonanno's son, Salvatore "Bill" Bonanno. The two sides went to what the media called the Banana War. The war, which lasted four years, pitted those loyal to Bill against those loyal to DeGregorio.

Before the war even started, the rank and file of the Bonanno family had been unhappy when Joseph Bonanno appointed his son as consigliere of the family. Bill had been a university student; he was not a street guy. He didn't know how to speak with the street guys on their level. At best, he was perceived as a dilettante; at worst a completely inexperienced mobster wannabe who was appointed simply because he was his father's son.

DiGregorio, however, was the real deal, a hardened Mafioso. He did not look kindly on someone who was given his button without earning it. As Machiavellian as any boss, he invited Bill to a peace meeting. Bill agreed and suggested what he thought would be a safe place; it was his granduncle's house on Troutman Street in Brooklyn. On the night of January 28, 1966, Bill and his entourage drove to the house; as they were exiting their car, they were met by a storm of bullets. Bullets from rifles and shotguns rained down from building roofs and whizzed by from doorways, windows, and from behind a lamppost. Bill and his men attempted to retaliate, firing into the darkness, in the general direction of the attack. But it seemed to be coming from every direction. "More than one hundred rounds were fired." [3]

Bill and his men finally dove back into the car and sped off, bullets pinging the roof and hood of the car. No one was injured. The incident became known as "The Troutman St. Ambush." Though DiGregorio was thought to be the mastermind behind the attack, Paul Sciacca and Frank Mari were thought to have managed it. The bosses of the other Mafia families were furious. The ambush resulted in just the kind of notorious publicity that the Mafia had always attempted to avoid. And that publicity would put pressure on police and FBI agents to launch investigations. Just what the mob hated.

Regardless of Mafia disapproval, the Banana War continued; bullets flew, bodies fell. Though only about a dozen men were killed, dozens more were shot, beaten, knifed, and nearly strangled, and surprisingly, they all survived and continued fighting. DiGregorio and Sciacca continued to map out battles and ambushes. No one was safe, including Sciacca, who narrowly avoided an attempt on his life. The two men were like a pair of allied generals. Sciacca needed another tough warrior at his side and promoted Frank Mari as his second-in-command; it was a decision he would later come to regret.

Usually when a boss is taken off the field of battle, the war winds down. However, after Joe Bonanno had a heart attack in 1968, nothing changed. The gunfire continued. Not only did Joe have a heart attack, but he offered to resign as boss and move to Tucson, Arizona. He promised not to interfere in business in the East. As if that were not enough, in 1968 DiGregorio was wounded by machine gun fire and his health rapidly deteriorated, so much so that he gave up his position as boss. He died two years later. The Commission, which had been angry at DiGregorio, was relieved that he relinquished his position. They welcomed Sciacca as Bonanno family's new boss. Now there could be peace.

Bill, glad the war was over, resigned as consigliere and agreed to move to Tucson with his father. He hoped that the move would put him out of harm's way. Regarding his time as a warrior, he commented, "I always say I had only one goal in the '60s—actually two goals. When I got up in the morning, my goal was to live to sunset. And when sunset came, my second goal was to live to sunrise." [4]

Frank Mari, Sciacca's second in command, began to plot against his boss. He was joined by Michael "Mike" Adamo. Both men were betrayed to Sciacca, and on the night of September 18, 1968, the two plotters disappeared from the face of the earth. That left Philip "Rusty" Rastelli as another possible usurper. He had initially been loyal to the Bonannos, then switched his allegiance to the DiGregorio and Sciacca team. Sciacca promoted him to consigliere and Natale "Joe Diamonds" Evola, a former Bonanno loyalist, to underboss. One would have thought that would have been the end of the conflict, but it continued among the two sides that had gone to war against one another. One more man chewed on the dust of death; he was soldier Thomas Zummo, a former member of the DiGregorio and Sciacca faction. He was shot on May 6, 1969. Another blow to the reorganized family occurred on May 13, 1971, when Sciacca was indicted for selling $100,000 worth of heroin. The blow to the family was short-lived, for the case was dismissed. He died on August 27, 1986, age seventy-seven. No one had attempted to kill him. His death came as naturally as night.

No one individual seemed able to herd the disparate warriors into a coherent army, so the Commission appointed a three-man panel, consisting of Rastelli, Joseph DiFilippi, and Evola.

Evola, of the three, had the most respect, which made him a likely candidate for eventually being the sole boss. Of course, it would depend on the other two going the way of all flesh. Evola knew that if the other two vanished from life, he would have the Commission's vote of confidence. He had been a stand-up guy, loyal to the Mafia code of silence. The bosses admired him, especially after he was sentenced to a ten-year prison term on April 17, 1959. He had been convicted of conspiracy to distribute drugs while being the manager of a scheme to import large quantities of heroin into the United States from Sicily. He refused to flip under government pressure and never implicated any of those involved in the conspiracy. Following his release, the esteem in which he was held increased, for he added considerable wealth to the Mafia's income by getting deeply involved in garment trucking and bringing in Carlo Gambino and Vito Genovese. Nevertheless, even with those two powerhouse partners, Evola could not bring peace to the Bonannos.

"In 1971-72, investigators gained significant information on Evola's operation, as well as that of then-Lucchese-boss Carmine Tramunti, by bugging a trailer used by the bosses and their lieutenants as a meeting place. Evidence suggested that Evola was engaged in garment district labor racketeering, drug trafficking and hijacking.

"Evola's health was failing by then. He died of cancer [on August, 29, 1973 in Columbus Hospital in the Bronx. And is buried in Calvary Cemetery in Woodside, Queens, New York]. He was reportedly unmarried and lived at the time of his death with his elderly mother in Brooklyn.

"Evola was replaced for a time by his underboss Philip 'Rusty' Rastelli. (Rastelli, not yet popular with the Bonanno capos, was merely keeping the seat warm. Former Bonanno underboss Carmine Galante, a genuine power in the family, was finishing a jail term for drug trafficking.)" [5]

Rastelli's time in wearing the crown was not without honor. He enjoyed the power of his position, for which he believed he was entirely qualified. He, like Evola, had always been a stand-up guy, who participated in the standard Mafia rackets, such as extortion, drug dealing, and loan sharking. Though many Mafiosi owned highly profitable restaurants, Rastelli may have been the only one to own a lunch wagon, which inspired him to form a trade association of lunch wagon operators; they were a rich source for his extortion efforts.

It was not lunch wagons, but murder that the FBI had been trying for years to nail Rastelli. The murder they wanted to nail him for occurred on December 3, 1953, and the victim was Michael Russo. Russo, much to Rastelli's disappointment, survived, but only because he was rushed to a hospital emergency room where doctors intensely worked to save his life.

As commendable as were the actions of the doctors and nurses who saved Russo, his survival was not something that Rastelli approved of. If Russo talked, Rastelli was sure to have been indicted. Rather than wait around to see if handcuffs were in his immediate future, Rastelli went into hiding. Though in hiding, he was still able to operate as a gangster. Threats and bribery were two tried-and-true means of influencing witnesses. Rastelli determined to try a softer approach, and he deputized his wife, Connie, to offer Russo's wife, Rose, $5,000 for her husband's silence. Rose figured that Rastelli offered too low a price for his freedom and refused the offer. It was upped, and Rose still refused. A third offer was presented to the angry wife, and she refused that as well. Not only did she refuse the offer, but she visited the office of the local district attorney and complained about the bribe and lack of justice in arresting Rastelli. This was too much for an exasperated Rastelli. But if that wasn't bad enough, Connie became a confidential informant. Then, to make sure that Russo would never talk, he was shot and killed in December 1954. That same year, Connie was indicted for her attempts to bribe Rose Russo. Bad enough to be hit with an indictment for only trying to protect her husband, but then she was murdered. However, news of the murder spread only as a rumor, and since her body was never found, the rumor of murder turned into a non-prosecutorial fact. Not only was no one prosecuted for the murder of Connie, but no one was indicted for the shooting of Michael Russo. The Mafia's esteem for Rastelli went up several notches.

Though no one hung the Russo murder rap around Rastelli's neck, he didn't get a long period to enjoy his freedom. He was indicted for loansharking in 1971, followed by a conviction in 1972. Nevertheless, at a meeting at the Americana Hotel on February 24, 1974, the Commission unanimously chose Rastelli as the boss of the Bonanno family. He was a top earner, and his loansharking alone generated one million dollars a year. Nevertheless, the real power went to Carmine Galante, who was released from prison in January 1974.

Though Rastelli had beat a murder rap, he was not as lucky in being indicted for less mortal crimes. On March 6, 1975, he was indicted for extorting those whom he forced to join his lunch wagon trade association. To succeed as an extortionist, Rastelli used threats, vandalism, and violence. The trial that followed his indictment led to a conviction on April 23, 1976. The sentence was ten years in prison to be served consecutively with a four-year sentence for usury and contempt of court.

With Rastelli in prison, Galante was able to exercise his ambition to being boss of the Bonannos. Galante didn't give a shit about the other bosses, and he practiced his contempt for them as if they were harmless insects.

A symbolic demonstration of Galante's contempt for the bosses, dead or alive, occurred when Frank Costello's mausoleum was bombed in 1974, following Galante's release from prison. He allegedly ordered the bombing because Costello had ordered members of his Borgata not to deal in drugs, and Galante was deeply involved in the importation and distribution of drugs. In addition, Galante had contempt for Costello for retiring from the Mafia. Galante, like many Mafiosi, believed that membership was a lifetime commitment and no one had the right to retire. Anyone who retired from the mob invited a death sentence, though Joe Bonanno would suffer no such threat to his well-being.

Not only did the bosses regard the bombing as a sacrilege, but they were also alarmed that Galante's brazen drug dealing would bring down intense law enforcement scrutiny on all of their illegal activities. Frank Tieri, boss of the Genovese family, was the first to suggest to the other bosses that Galante should be eliminated. While still in prison, Rastelli also pushed for Commission approval for a Galante hit. Next came Joe Bonanno's suggestion that Galante be hit. After all, if Galante ordered the bombing of Costello's mausoleum because Costello had retired from the mob, what might he have in mind for Bonanno? No one on the Commission objected. After all, who knew what crazy actions Galante was capable of?

On July 12, 1979, Galante was having a pleasant lunch with Leonard Coppola, a Bonanno capo, and Giuseppe Turano, a Bonanno soldier on the patio of Joe and Mary's Italian American Restaurant in Bushwick, Brooklyn. For protection, Galante was joined at the table by two of his Sicilian bodyguards, Baldassare Amato and Cesare Bonventre. All five men were enjoying platefuls of pasta and the warm summer sunshine on the patio of the restaurant. Suddenly, at 2:45 p.m., as Galante was enjoying a postprandial cigar and espresso, three men rushed through the restaurant and onto the patio, shotguns and pistols blazing. Galante, Coppola, and Turano were immediately hit, their bodies decorated with bloody holes. The two bodyguards were unharmed. Amazing that none of the shotgun shells hit them! Galante, not so lucky, was hit by several blows that shot him out of his chair, landing him face up on the floor of the patio, a cigar still clenched between his teeth and blood smeared over his shirt. In the shocked silence in the restaurant, the gunmen rushed out as fast as they had rushed in. They got into a hot car and were driven to safety. Their ski-masked faces provided no identities for the police to investigate.

On April 21, 1983, Rastelli became a free man and still boss of the Bonanno family. However, his freedom was again brief: on August 16, 1984, he was arrested for violating his parole by associating with (to use a parole board's phrase) "known criminals." He may have felt that some ancient gods had provided him with a haphazard fate, cursedly designed to let him make steps forward, then steps backward. However, for another brief time, he may have thanked the gods of fate, for the government indicted the Mafia bosses in what became known as the Commission Trial of 1985. And since, the Bonannos had been kicked off the Commission for inviting FBI undercover agent Donnie Brasco to join the family. Rastelli was saved from a trial that sent the bosses to prison for life. Just as Rastelli thought he was home free, surprise of surprises, he was indicted on October 14, 1986, on twenty-four counts of labor racketeering. He was convicted on January 16, 1987, and sentenced to twelve years in prison. It was a better sentence than the ones handed out at the

Commission Trial, but Rastelli would be betrayed by his failing health. He had developed liver cancer, which became so deadly and painful that he was given compassionate release from prison on June 4, 1991. Twenty days later, he died in a hospital in Queens, New York.

Joseph Massino became the boss of the family, and he is primarily remembered by friends and foes as the first boss to testify against his cohorts and go into the Witness Protection Program. Galante, no doubt, would be cursing such a betrayal.

Notes

1   https://crimelibrary.org/gangsters_outlaws/family_epics/bonanno/3.html
2   Gay Talese, *Honor Thy Father* (New York: World Publishing, 1971), 385–6.
3   https://crimelibrary.org/gangsters_outlaws/family_epics/bonanno/3.html
4   https://www.latimes.com/archives/la-xpm-2008-jan-03-me-bonanno3-story.html
5   https://onewal.com/w-evola.html

19

Flippers, Informants, Rats, Explainers

Omerta was to the Mafia what the US Constitution is to presidents: something to be obeyed with utter devotion. Though a few presidents have been found to be less than loyal to their oaths to uphold the Constitution, numerous Mafiosi have chosen to abandon their adherence to omerta, testifying against their cohorts, and finding refuge in the Witness Protection Program.

Such apostasy was abhorrent to the bosses as stated by Paul Castellano, the assassinated boss of the Gambino crime family: "There are certain promises you make that are more sacred than anything that happens in a court of law, I don't care how many Bibles you put your hand on."[1]

For years, the FBI, Justice Department prosecutors, district attorneys, and organized crime detectives disagreed: they knew that the best way to get convictions of Mafia bosses is to offer their underlings get-out-of-jail cards for testifying against those who give the orders. The ones who accept such offers are said to have flipped. Those who flip, while in prison, and agree to testify against bosses, capos, soldiers, and associates, are granted reduced sentences or commuted ones. Prior to arrest, some future flippers had acted as confidential informants, operating in secret. When their covers were blown, they were called rats, and contracts to have them killed were issued. It's not easy to betray one's crime family, and many of those who did so twisted themselves into knots of self-exculpatory non sequiturs to justify their acts. These explainers, when called rats by defense attorneys, often muttered tortuous explanations for their actions. Those who became flippers, informants, rats, and explainers fit into a FIRE acronym, for they set their Mafia families on fire, leaving behind burnt offerings from which new men resurrected edifices of criminality. But, it often went up in smoke again. It was one of the risks of being in the Mafia. Paul Castellano, who in addition to being a boss was something of an oracle, ruefully commented: "This life of ours, this is a wonderful life. If you can get through life like this and get away with it, hey that's great. But it's very [un]predictable. There's so many ways you can screw it up." [2]

Those who chose to testify against their bosses and cohorts are not just members of a rogue's gallery; they are the ones who helped to reduce the Mafia to its current diminished status. What follows are profiles of some of the most consequential flippers, informants, rats, and explainers (FIREs).

- "Handsome" Phillip Leonetti.

Leonetti looked like a Hollywood stereotype of a smooth operator. He was considered Mafia royalty in Philadelphia, for he served as underboss of the Philadelphia crime family under his uncle Nicodemo "Little Nicky" Scarfo.

Leonetti had become his uncle's underboss after Scarfo arranged for the murder of crime boss Philip Testa, who had been blown to pieces by a bomb filled with nails. The FBI suspected Scarfo of ordering the attack, and Scarfo's quick ascension to the position of boss of the family did nothing to dissuade the FBI of its conclusion. Once established as boss, Scarfo then quickly promoted Leonetti to be his underboss.

Leonetti reportedly made millions of dollars from skimming Atlantic City casinos, loansharking, and extortion. As Scarfo's protégé and nephew, Leonetti walked on water: no other mobsters interfered with his operations. If he needed to mention his uncle, who had a reputation as an exceedingly vicious killer, people parted the seas for him. Scarfo had given Leonetti contracts to commit murder, and his nephew did what was on the menu. He earned his button and was inducted as a made man into the Mafia. His life was filled with fears of being killed, fears of being arrested, and fears of his uncle, whose paranoia could result in a contract on Leonetti's life.

Leonetti, like all other made men in Philadelphia and Atlantic City, knew that you had to pay obeisance to Scarfo: it was a passport to go on living. Show Scarfo disrespect, and he might kill you. For one such disrespectful Mafioso, Scarfo ended his life with an ice pick. Scarfo was not alone in killing people who got in his way or betrayed him or failed to pay a debt. For example, in 1978, Scarfo and Nicholas "Nick the Blade" Virgilio murdered a judge named Edwin Helfant, who had accepted a bribe to convince another judge to provide a light sentence for Virgilio, who was on trial for murder. Scarfo and Virgilio had given Helfant $12,500 to pass on to the sentencing judge. However, the sentencing judge was just short of being a hanging judge: he sentenced Virgilio to twelve to fifteen years in prison. Virgilio raged against the judge and against Helfant. The latter challenged fate by refusing to return the bribe. It was a case of suicidal chutzpah. Helfant may have felt safe. After all, he was a respected judge, and the Mafia had an unwritten rule (of course, all their rules were unwritten) about not killing judges, cops, district attorneys, FBI agents, etc. On February 15, 1978, Helfant—oblivious to the rage he had stirred up—took his wife for dinner and drinks in the Lounge of the Fountain Hotel in Atlantic City. Scarfo drove a vengeful Virgilio to the Lounge. Wearing a ski mask, Virgilio angrily strode into the restaurant and over to Helfant. He stopped in front of the judge and his wife, then pulled out a gun and fired five bullets into the judge. Screams and shrieks echoed through the restaurant as shocked diners dropped their forks. Virgilio, having satisfied his appetite for vengeance, strode out of the restaurant. He got into Scarfo's getaway car, and the two men sped into the night. Scarfo dropped off Virgilio at his girlfriend's apartment. After entering the apartment, Virgilio's greeting was an announcement of his alibi: "I'm glad I was here since 8 P.M."[3] It was well past 9 p.m.

The two men may have felt that they walked on water as fearsome Mafia bigshots, but they were ultimately indicted in 1987, and at trial, they were convicted of murder.

Leonetti was not destined to be an underboss for long, and he was certainly not destined to ever become a boss; Scarfo, his paranoia always on the boil, at times suspected his nephew might try to kill him and take over. Leonetti walked on a tightrope, and the only net that could break his fall would be provided by the government. They gave Leonetti a choice: flip or spend years in prison. Leonetti made a sensible choice and flipped. His uncle had a new reason for killing him.

Leonetti commented: "[Scarfo] always told me, he says, 'You gotta kill people. And you gotta keep on killing 'em. That's how this thing works, La Cosa Nostra. That's how he looked at a problem. They would have to kill him not to be killed. But there was no more brotherhood. I mean, my uncle took over. And the way he was acting, it wasn't the same. It was—he was—breaking all the rules that he taught me to obey. And I just—I was disgusted. I couldn't take it anymore." [4]

Asked by John Miller on *CBS News* what he liked about being in the Mafia, Leonetti responded: "I liked the respect that I received from everybody in our family because I had quite a reputation, you know, from being taught by my uncle the rules of the mob. He taught me how to kill people." [5]

And when had he first killed someone? By the age of twenty-three, Leonetti—out to prove himself—committed his first Mafia murder. Of it, he said, "I remember the feeling I had; I felt cold and I didn't feel any remorse. I ran behind him. . . . And I stuck the gun to his—behind his head. And I fired. And I thought he was running away because the force of the gun moved him forward, you know? And then he fell down. And I emptied my gun into him."

Leonetti added: "I hate to say, but it felt natural. I mean, I didn't feel anything. I just did it. I thought it was my job. And—and that was it. To me they were all bad people," he said. "I mean, they could have killed me, too; I could have got killed. So I'm not—I—I can't worry about the past." [6]

The respected and feared killer had notched ten murders. He was one of the boys. But then, the feds dropped a net on him (not under him) and his career was over. He faced a forty-five-year prison sentence. If he lived to breathe outside prison walls, he would be an old man. There was nothing tempting about growing old in prison. He reached for the only brass ring made available to him. He would admit to all of his crimes and testify against his cohorts, including his uncle. As might be expected when his paranoia proved to be no fantasy, Scarfo placed a $500,000 bounty on his nephew. Of the forty-five years, Leonetti served a mere five. Scarfo, however, was sentenced to fifty-five years and died there in 2017, at age eighty-seven. His seventeen-year-old son, Mark, taunted by classmates about his father's criminal career, hanged himself. He was found by his mother, who called 911. Medics provided CPR, but Mark had been deprived of necessary oxygen. He remained in a coma until his twenty-third year, then died.

How did Leonetti feel about flipping? He told interviewer Paul Davis: "Becoming a witness is not a nice thing. You go up on the stand and testify against people that you know. I didn't enjoy that at all. But I made an agreement with the government and I testified truthfully about everything." [7]

Leonetti offered a conclusion to his life of crime and his subsequent freedom: "It's justice for me. I'm happy I'm out of jail. I think I did a good job with my family that I'm raising. I'm not looking to be in the mob. I never got in trouble after I got out of prison. So I think I'm doing pretty good. I think I'm a success story." [8]

Following his release from prison and tucked away in the Witness Protection program, Leonetti wrote his life's story titled *Mafia Prince*. The book was a terrific success, resulting in major television interviews and numerous newspaper and magazine stories. Leonetti, now seventy-one years old, continues to enjoy his life with his family. He is prosperous and, unlike others who emerged from the Witness Protection, he has remained crime-free.

- Sammy "The Bull" Gravano.

Another former underboss who flipped is Sammy "The Bull" Gravano. After serving a long prison term, he too has managed to shed his skin as a career gangster.

Before he disrupted the Gambino crime family and his relationship with its boss John Gotti, Gravano enjoyed an accelerated rise within the crime family. Soon after Gotti had engineered the assassination of his predecessor Paul Castellano, he promoted Gravano to be a capo, which followed the demotion of Salvatore "Toddo" Aurelio. Gotti's bull was promoted again in 1987 to become consigliere. From there, he ascended to being Gotti's underboss. And it was from that lofty position that he changed the course of his life, that of Gotti, and fellow gangster, Frank "Frankie Loc" LoCascio.

Prior to Gravano's apostasy, none of the mobsters realized that their conversations in the Ravenite Social Club, at 247 Mulberry Street in Little Italy, had been recorded. The three had provided prosecutors with enough evidence to warrant an arrest. And on December 11, 1990, New York City detectives and FBI agents raided the club and arrested the three gangsters. Gotti was the prize catch, subsequently being charged with five murders: Boss Paul Castellano, Thomas Bilotti (Castellano's driver), Robert DiBernardo (a producer and distributor of pornography), Liborio Milito (soldier), and Louis DiBono (a Gambino capo). In addition, Gotti was charged with illegal gambling, bribery, and tax evasion. The FBI's tapes were so dispositive of guilt that the three gangsters were denied bail. Then to top it off, the gangsters' attorneys, Bruce Cutler and Gerald Shargel, were disqualified from serving as counselors because prosecutors asserted they were "part of the evidence" and could be called as witnesses. Gotti then hired well-known criminal defense attorney Albert Krieger.

Now the tapes were about to do damage that could not be undone: the tapes, which were heard by the defendants, indicated Gotti's intention to blame the murders of DiBernardo, Milito, and Dibono on Gravano. He also fulminated that Gravano was excessively greedy. Denied the services of his attorney Gerald Shargel, Gravano figured that he would be found guilty, and so to save himself, he chose to flip and testify against Gotti. Following Leonetti, he now became the second underboss to testify against his crime family. Where was omerta now that it was so desperately needed? Or as columnist Murray Kempton bemoaned, "where are the scungilli of yesteryear?" [9]

Gravano was not about to be sacrificed and so requested a meeting with prosecutors. Brought into their presence, he announced: "I want to switch governments."[10] It was a strange comment: it wasn't as if he were a secret Soviet agent during the Cold War, who wanted to defect to the United States. He was a member of Cosa Nostra, which many members apparently believed was a separate government with laws and rules not shared by the United States. After agreeing to testify for the government, Gravano was taken from the Metropolitan Correctional Center to a US Marine base in Quantico, Virginia. There, he negotiated with his handler, prosecutor John Gleeson. He agreed to allocute to his crimes, including his participation in nineteen murders. In addition, he would have to testify for two years and would not be sentenced to more than ten years in prison.

Gravano's new status became publicly known on November 12, 1990. He was immediately vilified as a rat and was accused by Gotti's allies of being a serial killer, a sexual deviant, a drug dealer, and a terrorist. To protect their prized witness, the FBI's Hostage Rescue Team guarded Gravano day and night. The media became as excited as teenage groupies when it was announced that Gravano would be called to testify on March 2, 1991. On the witness stand, Gravano, with the poise of a movie tough guy, testified for three days. His words were daggers driven into the hearts of Gotti and Frank Locascio. Next, Gravano was bombarded for five days of aggressive cross-examinations by a team of defense lawyers. He never lost his tough guy poise and responded with unshakeable certainty, never faltering, never failing to live up to his agreement with prosecutors. Then, on April 2, after thirteen hours of jury deliberations, Gotti and Locascio, as expected, were found guilty of murder and racketeering. They were each sentenced to life in prison. Gravano's testimony had also nailed numerous members of the Gambino crime family as well as Colombo acting boss Vic Orena; his consiglieri, Benedetto Aloi; Genovese boss Venero Mangano; and DeCavalcante boss Giovanni Riggi.

When it came time for Gravano to pay for his crimes in 1994, he was sentenced to five years in prison, followed by three years of supervised release. However, since he had already served four years, his actual sentence was reduced to one year. The tabloids, which had for years carried flattering stories that in some cases seemed to have paid homage to John Gotti, the debonair Teflon Don, now screamed in dismay that a snitch who had admitted to nineteen murders should only have to serve one additional year in prison. In 1995, Gravano was released from prison and disappeared into the Witness Protection Program. Then, after eight months, he left the program and moved to Phoenix, Arizona, and opened a swimming pool company under his new name, Jimmy Moran. He began dealing the drug ecstasy, was arrested, served a long prison term, and was released on September 18, 2017. In December 2020, he began a popular podcast called *Our Thing* and has been crime-free.

- Frank Coppa.

Next on the hit parade of those who chose to flip was Frank Coppa, a Bonanno capo, who set the stage for his boss, Joseph Massino, to flip.

Like most Mafiosi, he was an entrepreneur; he owned a chain of chicken rotisserie restaurants and a school bus company named Three Brothers. Through his political connections, he won a New York City contract to bus children with disabilities to and from schools. Among his other holdings were parking garages and vending machines. With his income from all those sources, he was not driven by necessity to be a gangster.

But he had been a criminal since his late teenage years, and larceny had become a habit. He eventually moved on from thievery to drug dealing, and by the 1970s, he had moved on to Wall Street, where he proved to be an expert at pump and dump schemes. He and his associates bought stock in Tucker Drilling, then promoted it as a hot oil drilling company whose earnings would soon shoot up like an oil geyser. Bribed stock brokers sold shares to naïve and gullible customers. If a broker refused to go along with the scheme, he would be threatened; and if that didn't work, a beating would follow. As in all pump and dump schemes, as soon as the stock reached a high point, the schemers sold out; only the suckers remained, and they were left with worthless dry holes in the ground.

The good times for Coppa went on for years, but then his crooked dealings were exposed; he was arrested, tried, and imprisoned. Nobody likes prison, and though a mobster might say he can do his time standing on his head, when that time is extended and too much blood has rushed to the head, there is a desire for a more comfortable posture. In 2002, while serving time for stock fraud, Coppa was hit with an indictment for racketeering and extortion. If he was convicted under the RICO statute, he might spend the rest of his life in prison. Neither a head-stander nor a grandstander, Coppa contacted the FBI: he was ready to make a deal, to flip. It was a radical break with tradition, for no one in the Bonanno family had previously flipped. In fact, the bosses of the family had historically taken pride in the fortitude of its members never to rat on any member of the family.

Coppa, a radical uprooter of tradition, was taken to the FBI's training facility in Quantico, Virginia, where he spent two weeks pouring out information about the deeds of the Bonanno family. It was a history lesson that kept the agents transfixed. Once Coppa's testimony was heard in court, Bonanno members began tripping over themselves to make deals. In fact, ten members of the family escaped the cold doom of prison by following in Coppa's footsteps and sang songs of regret about their nefarious activities.

Meanwhile, the family's boss Joseph Massino may have raged against his turncoat pal, not just for breaking the sacred tradition of omerta, but also because Coppa's testimony would suck all the air out of the family. Massino alone would later be hit with indictments for seven murders.

Coppa spent two days testifying in court about characters with names that could have been invented by Robert Louis Stevenson if the author had written about Mafiosi rather than pirates named Billy Bones, Black Jack, and Long John Silver: the objects of Coppa's testimony included Bobby Wheelchairs, Gene the Hat, Little Nicky Eyeglasses, Sally Bagel, and Patty from the Bronx.

"Coppa's cooperation as well as his failing health played a role in a lenient sentence, [Judge Nicholas] Garaufis said. Coppa entered the courtroom on a mobility scooter, dressed in a red tie, white shirt, and black cardigan. He stood up from his scooter, despite the judge's opposition. "I'm really sorry for the people that I've hurt," he told the court. Coppa was associated with the Bonanno crime family for more than thirty years and eventually became one of its captains, according to the US Attorney's Office for the Eastern District of New York.

"Coppa's cooperation was the first major development in a series of prosecutions which, during their course, resulted in the indictment of virtually every high-ranking member of the Bonanno family," Amy Busa, a federal prosecutor, wrote in court papers. "Coppa's cooperation with the government has been truly historic." [11]

"Though he carried a .38-caliber revolver most of his life, Mr. Coppa was never accused of pulling the trigger in a murder. His toughness, especially when it came to doing time, was questionable. He acknowledged in court that when he went to prison for the first time, in 1992, he cried uncontrollably for days. 'He was one of the smartest mob guys you're ever going to meet,' a former F.B.I. agent involved in the case said in an interview on the condition of anonymity so that he could speak about the investigation. 'He understood how to engineer these financial frauds. He was at a completely different level when it came to most of these guys.' The former agent said he believed that Mr. Coppa had been remorseful. 'One of the reasons he cooperated is that I think he regretted his participation in the violent stuff when he was younger,' the official said. 'He lived off that reputation for many years. But he was actually likable in a way.'" [12]

One of the more fascinating stories that Coppa told was about his role in the murder of Dominick Napolitano, also known as Sonny Black, who was executed in 1981. "He was executed, for 'unwittingly connecting the family with an undercover F.B.I. agent, Joseph D. Pistone, who used the alias Donnie Brasco. Mr. Pistone later wrote a book about that experience and was played by Johnny Depp in *Donnie Brasco*, a 1997 film adaptation. 'The night of Mr. Napolitano's murder, Mr. Coppa testified, he had bought fried chicken for the hit men as they prepared for the execution, at a Bonanno member's house in Queens. 'It happened while Mr. Massino waited in a car nearby. Mr. Coppa, guarding the home's front door, let Mr. Napolitano in for a prearranged meeting in the basement. Mr. Coppa testified that he heard three shots soon after they descended the stairs—one, then a pause, then two more. It turned out that one of the assassin's guns had jammed. The other Bonanno associate finished the job. 'He died like a man,'" Mr. Coppa testified. [13]

Coppa wound up serving twenty-four months in prison from 2002 to 2004. Thereafter, he entered the witness protection program. According to an obituary in *The New York Times*, after testifying against Massino, "Mr. Coppa said he hoped the government would let him keep about $2 million that he had stashed away along with several homes and vehicles. It is believed that Mr. Coppa left the witness protection program a year ago, when the depleted Bonanno crime family was no longer a threat to his life."

"Public records listed him as residing in Sarasota, Florida in a high rise condominium, which his wife Marguerite Coppa, purchased in 2010 for

$457,500, according to the deed." Frank Coppa died on October 17, 2023, age eigty-two. [14]

- Joseph Massino:

The highest-ranking Mafioso to flip was Joseph Massino, whose choice to make a deal with the FBI led to execrations and excoriations: Bastard! Rat fuck! Son of a bitch! He was the last person Mafiosi would have considered breaking the law of omerta. So who was Massino?

His career in the mob did not portend either a rapid rise or a willingness to rat on his cohorts. He was such a devout believer in omerta that he had even instructed his children never to tattle. He was a man who valued his secrets and kept his own counsel. His wife was kept in darkness about her husband's business dealings.

He started out as a tough guy truck hijacker. He was conservative with his money and used his hijacking profits to open a catering business. His truck hijacking proved so prolific and profitable that he was seen as a likely recruit for the Bonanno family. It was not long before he became a protégé of Bonanno capo Rusty Rastelli, who set him up in Maspeth, New York, with a lunch wagon that became a front for a numbers racket and selling stolen merchandise. Rastelli inducted him into his own racket, the Workmen's Lunch Wagon Association. As a member, Massino had the privilege of not having to compete with other lunch wagon operators, but he also had to pay extortionate dues. Money was money, regardless of being a protégé. He was soon a made member of the Bonannos. Rastelli, who had a revolving door relationship with prison, departed from the lunch wagon trade and was sent to prison.

Meanwhile, Massino was rising swiftly in the family. His power and influence were unbeatable. As he rose, his girth increased. As a young man, he had been a well-muscled lifeguard and athlete. As a Mafia boss, he seemed to have ingested all of his power. His stomach ballooned and began to pour over his belt. Regardless of girth, Massino was determined to bring respect to the family. He cursed the day that FBI agent Joe Pistone (Donnie Brasco) brought disarray and disrespect to the family. Following the murder of capo Sonny Black Napolitano, who paid the ultimate price for proposing that Donnie Brasco become a made man, the family's reputation had fallen down a well.

But the decline of the Bonanno family had started before the Donnie Brasco fiasco; it occurred after Joe Bonanno published what Massino considered a self-aggrandizing memoir titled *A Man of Honor*. Its revelations, said Massino, amounted to ratting out the family. After the book and the revelations about Donnie Brasco's infiltration had become known, Massino announced to his men that from now on the family would be known as the Massino family. There was too much stigma associated with the name Bonanno. Yet, the media and FBI, police, and prosecutors continued to call it the Bonanno family.

Regardless of what the family was called, no one denied that Massino was its boss. He was indeed a Mafia boss, but not one out of the typical boss mold. *Time* magazine wrote: "Massino is an anomaly, an anachronism—the Masto-Don. He does not frequent posh nightclubs, Vegas high-roller rooms, designer-clothing stores or the front page of the *New York Post*. He does not care to give interviews (though he seemed amused when asked for one, and told a TIME reporter, 'Have a nice day'). His couture is less dapper than schlepper: jeans and T-shirts (he doesn't like wearing a tie), without the usual mobster adornments of a siliconed blond on each arm. He has never been accused of swagger. About as close as he got to being a public figure was in '87, when he was tried and acquitted for the slaying of three rival captains. (The charge was only conspiracy, so he can now be tried for the actual murders.) One day in the courtroom he joked with Pistone, who was about to publish a best seller about his exploits. As Pistone recalls it, 'So he asks me, 'Hey, Donnie, who's gonna play me in the movie?' I say, 'Joey, we're having a problem. We can't find an actor as fat as you.' He just started laughing." [15]

He may have appeared to be a shlepper, but he was meticulous when it came to security and not talking on wiretapped phones. His men were instructed to never use his name when discussing family matters. Taking a leaf from Chin Gigante's playbook, the boss who insisted that his men point to their chins when discussing him, Massino instructed his men to touch their ears rather than say the name of Massino.

He further enhanced security by closing many of the family's social clubs, a haven for indiscreet, wiretapped talks. Business meetings were to be held in out-of-the-way locations throughout the country, hundreds—if not thousands—of miles away, if necessary. He even held meetings on Caribbean islands and in European countries; his men were told to bring along their wives, so their trips would be seen as vacations. And no associate was to be even considered for membership in the family until that associate had contributed to the family's coffers for a minimum of eight years. Such a policy was to deter the infiltration of another Donnie Brasco. To further reduce the chances of inducting a potential traitor into the family, Massino encouraged members to induct their sons into the family. And like secret underground terrorist groups, the members were organized into secret cells where they would have limited or no information about other members. Following his shrewd and careful planning, Massino was able to restore the reputation of the family. He became a respected leader known as Big Joey, and no wonder: his weight had reached nearly 400 pounds.

Nevertheless, the Mafia is a very fluid organization. One day you're on top, the next day you may be killed or indicted. No gangsters were gunning for Massino, but the FBI had him in their sights. How ironic that the man who so valued omerta would be betrayed by his own underboss, capos, and soldiers in order to spare themselves long prison sentences.

And it wasn't just Coppa that led the way to Massino's downfall. There was also acting underboss Richard (Shellackhead) Cantarella, a participant in several murders, who was facing racketeering and murder charges. Next came Joseph (Joey the Mook) D'Amico, who flipped believing that Cantarella could implicate him for murder. Defections to the right of him, defections to the left of him, put Massino in a crossfire of damning testimonies. On January 9, 2003, he was arrested following a comprehensive racketeering indictment. To make sure that jurors would have no doubts about Massino's guilt, prosecutors were able to assemble a fraternal firing squad of Bonanno members who wanted get-out-of-jail cards. The most shocking turncoat was Salvatore Vitale, the brother of Massino's wife, Josephine.

Who was Sal Vitale and why did he turn on his brother-in-law? He was a boy when he met Massino, who took a paternal interest in his brother-in-law. He taught Vitale to swim and along the way instructed him in the skills and tactics of being a criminal. As he grew older, he was invited to participate in burglaries and truck hijackings. He was given a no-show job as a food consultant with a mob-run catering company.

He was now a full-fledged gangster and was inducted into the Bonanno family. With Massino as his mentor and brother-in-law, Vitale received rapid promotions and was eventually declared an underboss. Other members of the crime family were not enthusiastic about their underboss, but what could they do?

In 2001, Vitale was sentenced to house arrest following his guilty plea to participating in an extortion scheme. A year later, he pleaded guilty to being a loan shark. Massino, upon learning of Vitale's house arrest immediately became suspicious. Why was he given such a mild sentence? It must be that he agreed to make a deal with prosecutors. Massino then ordered two of his men to kill Vitale if his suspicions proved true. Then, on January 9, 2003, Massino was arrested along with Frank Lino and capo Daniel Mongelli. Vitale was also netted in the same arrest. He was in for a major surprise: on the day of his arrest, FBI agents informed him that Massino believed he was a rat and issued a contract on his life.

Before learning of his death sentence, Vitale had been harboring a grudge against Massino: while Vitale was in prison, Massino had not provided any support for the Vitale family. His anger no longer contained, the dam broke, and Vitale poured out his grievances and made a deal with prosecutors. Though Vitale admitted to eleven murders, he would get to become a new citizen in the Witness Protection Program if he testified against Massino. Vitale performed as he promised, and in October 2010, he was sentenced to time served.

Dark clouds formed over Massino's fate: he was indicted not only for racketeering, but for conspiracy to commit murders or for participating in several murders. Being indicted under the RICO statute would be bad enough, but Massino also faced a possible death sentence for the murder of Gerlando Sciascia, a capo in the Montreal Rizzuto crime family.

Massino's trial began on May 24, 2004, with Judge Nicholas Garaufis presiding. Those testifying against Massino sealed his fate. But the words of Vitale alone may have been enough to end Massino's career as boss.

Vitale was the last witness to testify against Massino. He had been a member of the family for about thirty years, and his knowledge of Massino's crimes was encyclopedic. It was devastating for Massino. There was his trusted protégé, the final witness for whom he had been a big brother. Et tu, Vitale? *Time* magazine wrote: "What must Big Joey think of this fraternal betrayal? Perhaps his emotions echo those famous words from The Godfather: Part II: 'I know it was you, Fredo. You broke my heart. You broke my heart!'" [16] After the defense and prosecutors had given their summations to the jury, Massino was a beaten man. Jury deliberations went on for five days. On July 30, 2004, Massino was found guilty of eleven counts. His sentencing was set for October 12. He glumly expected a life sentence, one with no opportunity for parole. He was right. As depressing as that was, he was also ordered to forfeit ten million dollars worth of assets and fined two hundred and fifty thousand dollars. And the law was still not finished with him. He faced another trial for the murder of Sciascia. Massino had always been resourceful; he had no intention of accepting the fate that the court had decided on. Immediately after his conviction, he requested a meeting with Judge Nicholas Garaufis. If Massino couldn't make a deal, there was a good chance he would be executed for the murder of Sciascia, for Attorney General John Ashcroft had ordered federal prosecutors to seek the death penalty for Massino.

On June 23, 2005, Massino finalized his deal with the government. He pleaded guilty to ordering the murder of Sciascia. He was sentenced to two consecutive life sentences with the possibility of early parole if his services as a witness proved valuable. When news of it leaked out, the other Mafia families could hardly believe it; Massino had a reputation as a stand-up guy; he had always bragged that the Bonanno family, unlike the other families, never had a rat and never would. The Bonannos were a family bound by old-world traditions, of which omerta was an essential ingredient.

As Jimmy Breslin writes in *The Good Rat*, "All his life Joe had a religious belief in omerta, a stop on his own personal stations of the cross." [17]

Massino's deal distinguished him as the first Mafia boss of a New York family to become a prosecutorial witness. In Philadelphia, he had been preceded by Ralph Natale, who had flipped in 1999. Massino's testimony against the mob was everything prosecutors had wanted. As a result, the Justice Department filed a request with Judge Garaufis for a reduction of Massino's sentence. The judge agreed to the request and granted Massino a reduction of his sentence to time served, plus close supervision for the remainder of his life. He, like other flippers, became a guest of the Witness Protection Program, living in an affluent retirement community in a Cleveland suburb. He was known to his neighbors as Ralph Rogers. On September 13, 2023, he died at a rehabilitation facility in Glen Cove, New York. He was eighty years old.

Notes

1 https://www.brainyquote.com/quotes/paul_castellano_211473
2 https://www.brainyquote.com/quotes/paul_castellano_211470

3   http://articles.philly.com/1995-03-18/news/25702337_1_virgilio-mob-boss-angelo-bruno

4   https://www.cbsnews.com/news/mafia-prince-phil-leonetti-says-murder-felt-natural/

5   https://www.cbsnews.com/news/mafia-prince-phil-leonetti-says-murder-felt-natural/

6   https://www.cbsnews.com/news/mafia-prince-phil-leonetti-says-murder-felt-natural/

7   https://www.cbsnews.com/news/mafia-prince-phil-leonetti-says-murder-felt-natural/

8   https://www.cbsnews.com/news/mafia-prince-phil-leonetti-says-murder-felt-natural/

9   Murray Kempton, *Rebellions, Perversities, and Main Events* (New York: Timed Books, 1994), 247.

10 Peter Maas, *Underboss* (New York: HarperCollins, 1997), 289.

11 https://dnyuz.com/2024/09/26/frank-coppa-first-bonanno-mafia-family-member-to-flip-dies-at-82/

12 https://dnyuz.com/2024/09/26/frank-coppa-first-bonanno-mafia-family-member-to-flip-dies-at-82/

13 https://dnyuz.com/2024/09/26/frank-coppa-first-bonanno-mafia-family-member-to-flip-dies-at-82/

14 *New York Times*, "Frank Coppa, 82, First Bonanno Capo To Flip on the Mafia Is Dead," Michael S. Rosenwald, September 25, 2024, B12.

15 http://www.time.com/time/magazine/article/0,9171,993685,00.html#ixzz25AsDnReQ

16 http://www.time.com/time/magazine/article/0,9171,993685,00.html#ixzz25AsheNUI

17 Jimmy Breslin, *The Good Rat* (New York: ECCO, an imprint of HarperCollins Publishers, 2008), 12.

20

Friends of the FBI

If you're a gangster and you don't want to be arrested, indicted, and wind up in prison, the best protection insurance you can buy is from the FBI. Two of the most murderous gangsters in America, who were given carte blanche by the FBI to be criminals, were James Joseph "Whitey" Bulger and Gregory "The Grim Reaper" Scarpa.

Whitey Bulger, though not a member of the Italian Mafia (he was an Irish American), was the boss of the Irish Winter Hill Gang that controlled Boston in the 1970s, 1980s, and 1990s. Thanks to the FBI, he was one of the longest-serving crime bosses in America. The arrangement proved to be a great deal for Bulger, but not so great for his FBI handler.

With Bulger, the FBI had a tiger on a leash. He was brutal and bloodthirsty, unlike his brother William, a powerful Massachusetts politician who served in the state senate for twenty-five years. Anyone who spoke with Whitey would quickly experience his brusqueness, which could suddenly become threatening. There was none of a politician's evasive malarkey. He was a gangster, a killer, who didn't take shit from anyone. Whitey killed anyone who didn't acquiesce to his demands, anyone whom he suspected of being a rat. Killing was as natural to him as to any predatory animal.

He grew up a poor, young kid from the streets of South Boston. And as a tough young Southie, he proved to be the toughest kid in his neighborhood on his way to maturing into a major gangster.

His life as a criminal began when he was fourteen years old. His thievery and threatening ways brought the law down on him, and he wound up in an ironically misnamed institution called a reformatory. There, he learned new criminal skills while feeding his contempt for authority, especially cops.

As his criminality progressed, prisons became his universities; he was in and out for thievery and assaults. Even when serving in the US Air Force from 1948 to 1952, his violations led to numerous criminal charges. Yet, he was honorably discharged, but still a dyed-in-the-wool criminal. He could have gone straight after his discharge, but straight into what? Being a legit civilian was not for him. There was nothing duller than a nine-to-five job. Truck hijacking, however, was exciting. It was also easy and profitable. Loads of swag could be easily fenced, and the cops never got wind of Whitey. However, that changed: Whitey decided on an even more exciting and dangerous profession: bank robber. After robbing some banks in Rhode Island, he was finally arrested, indicted, tried, and convicted. Excitement turned to anti-cop fury as he was sentenced to twenty-five years in prison. For the twenty-seven-year-old bank robber, a sentence nearly as long as his age was motive enough to lash out at cops, guards, and other inmates. Whitey had moved into the upper echelons of felons. He would be an inmate at such prisons as Alcatraz, Leavenworth, and Lewisburg, all graduate schools of criminality. If there were PhDs awarded in gangsterism, Bulger would have received more than one. He had the perfect transcript for being a boss. In fact, he so much valued his time in prison that he told a CNN interviewer: "If I could choose my epitaph on my tombstone, it would be 'I'd rather be in Alcatraz.'" [1]

While in a federal prison, he volunteered to participate in the MK-Ultra project, an experimental program conducted by the CIA; he was told the experiment was designed to find a cure for schizophrenia, and he would receive a reduced sentence for his participation. He was dosed fifty times with large quantities of LSD and other hallucinatory drugs. However, being a CIA guinea pig and receiving large quantities of those drugs proved to be a dangerous diet for Bulger. There is some evidence that the experiment aggravated Whitey's bloodthirstiness.

Many criminals, following their convictions, either claim they are innocent or cite powerful outside forces that caused them to commit crimes. Whitey was no exception. Following his 2013 conviction, he wrote to juror Janet Uhlar informing her that because he had been pressured to participate in the MK-Ultra project (which his lawyers did not mention during his trial), he believed that the drugs made him a violent man. In one of his many letters to Uhlar, he wrote: "On the Rock at times felt sure [I was] going insane." In another letter, he wrote: "Auditory & visual hallucinations and violent nightmares—still have them—always slept with lights on helps when I wake up about every hour from nightmares." [2]

"MK-ULTRA, which operated from the 1950s until the early '60s, was created and run by a chemist named Sidney Gottlieb. Journalist Stephen Kinzer, who spent several years investigating the program, calls the operation the 'most sustained search in history for techniques of mind control.'

"'Gottlieb wanted to create a way to seize control of people's minds, and he realized it was a two-part process,' Kinzer says. 'First, you had to blast away the existing mind. Second, you had to find a way to insert a new mind into that resulting void. We didn't get too far on number two, but he did a lot of work on number one.'

"Kinzer notes that the top-secret nature of Gottlieb's work makes it impossible to measure the human cost of his experiments. 'We don't know how many people died, but a number did, and many lives were permanently destroyed,' he says.

"Bulger wrote afterward about his experiences, which he described as quite horrific. He thought he was going insane. He wrote, 'I was in prison for committing a crime, but they committed a greater crime on me.' And towards the end of his life, Bulger came to realize the truth of what had happened to him, and he actually told his friends that he was going to find that doctor in

Atlanta who was the head of that experiment program in the penitentiary and go kill him." [3]

As horrible as the result of what Whitey endured, there were others who seemed to thrive on the use of LSD. Ken Kesey, the author of *One Flew Over the Cuckoo's Nest* and other novels, experienced the effects of the drug as pleasurable.

"The [CIA] was secretly funding a research project on hallucinogenics at the VA hospital near the Stanford campus. The researchers needed observable subjects—needed them so badly they were offering volunteers $75 a day. So Kesey signed up. Kesey was feeling an overwhelming sense of freedom. 'We were beautiful,' he said of his first LSD trips. 'Naked and helpless and sensitive as a snake after skinning, but far more human than the shining knightmare that had stood creaking in previous parade rest. We were alive and life was us.'" [4]

Robert Hunter, lyricist member of the Grateful Dead, was another celebrant of LSD. Tom Taylor wrote in *Far Out*: "The songs in question were, in essence, borne from his days in MK-ultra—a flowing stream of colourful nonsense.

"This further highlighted the possibilities of musical freedom to the [Grateful Dead] band, and they signed him up as a lyricist. His acid-infused anthems emboldened the band, made them a full-formed beast, a travelling road show now with poetry in their ranks—an odd form of poetry strangely conceived in a CIA laboratory.

"So, does that mean that, in some way, the success of MK-ultra was in producing the most counterculture band of all time? Was the organisation hoisted by their own petard in the most glorious fashion? Hunter simply says, 'Who can say' but there's no doubt that LSD gave the band their voice, and it was a weird one that still echoes." [5]

And Beat poet Allen Ginsberg "strongly advocated the use of psychedelic drugs, particularly LSD and psilocybin, as a means of self-discovery through the expansion of consciousness." [6]

Nevertheless, there were plenty of others who had extremely negative experiences after consuming LSD. I know, for example, of a young man who tried to throw himself out of a speeding car. Fortunately, he was hauled back before he could be broken into pieces and crushed under the wheels of speeding cars. There were also accounts of people who flung themselves off of high buildings. As Kinzer wrote, "The CIA mind-control program known as MK-ULTRA involved the most extreme experiments on human beings ever conducted by any agency of the US government. During its peak in the 1950s, that program and its director, Sidney Gottlieb, left behind a trail of broken bodies and shattered minds across three continents." [7]

So, it's entirely possible that Whitey was one of the unfortunate victims of the failed experiment. Mt. Sinai Health Systems in New York includes the following about LSD on its website: "Fears that you normally can control may become out of control. For example, you may have doom and gloom thoughts, such as thoughts that you will soon die, or that you want to harm yourself or others." [8]

In addition, "Hallucinogens like acid can make you do things you wouldn't normally do. For some folks, it causes extreme mood swings that may lead to aggressive and violent behavior." [9]

Regardless of whether Whitey's life as a violent criminal was the result of LSD, he became a murderously powerful force in the Winter Hill Gang. He was using murder to ensure his position and was implicated in three murders. Murders lead to investigations, and investigations may lead to arrests, convictions, and long prison sentences. Whitey had spent enough time in prison; as an ex-convict, he was determined to cash in on his criminal knowledge and skills. To do so, he needed protection, not from gangsters who might challenge his leadership, but from cops and the FBI. In 1974, he was approached by FBI agent John "Zip" Connolly to become a confidential informant for the FBI. Though Whitey had known Connolly since childhood (they grew up in the same zip code, hence the nickname), he was suspicious of the offer and did not agree to it for several years. However, it was frequently on Whitey's mind as an option. By 1979, Whitey felt the law closing in: twenty-one members of the Winter Hill Gang, including its bosses, members, and associates, were arrested. Whitey quickly moved to fill the void, and by doing so, he put a target on his back. Who better for the FBI to take down than a boss? The ensuing publicity alone would enhance one's career.

Whitey had leverage: the FBI wanted information on the Patriarca crime family, and Whitey did deals with them. In exchange for dropping a dime on the Patriarcas, Whitey could get immunity from the FBI. He could sail through his crimes with the wind at his back. Whitey saw a future without handcuffs, indictments, and prison sentences. And he wouldn't have to worry about revenge from the Patriarcas because they would never know of his role as a confidential informant.

Connolly received approval to use Whitey as his C.I. Connolly told fellow agents that he had recruited Whitey by promising to help him against his rival, the Patriarca crime family and its underboss, Gennaro Anguilo. Whitey supposedly responded by saying, "All right, deal me in. If they want to play checkers, we'll play chess. Fuck 'em." [10]

Whitey wasn't the only member of the Winter Hill Gang who made a deal with the FBI; the other was Stevie "The Rifleman" Flemmi. "Flemmi would scrape up intelligence on the Italians, and Whitey would pass it along to the feds. As Flemmi later described it, this relationship produced a perverse alchemy: 'Me and Whitey gave [the Feds] shit, and they gave us gold.'" [11]

The FBI had, in effect, become a partner of a murderous mob in an effort to destroy the Patriarca crime family. Whitey and Stevie's work with the FBI would more than tarnish the image of the FBI. "[The] business arrangement was nothing less than a license for Bulger and his cronies to murder, extort, and rape with impunity. They also seized control over the local narcotics trade even as Bulger was heralded in the *Boston Globe* as a kind-hearted Robin Hood who was 'keeping drugs out of Southie.'" [12]

The Winter Hill Gang not only got protection from the FBI, but it helped the FBI decimate the Patriarca crime family. Though sometimes, things worked out unexpectedly for Whitey and the FBI. In the summer of 1983, an employee of Coin-O-Matic, a Patriarca-owned company, was kidnapped. Someone called the Boston cops, telling them where they could find the kidnap victim. The cops then raided a butcher store partially owned by Whitey. There, the cops found the tortured kidnap victim hanging from a meat rack. His freezing body was taken down and wrapped in a blanket. Cops attempted to convince the shivering, teeth-chattering victim to testify against Whitey and his cohorts and then go into the Witness Protection Program, but he refused. Revenge was on the menu: the Patriarcas were not about to sit still after one of their own had been so badly treated; over the next few months, the Italians killed three members of the Irish gang. Many in the media spoke of an ethnic rivalry. This was not in the FBI's scenario. The killings set off alarm bells at FBI headquarters. An investigation commenced. Connolly's supervisor, John Morris, was held responsible for his incompetence in handling Whitey.

As a further embarrassment to the FBI, the *Boston Globe*, after an intensive investigation, revealed that Whitey was an FBI informant. The paper also reported on the many crimes attributed to Whitey. Readers were left asking, how could one man commit so many crimes while being an FBI informant? Why was the agency protecting him? If the agency was, indeed, protecting him, Whitey could go on killing sprees and no one would arrest him. There certainly would be no one willing to testify against him. And any witnesses to his crimes would be committing suicide if they reported those crimes to the FBI.

While the FBI was in bed with Whitey and Stevie, other law enforcement investigating agencies were convinced that Bulger was a top criminal and was responsible for some of the most vicious murders in Boston. He had to be stopped. In 1994, the Drug Enforcement Administration, the Massachusetts State Police, and the Boston Police Department, without informing the FBI, launched their own investigations. Throughout the investigation, they did not share results with a compromised FBI.

However, Connolly had his sources and having learned what was in store for Whitey, he informed him what to expect. In 1994, Whitey fled from Boston, abandoning his gang to the coming storm of indictments.

In 1995, Whitey and Stevie, as well as Mafiosi Frank Salemme and Bobby DeLuca, were indicted on racketeering charges. During pre-trial discovery, the two Mafiosi and their lawyer Tony Cardinale listened to an FBI-bugged conversation during which two agents discussed an informant. Cardinale requested that federal judge Mark L. Wolfe demand that prosecutors reveal information about the informants. On May 22, 1997, the judge did so. On June 3, Paul E. Coffey, head investigator of organized crime and racketeering in the Justice Department, provided sworn testimony that Whitey was an informant. He added that since Whitey was indicted for leading a criminal enterprise while acting as an informant, he was now considered a fugitive and his identity no longer had to be concealed.

Whitey, the fugitive, was as elusive as a phantom for sixteen years, much of the time accompanied by his girlfriend Catherine Greig. A chagrined FBI, determined to redeem itself, was now on the hunt for the fugitive who was allegedly spotted in cities around the world. Finally, in 2011, a neighbor of the couple in Santa Monica, California recognized the fugitives and informed the agency that Whitey and Catherine were using the names Charles and Carol Gasko. The fugitives had been living in a rent-controlled apartment in which the arresting officers found thirty high-powered weapons that had been concealed in the walls, and $822,000 in cash. Catherine and Whitey were shackled and brought back to Boston. There, the prize catch was, of course, Whitey. He had been the subject of a well-publicized manhunt for years. He was arraigned on July 6, 2011, and faced forty-eight federal charges, including nineteen for murder. Following a highly publicized trial that provided TV news viewers and tabloid readers with a detailed daily diet of Whitey's crimes, the boss of the Winter Hill Gang was found guilty on thirty-one charges and sentenced to life, plus five years, in prison.

Catherine was tried separately. In court, she appeared in a smart black sweater, and her silver-white hair was cut stylishly short. She periodically smiled at her twin sister; otherwise, her expression was that of a stoic. The judge sentenced her to eight years in prison. Then, in 2015, she was sentenced to an additional twenty-one months on a contempt charge for refusing to testify about others who may have helped the fugitives while on the lam. Following the completion of her sentence, Catherine moved in with her twin sister.

Whitey would never breathe again as a free man. He had served years in a prison in Colean, Florida; then on October 30, 2018, the 89-year-old Whitey, dependent on a wheelchair, was moved to Hazelton Federal Prison in West Virginia, where he was beaten to death in his cell hours after arriving. He was beaten with a padlock that had been stuffed into a sock. His eyes were also gouged out. Prison officials named Fotios ("Freddy") Geas, a mob hitman, who was serving a life sentence for the murder of a Mafioso member of the Genovese crime family. A second suspect was Paul DeCologero, serving a 25-year sentence for racketeering and conspiracy that led to a 1996 murder.

Whitey's partner in crime, Stevie Flemmi, pleaded guilty in US District Court in Boston to ten counts of murder and accepted a sentence of life in prison without parole. He did so in exchange for a reduction of the prison sentence of his brother Michael, a retired Boston cop, who had been arrested for having seventy weapons stored in a shed on his mother's property. Michael was convicted in 2002 and sentenced to ten years in prison. Stevie had turned against Whitey, and in 2013, he testified against him, confirming Whitey's role in murders and racketeering.

Howie Carr, a Boston radio show host, commented: "The only time Flemmi left prison was when he testified against other gangsters. But those days are over now because everyone he could have ratted out is dead. On what was probably his final snitch assignment back to Boston in 2018, Stevie was asked on cross-examination how many murders he'd been involved in. It took him a while to add everything up in his head. 'Probably about 50,' he finally said, 'either as an actual participant or the conspiratorial aspect.'" [13]

And what of John Connolly? He was indicted in December 1999 for providing confidential information to Whitey and Stevie (not for receiving confidential information from his C.I.s) and taking bribes and prevaricating in FBI reports.

Connolly was not helped when Stevie testified that he and Whitey paid their FBI handler $235,000 over several years. Much of that money was itemized by FBI agent Sandra Lemansky, who testified that during the 1980s Connolly bought a 27-foot Sea Ray for $46,567, a Boston condo for $63,000, another condo in Brewster for $80,000, and land in Chatham for $98,000, then built a house on the property for $132,000. Not bad on a salary that started at $45,000 in the 1980s and went up to $65,000. Connolly wasn't the only FBI agent whose reputation was tarnished; his superior, John Morris, admitted that he had accepted $7,000 in bribes from Whitey and Stevie, plus a case of wine and a thousand dollars from the two gangsters.

However, not everyone set fire to Connolly's funeral pyre. Edward F. Harrington, a former US attorney and later a US district judge, testified that Connolly was credited with using his informant to weaken the Patriarca crime family. And retired FBI agent Joseph D. Pistone (aka, Donnie Brasco) wrote in his book *The Ceremony* that "The reign of the Patriarca Family is virtually ended. A substantial amount of the credit for the demise of that mob Family must be given to one man, Special Agent John Connolly." [14]

Connolly was indicted again in 2005 and tried in 2008 on murder and conspiracy to commit murder charges in the 1981 murder of Roger Wheeler, owner of World Jai Alai sporting corporation, and the 1982 murder of John B. Callahan, former president and CEO of World Jai Alai. Wheeler had been murdered on the orders of Whitey and Stevie, who learned that Wheeler had uncovered their embezzlement scheme at World Jai Alai. Callahan was murdered because Whitey and Stevie were concerned that he might be an FBI informant and could testify against them. His bullet-ridden, decomposing body was found in the trunk of a car at a Miami airport.

Callahan and Wheeler were in fact murdered by John Martorano, a former hitman for the Winter Hill Gang, who admitted to twenty mob murders. In return for confessing to those murders, he received a reduced prison sentence of twelve years. In 2007, he was released from prison and given $20,000 and a new identity.

On June 28, 2011, Connolly was released from federal prison and transferred to Florida State Prison to serve out his 2008 sentence of forty years. He has always contended that he had nothing to do with Callahan's murder. In fact, after Whitey was captured, Connolly hoped that Whitey would confirm his contention.

Nevertheless, on May 28, 2014, Connolly's murder conviction was overturned by a panel of judges on Florida's Third District Court of Appeals. Two out of three judges voted that Connolly had neither carried nor discharged that gun that had killed Callahan. Therefore, he could not be convicted of murder. Unfortunately for Connolly, the court's decision was reversed by the full court in a six to four decision on July 29, 2015. Judge Leslie B. Rothenberg, who had dissented from the earlier decision to find Connolly innocent, wrote, "It now no longer matters whether the defendant hired (procured) a hit man, turned to his mob friends to murder Callahan, served as a lookout, provided the gun, or pulled the trigger himself, he is a principal in the first degree." [15]

In 2021, prison doctors determined that the eighty-one-year-old Connolly was gravely sick and might only live for another year. He was paroled from a Florida prison and lives under strict conditions of supervision in Massachusetts. Callahan's wife did not object to the parole, though some in the media wondered why Connolly was permitted to receive his FBI pension.

Another, even more vicious killer than Whitey was Gregory "The Grim Reaper" Scarpa. Police officials estimate that he killed between 80 and 120 people while serving as a CI for the FBI. He loved killing so much that he once said he was going to dig up one of his victims and kill him again.

He rose from Mafia soldier to capo in the Profaci crime family in Brooklyn, New York. As a gangster, he ventured into anything that was profitable: truck hijacking, extortion, loan sharking, and murder for hire.

He was also a man of many contrasts: he was a loving father and husband, but also an inveterate womanizer and a bigamist. While many street thugs are almost illiterate, Scarpo spoke in grammatically exact sentences and spoke knowledgeably about world affairs, domestic politics, and sophisticated financial matters. He dressed elegantly, wore an expensive toupee that matched his remaining black hair, and had a neatly trimmed mustache.

Jay Goldberg, a deceased criminal defense lawyer and former client of my marketing company, wrote: "When Greg walked in [to a restaurant], it was apparent to me that he was a person of class. He dressed impeccably, wore a well and expensive toupee, and had a deep suntan. Greg, apparently with me, wearing his toupee, was a person of class, but when he returned to Brooklyn to support a crime family boss [Carmine Persico], he removed his toupee and became a notorious killing machine—supposedly aided, shockingly, by members of the FBI." [16]

When Scarpo was arrested (which wasn't often) by the NYPD, an FBI agent would let the judge know of Scarpa's valuable services to the FBI. If Scarpa wasn't immediately released (which rarely happened), he was given a small fine and immediate probation.

As I wrote in *Big Apple Gangsters: The Rise and Decline of the Mob in New York*:

"Scarpa's involvement with the FBI had one salutary benefit: on June 24, 1964, three civil rights workers were murdered in Mississippi. They were Andrew Goodman, James Chaney, and Michael Schwerner. They had gone to Mississippi to register African-Americans to vote during what was known as Freedom

Summer. There existed in the state an organization with the bland name of the Mississippi State Sovereignty Commission, which was determined to thwart the efforts of civil rights workers, whom the commission described as outside agitators. The commission did so by paying spies to infiltrate groups of civil rights workers. Spies provided names, license plate numbers, and descriptions of civil rights workers to the commission, which passed along the information to local authorities. The case of Goodman, Chaney, and Schwerner, was given to the Neshoba County Sheriff, who was later implicated in the murders of the three, all of whom had earlier gone to Philadelphia, in Neshoba County to investigate the burning of a church that been the site of voter registration. After they left the church in their station wagon, they were stopped by Ku Klux Klan members and deputy sheriff Cecil Price. They were arrested for exceeding the speed limit by 5 miles per hour and taken to jail. Chaney paid a $20 fine, and all three were released from jail. Driving out of town, the boys were stopped again by Deputy Price, who ordered them to get into his car. Followed by two car loads of Klansmen, Price drove the three workers to a deserted area and ordered them out of the car. Chaney was viciously beaten and then shot in the head and abdomen. Seeing the gruesome murder of Chaney, Goodman and Schwerner knew they were next. 'Are you a nigger lover?' shouted one of the Klansmen at Schwerner and then shot him; Goodman met the same fate. Their bodies were buried in an earthen dam. After their bodies were discovered, autopsies were performed, and the medical examiner determined that Goodman was still alive at the time of his burial." [17]

When the FBI entered the case, they were met by locals with either misinformation or no information. The people they interviewed observed their own code of omerta. Stumped, the FBI decided to hire Scarpa; they knew he would use his own violent methods to reach conclusions. The agents rightly believed that they could not use those violent methods without breaking numerous laws. Their sense of irony was non-existent. Scarpa was given

$100,000 and a gun: the incentive and the means. He quickly located a weak-willed squealer and Klansman named Lawrence Byrd, who ran an appliance store.

Scarpa entered the store and was immediately taken for an affluent potential customer. Byrd approached him and asked if he could be of assistance. Scarpa said he wanted to buy a TV and soon identified the model he wanted. He paid cash for the TV, then asked Byrd to help him get the TV into his car, which was parked in an alley behind the store. After Byrd had pushed the TV onto the back seat, he felt the barrel of a gun against the right side of his head. Scarpa, with his free hand, opened the passenger door and curtly told Byrd to get in or he would blow his head off. Scarpa then drove a terrified Byrd to a local army base called Camp Shelby. Once inside, Scarpa forced Byrd onto a chair, then suddenly pistol-whipped him. He warned Byrd that he wanted to know where the three civil rights workers were buried, or he would whip him again. Though whimpering, Byrd refused to answer. A furious Scarpa pulled off Byrd's pants and underpants, then pulled a straight razor from a jacket pocket, unfolded the blade from its handle, and held the blade to Byrd's throat. He told Byrd that he would not slit his throat, but he would cut off his balls in five seconds if Byrd didn't give him the information he wanted. The still whimpering Byrd quickly told Scarpa the location of the burials and named some of the men who had killed the workers. Without public fanfare, Scarpa became the real-life hero of *Mississippi Burning*.

Scarpa, an FBI darling, returned to Brooklyn, where he went back to work supporting the imprisoned Carmine Persico in the ongoing Colombo war. Scarpa had attempted to gun down Persico's rival, Vic Orena, and as a result of his failure, Scarpa became the hunted.

On November 18, 1991, Scarpa escorted his daughter to her car; she was carrying her infant son. Before getting into his Mercedes, Scarpa told his daughter to follow him in her BMW. As they started to drive, a white van suddenly screeched into the road, blocking both Scarpa cars. Gunmen leapt from the van, their machine guns blasting away at the Scarpas. The Scarpas floored their cars, driving on sidewalks, over front yards, knocking down garbage pails and lawn ornaments. They managed to escape without any bullets hitting them.

Scarpa, raging and filled with a need for revenge, shouted that no one would get away with trying to kill him and his daughter. He called his FBI handler, Lin DeVecchio, who headed an FBI squad that surveilled the members of the Colombo crime family. Scarpa had been DeVecchio's confidential informant.

Scarpa had assumed too much. DeVecchio was incorruptible. And when others accused the FBI agent of misdeeds regarding his relationship with Scarpa, the FBI investigated DeVecchio and concluded he had done nothing wrong. In fact, he had acted exactly as one handling a CI should.

When accused of providing secret information to Scarpa, "DeVecchio vehemently denied that he had spilled secrets to Scarpa or had undermined investigations of the Colombo family. An agent with a distinguished record he retired from his $105,000 a year job soon after the Justice Department found insufficient cause to prosecute him for misconduct. 'The bottom line is that I never gave Scarpa any confidential information about the [Colombo] war or any other matter,' DeVecchio insisted in an interview. He attributed the agitation over his relationship with Scarpa to agents and prosecutors inexperienced in organized-crime investigations, and who misinterpreted justified and legal techniques in dealing with informers." [18]

Worse for Scarpa than Vic Orena's planned revenge tactics and the Colombo war was his dramatically failing health. Scarpa, who munched aspirins the way barflies munch peanuts, was suffering from abdominal bleeding. The aspirins had destroyed his stomach. Scarpa would need a blood transfusion during surgery, and he refused to accept any blood from people he did not know. It was the time of the AIDS epidemic, and patients were fearful of being transfused with infected blood. So Scarpa chose a member of his crew to be his donor; the man whom Scarpa had instructed to donate blood was a weightlifter who bulked up by regularly injecting himself with steroids. The man, unfortunately, used dirty needles. Neither Scarpa nor his surgeon knew that the donor was

HIV positive. He selflessly, but ignorantly, passed his diseased blood into Scarpa's body.

When Scarpa learned that he was HIV positive, he and his mistress blamed the surgeon and the hospital for permitting untested, infected blood to be used for his transfusion during the surgery.

"Linda Shiro [Scarpa's mistress] claimed that the resident surgeon who had performed the operation, a Filipino named Angelo Sebollena, insisted that everything was all right, but she was unnerved one day when she caught him shaving Scarpa's face, in order to, as the doctor put it, 'make him look nice.' She had Scarpa transferred to Mt. Sinai Hospital in Manhattan. There his stomach, which was hemorrhaging beyond repair, was removed. Scarpa finally went home in October, with the aid of a walker.

"Scarpa blamed Sebollena for making a faulty decision and Victory Hospital for exposing him to AIDS. He filed a law suit. Before long Sebollena was in further trouble. In 1991, he injected two male patients with the drug Versed, a central nervous system depressant that leaves a person conscious but immobile, and performed oral sex on them. Gary Pilledsdorf, the lawyer who represented Scarpa at the medical-malpractice trial, in August 1992, recalls that on the morning of the opening statements the judge motioned him to the bench and said, 'Let me get this straight. You're representing a hit man with AIDS against a doctor who sodomizes his patients. Am I on the right page?'" [19]

As expected, Scarpa won the case. The jurors were prepared to award him more than a million dollars. However, the insurance company, also as expected, wanted to negotiate a settlement. Believing that he did not have long to live, Scarpa agreed to accept a settlement of $300,000. He wanted it all in cash and sent a member of his crew to collect the payoff from a branch of Citibank. The man arrived at the bank with a duffle bag; he opened the bag and tossed it to a banker, who instructed the tellers to fill the bag with cash. Scarpa's emissary warned the tellers that if the amount turned out to be even just a few dollars short of $300,000, he would be back, and they better watch out.

Not long after his release from Mt. Sinai, Scarpa killed four of Vic Orena's men. Scarpa was on a warpath, and neither the law nor disease nor his coming death could deter him. He was a hitman through and through.

One day, Scarpa's son, Joey, came home after a failed drug deal and told his father that two of the dealers had threatened to kill him. One of them pointed a gun at Joey. Scarpa's anger went into high gear. He and his son drove to the site of the failed drug deal. Upon seeing the two targets, Scarpa stopped the car and fired shots at them. One man fired back, wounding Scarpa in his left eye. He sped home, rushed into his house, and poured a glass of Scotch into the bloody wound. All the while, he had been wearing an electronic monitoring device on one ankle so the FBI could follow his movements. He had been warned not to leave his house without getting permission from the FBI. Minutes after he poured the Scotch whiskey into his eye socket, the telephone rang. It was an FBI agent. What's going on? the agent demanded. Scarpa assured the agent that everything was all right; he had just stepped out to pick up a prescription. He hung up the phone and was rushed to a hospital.

Scarpa was blind in one eye; his once robust physique was now emaciated. On May 6, 1993, he pleaded guilty to three murders and conspiracy to murder. He was sentenced to life in prison and knew he was soon to step off life's precipice. The court also knew and so reduced his life sentence to ten years. Even that was far too optimistic: on June 4, 1994, he died of AIDS in the Federal Medical Center for prisoners in Rochester, Minnesota. He was sixty-six years old.

In 1996, DeVecchio retired from the FBI and opened a private investigation business in Florida. In 2011, Lin DeVecchio wrote about his experiences as an FBI agent and about his relationship with Scarpa. The book is titled *We're Going to Win This Thing: The Shocking Frame-up of a Mafia Crime Buster*.

Notes

1. https://www.biography.com/crime/whitey-bulger
2. https://apnews.com/article/us-news-ap-top-news-whitey-bulger-crime-weekend-reads-8dff185e1324cb7079b8a86c48c2ec56
3. https://www.npr.org/2019/09/09/758989641/the-cias-secret-quest-for-mind-control-torture-lsd-and-a-poisoner-in-chief#:~:text=Whitey%20Bulger%20was%20one%20of%20the%20prisoners%20who,LSD%20every%20day%20for%20more%20than%20a%20year
4. https://lithub.com/we-were-alive-and-life-was-us-how-ken-kesey-created-lsd-subculture/
5. https://faroutmagazine.co.uk/robert-hunter-and-the-cia-how-mk-ultra-gave-the-grateful-dead-their-voice/
6. https://www.alternet.org/2017/02/why-leading-beatnik-poet-allen-ginsberg-was-crusader-legalizing-lsd
7. https://www.npr.org/2019/09/09/758989641/the-cias-secret-quest-for-mind-control-torture-lsd-and-a-poisoner-in-chief#:~:text=Whitey%20Bulger%20was%20one%20of%20the%20prisoners%20who,LSD%20every%20day%20for%20more%20than%20a%20year
8. https://www.mountsinai.org/health-library/special-topic/substance-use-lsd
9. https://www.healthline.com//health/lsd#risks
10. https://archive.nytimes.com/www.nytimes.com/books/first/l/lehr-mass.html
11. https://www.theamericanconservative.com/how-whitey-bulger-bought-boston/
12. https://www.theamericanconservative.com/how-whitey-bulger-bought-boston/
13. https://howiecarrshow.com/happy-90thninetieth-birthday-to-stephen-the-rifleman-flemmi-bostons-most-prolific-serial-killer/
14. Joseph Pistone, David Fisher, and Sara Caudwell, *The Ceremony: The Mafia Initiation Tapes* (New York: Dell Publishing, 1992), xxvii.
15. https://www.bostonglobe.com/metro/2015/07/29/florida-court-reinstated-john-connolly-murder-conviction-ruling/TjssT3Q5KFhRLgS3QhVLpL/story.html
16. Jay Goldberg, *The Courtroom is My Theater* (New York: Post Hill Press, 2018), 279.

17 Jeffrey Sussman, *Big Apple Gangsters: The Rise and Decline of the Mob in New York* (Lanham, MD: Rowman and Littlefield, 2020), 168–9.

18 Selwyn Raad, *Five Families* (New York: Thomas Dunne Books, an imprint of St. Martin's Press, 20,016), 342.

19 www.newyorker.com/magazine/1996/12/16/the-g-man-and-the-hit-man

21

Decapitation

Rudolph Giuliani pursued the Mafia with the determination of a guided missile. Once he locked on to his target, he could not be deterred. Not since Robert Kennedy was attorney general had there been such a zealous prosecutor of the Mafia as Giuliani. He targeted the heads of New York's Mafia families, and he would use the RICO Act (Racketeer Influenced and Corrupt Organizations) to nail them.

It all began after he had read Joseph Bonanno's memoir, *A Man of Honor*, which describes Mafia Commission meetings with the bosses of New York's five Mafia crime families. Giuliani sought permission from the Justice Department to prosecute the Commission members and that permission was forthcoming. He believed that the mobsters were vulnerable under the RICO Act for contracting murders, drug trafficking, loan sharking, extortion, and labor racketeering. His famous Commission Trial would be the first time that RICO would be used to prosecute a major federal Mafia case.

RICO was drafted by G. Robert Blakey and signed into law by President Richard Nixon. Before RICO existed, crime bosses could order their capos, soldiers, and associates to carry out crimes; if arrested for those crimes, the bosses could claim that they were innocent since they had not personally committed the crime. Under RICO, however, police could arrest, and prosecutors could indict and try the bosses of Mafia families. There was a list of thirty-five crimes (twenty-seven federal ones and eight state crimes) that if committed during a ten-year period, a perpetrator could be charged under RICO. Guilty verdicts could result in fines up to $25,000 and prison sentences of twenty years for each count of the conviction. In addition, the guilty party would have to forfeit all ill-gotten gains and any interests in businesses related to racketeering.

And Giuliani was the perfect vehicle for prosecuting mob bosses. In fact, he was raised to be a prosecutor. His father, an Italian immigrant, hated the fact that Italians were stereotyped as members of organized crime. He wanted his son to shatter that stereotype. The elder Giuliani believed that the negative stereotype was reinforced because there were no Italian federal judges. The first step to becoming a judge was to attend law school. And it was New York University Law School from which Giuliani emerged with his JD in hand in 1970 (the year RICO became law). Though not destined to be a judge, he was hired as an assistant US attorney for New York's Southern District. He proved to be a hard-driving prosecutor, who by age thirty was the third highest-ranking prosecutor in New York. He made a name for himself as a prosecutor in the famous Prince of the City case, which was made into a popular and critically acclaimed movie. The case garnered headlines for Giuliani as fifty-two New York City cops were convicted for corruption. One could say that Giuliani himself had become a prince of the city. His name was gold, and he enjoyed several prestigious appointments before being appointed as associate attorney general in the Justice Department during the Reagan presidency. From there, he went on to be US Attorney for the Southern District of New York in June 1983. And it was from that launching pad that Giuliani would wage war against the bosses of New York's Mafia families. Though not a judge, Giuliani would more than fulfill his father's ambitions.

Bosses were usually careful about being overheard talking about their crimes. And there was nothing prosecutors loved more than Mafiosi incriminating themselves on tape. So, Giuliani began to accumulate devastating evidence against the mob by placing recording devices in pivotal

Mafia locations. Each of the bosses was secretly bugged. One bug, for example, had been placed in Paul Castellano's kitchen, where he discussed payoffs from real-estate developers to the mob-run Concrete Club (anyone putting up an office building or apartment building in New York needed concrete, and the mob controlled the delivery and price of concrete). Anthony "Ducks" (ducks, because he had a record of successfully ducking indictments) Corallo thought his Jaguar would be a safe place to speak freely; he was surprised to learn that his conversations with capo Salvatore Avelino had all been taped while the two cruised around the city (so much for ducking). "Fat" Tony Salerno, who operated out of the Palma Boys Social Club in East Harlem, was taped discussing his crime family's involvement in the construction industry. The Casa Sorta Restaurant in Bensonhurst, Brooklyn, proved to be a perfect location for taping conversations about the Colombo family's various illegal enterprises; topics included extortion, loan sharking, labor racketeering, payoffs, murder, etc. Taken together, the recordings proved to be a sword of Damocles to be used by swordsman Giuliani.

In addition to the bosses, the following Mafiosi were taped and indicted by Giuliani: Aniello Dellacroce, Gambino family underboss; Gennaro "Gerry Lang" Langella, Colombo family acting boss/underboss; Salvatore "Tom Mix" Santoro, Lucchese family underboss; and Christopher "Christy Tick" Furnari, Lucchese family consigliere. Removed from the trial were Aniello Dellacroce, who died of cancer; and Paul Castellano, who was murdered on orders of John Gotti. Another individual who avoided conviction was Rusty Rastelli, the Colombo boss, since he had been kicked off the Commission as a result of Joe Pistone's (aka, Donnie Brasco) infiltration of the Colombo family.

By February 1985, Giuliani had assembled enough information to win indictments against Carmine (Junior or the Snake) Persico and Ralph Scopo; Gambino family crime boss Paul Castellano; Anthony Salerno, fronting as boss of the Genovese crime family, and his underboss, Gennaro Langella; Lucchese crime family boss Anthony "Ducks" Corallo and his underboss Salvatore Santoro and consigliere Christopher Furnari.

Working with Giuliani was Michael Chertoff, who would go on to head the Homeland Security Department and coauthor the Patriot Act. Two additional prosecutors worked on the trial: John Savarese and Gil Childers.

Time Magazine wrote: "The jewel in the crown is the 'Commission' trial, sometimes called 'The Case of Cases,' which is set to begin next month. In what could be the most significant assault on the infrastructure of organized crime since the high command of the Chicago Mafia was swept away in 1943, the dons of the five major Mafia families that dominate the East Coast are charged with operating a 'ruling council' that controls a variety of illegal enterprises. The case, which Giuliani will try himself, uses the Racketeer-Influenced and Corrupt Organizations Act to prosecute an entire organization, not just its leaders, and to confiscate its proceeds. 'Our approach,' he declares, 'is to wipe out the five families.'" [1]

The Mafia Commission trial began on February 25, 1985, and generated reams of banner headlines throughout its run. It was like a hit Broadway show, which true crime and Mafia fans attended with the enthusiasm of rock groupies. Jurors heard the presentation of twenty-five indictments, including charges for extortion, labor racketeering, narcotics, gambling, and murder. Prosecutors let jurors know that the Mafia Commission used "threats, violence and murder." Attempting to make light of the indictment, Samuel Dawson, attorney for Salvatore Santoro, commented: "The indictment includes the Chicago fire and the San Francisco earthquake. I intend to prove that Mr. Santoro did not play with matches, or have anything to do with the earthquake." [2] He incited smiles and laughter but not sympathy for his client.

When Magistrate Michael Dollinger warned the defendants not to threaten any witnesses or their bail would be forfeited, "Christie Tick" Furnari asked, "What witnesses?" [3] His attorney quickly escorted him from the courtroom.

Carmine Persico, who chose to act as his own attorney, told Judge Owen that the Mafia was not a criminal entity. It was a chimera hatched by the government. Then, as if to further educate the judge, Persico said, "Not too many of these jurors have a lot of education. I don't believe you should use this terminology questioning the jury. You should use more lay language. They don't understand this kind of language. I should put it in —plainer terms."

Judge Owen countered, "I'm accustomed to asking people questions in language that they can understand and answer." [4]

Defense attorney Samuel Dawson surprised reporters and attendees by stating, "This case is not about whether an organization is in existence, known as the Mafia or La Cosa Nostra. There is—right here in New York City. Yes, there is a Commission."[5] It was the first time that such an admission had been made in an American courtroom.

He added that the Commission was like a cross between an HR office and a mediation service, approving or disapproving of new potential hires and mediating disputes. And when it came to price fixing, jurors were told that the Commission only sets prices to minimize competition. At worst, the case should be an antitrust case. It was now Persico's turn, and he warned the jurors that those who would testify against the defendants included murderers and drug dealers. Would you trust such people? You certainly wouldn't hire them or even let them into your homes. He concluded that after hearing testimony from such untrustworthy criminals whose very words were self-serving lies, the jury would have no other choice but to acquit him. He smiled at the jurors, his eyes moving from one to another.

Prosecutors were then ready for the jurors to listen to the bugged taped conversations of mobsters discussing their criminal activities. Not only the jurors, but the entire courtroom was eager to eavesdrop on intimate mob conversations. Some attendees shushed others to be quiet. Whispers trailed off, and everyone in the courtroom sat up like meerkats on a termite mound. Please pay close attention, a prosecutor said to the jurors. The tape started rolling and soon could be heard Corallo and Avellino discussing problems with family members dealing in narcotics. Dealing drugs was not approved by the Commission (though many mobsters were making millions of dollars from the drug trade). How should these dealers be handled, Avellino asked. Corallo responded that they should be killed. Add to that came another: Salerno told Corallo how one of his underlings disrespected him by directly calling him "Fat Tony." Corallo was appalled and advised his boss to shoot him. Such disrespect was disgusting. Salerno agreed. Again, he made it clear that he had a definitive way of dealing with obstacles and insults.

In addition to the bugged conversations, the prosecutors used the testimony of 207 witnesses, including former Cleveland mob underboss Angelo Lonardo, whose testimony was eviscerating.

The combination of incriminating taped conversations and an extensive lineup of credible and persuasive witnesses were sufficient for the seven defense attorneys to realize they would be fighting a losing battle. Therefore, they asked Giuliani if he would negotiate plea deals if the defendants pled guilty to all charges. Giuliani was like a king facing a group of powerless commoners who were begging for his favors. What possible incentive would he have for making a deal? After all, he had the highest-ranking members of the Mafia on trial, and there was no one higher they could rat on. Plus, he had enough witnesses to fill an auditorium. No deal, he told the lawyers.

Unsurprisingly, Giuliani became the most hated man on the Mafia's enemies list. Carmine Persico and John Gotti urged the Mafia hierarchy to consent to a hit on the evil prosecutor. The suggestion was rejected. This was a repeat of the 1930s, when Dutch Schultz urged the Commission to whack prosecutor John Dewey. He was turned down, and his insistence led his colleagues to whack him instead of Dewey. Of course, if the gangsters had killed Dewey, two of his cases may never have gone to trial: one against Lucky Luciano, who was sentenced to thirty to fifty years in prison for pimping and pandering;

the other against Lepke Buchalter, who died in the electric chair at Sing Sing Prison. He was the only mob boss executed by the state.

Following Giuliani's refusal to plea bargain, the defense lawyers had no alternative but to set out their defensive arguments to the jurors. Their ongoing strategy of attempting to convince jurors that membership on the Commission was not evidence of any criminal activity seemed likely to be unconvincing. Though it was not a winning strategy, Judge Richard Owen confirmed to the jury that even if people belonged to the Mafia, that alone was not sufficient to reach a guilty verdict. He added that convicting the defendants required the jury to find not just that the Mafia Commission existed, but that the defendants conducted their affairs and those of the Commission in a pattern consisting of at least two acts of racketeering.

The bosses were walking on a loosely hanging tightrope that was being jerked like a jump rope by prosecutors: it would be easy for the defendants to tumble to their doom. In their precarious state, the defendants were faced with the question of whether they should admit there was a Mafia. No boss had ever publicly made such an admission. And certainly not in a courtroom. The rule of omerta was the basis of the Mafia's secretiveness. It was as integral to the Mafia as celibacy is to Catholic priests. If the rule was abrogated, the Mafia would become a society of plea bargainers, each member ratting on a higher-up to save himself from a long prison sentence. Yet, the prosecutors had hours of incriminating recordings that proved there was a Mafia. Jurors could hardly be expected to deny what their ears so clearly affirmed.

The bosses chewed over their predicament and finally swallowed their pride. They agreed to permit their lawyers to say that the Mafia existed, but the bosses would not be compelled to confirm what their lawyers admitted. Now that the lawyers admitted the existence of the Mafia, they achieved a milestone: it was the first time that the very existence of the Mafia had been indirectly confirmed by the bosses in a court of law.

On November 19, 1986, following six days of jury deliberations, the defendants were found guilty on all 151 indictments that included racketeering, conspiracy, and operating a commission that ruled the Mafia.

Less than two months later, on January 13, 1987, Judge Richard Owen sternly delivered the sentences: (1) Anthony "Fat Tony" Salerno was sentenced to 100 years and told by the judge that his sentence was imposed for devoting his life to terrorizing victims for financial advantage. (The gist of each sentencing message was the same for all the defendants.) (2) Carmine "Junior" Persico received a 100-year sentence for his role as a top member of the Mafia, whose success was built on murder and violence. (3) Anthony "Ducks" Corallo was sentenced to 100 years. (4) Gennaro "Jerry Lang" Langella was sentenced to 100 years. (5) Salvatore Santoro was next for sentencing. "Facing the judge, Santoro said, 'You're in the driver's seat, your honor.' Judge Owen stated he was just doing his job. Santoro responded with full sarcasm, 'And you're doing a good job' before adding, 'Give me my 100 years and we'll get it over with.' That's exactly what he got." [6] (6) Christopher "Christie Tick" Furnari Sr. was sentenced to 100 years. (7) Ralph "Little Ralphie" Scopo was sentenced to 100 years. (8) Anthony "Bruno" Indelicato was sentenced to forty years for the murders of Carmine Galante and his two bodyguards.

Though the judge told the defendants they would be eligible for parole after ten years in prison, he said he would recommend that none of them ever be granted parole.

True crime and Mafia fans, who had loyally attended the trial, were sorry it was over; it had been the best show in town. They filed out of the courtroom, doomed to live on repeated televised presentations of *Godfather I* and *Godfather II*.

Following the trial, Giuliani was celebrated not only in New York but throughout the country as newspapers from coast to coast published glowing articles about the greatest crime buster of the time. Editorialists compared him to Thomas Dewey, writing that the tough, successful prosecutor would likely ride his golden reputation into the governor's mansion and from there perhaps even into the White House. It was all within his reach. Giuliani, however, started a little lower down: he became Mayor of New York, the financial capital of the world, the city that never sleeps, and which has been celebrated in song as the crucible where if you can make it here, you can make it anywhere. Giuliani looked as if he was shooting into the stratosphere of politics. Years later, the prognosticators seemed correct; for after the shocking brutality of 9/11, Giuliani was celebrated all over again. The media crowned him America's Mayor. He would surely run for president. Those whom the gods raise up, they also cast down. And Giuliani would experience hard times in connection with his support of President Trump, but that's another story in the ongoing saga of the great prosecutor.

For an infuriated Mafia, the end of the Commission Trial was a pathetic epitaph for the lives of its tough bosses. The bosses had once exerted power over life and death like Roman Emperors. They made millions of dollars; they had controlled industries and politicians. They had been a government within a government. Many soldiers, capos, and associates angrily cursed Giuliani for bringing it all to an end. Some said he should be whacked. But what good would it do after the bosses were all found guilty? Unlike Roman emperors, the convicted Mafiosi—Salerno, Corallo, Santoro, Furnari, Persico, Langella, and Scopo—all died in prison, replaced by younger men who operated in the shadows, careful not to draw the attention of investigators.

Ralph Blumenthal wrote, in a *New York Times* article headlined, "Verdict is Termed Blow to the Mafia" that "[prosecutors] hailed the convictions as certain to disrupt long-entrenched patters of criminal activity and make it easier for authorities to fight racketeering in a host of industries long prey to traditional organized crime." [7]

Though reports of the death of the Mafia frequently arose after the trial, those reports dwindled to a trickle and then ceased as new members of crime families appeared. In my book *Big Apple Gangsters*, I reported the comments of prosecutors who believed that the Mafia was like a hydra-headed monster that grew new heads soon after an old one had been decapitated.

Robert Santucci, former chief of the Rackets Bureau, Office of the District Attorney of Bronx County and Special Assistant for the Southern District of New York Public Corruption Unit, stated: "the mob is in decline, but still active. Current mobsters are shadows of those who controlled organized crime decades ago. They are doing all they can to avoid being arrested and sent to prison under the RICO law." And Michael Vecchione, former chief of the Rackets Division of the Brooklyn District Attorney's Office and author of Friends of the Family, said: "To paraphrase Mark Twain the reports of the death of the American Mafia are greatly exaggerated. The mob is alive and well. It is as dangerous and profitable as it has always been. In my opinion, what has given the impression to mob observers that the Mafia is a thing of the past or a shell of itself, is the fact that there are no longer guys like 'the Teflon Don' John Gotti, or the 'Oddfather,' Vincent 'the Chin' Gigante, or Sammy 'the Bull' Gravano, in the spotlight of the press. These guys were headline makers, reporters' dreams and paparazzi followed them wherever they could. However, along with the spotlight came the searing interest of law enforcement, which was not good for business. The Mafia of today has learned a lesson from this past publicity and in many ways has gone back to the old style of flying under the radar. This allows them to do business and make money with little to no interruption. With the exception of an incident here and there that catches some agent's or reporter's eye, the American Mafia will likely remain in the shadows and thrive!" [8]

The shattered Mafia Commission was rebuilt; in 1988, its members assembled under the leadership of John Gotti, and attendees included Genovese crime boss Vincent "The Chin" Gigante and Lucchese boss Vittorio "Little Vic" Amuso. Another Commission meeting was held in 2000; there, the members agreed that both parents of anyone who was to become a made man had to be of Italian descent. According to investigators and prosecutors, the Commission has continued to be active and comprises the bosses of New York's five Mafia families and the Chicago Outfit. Secrecy, greater than at any time in the past, is a governing principle for ongoing meetings. New Mafia leaders, unlike John Gotti and Gigante, stay away from the media. Though complete anonymity and near invisibility are impossible, it's a goal of those who want to avoid the fate of the Commission Trial defendants.

Notes

1 http://www.time.com/time/magazine/article/0%2C9171%2C1101860210-143096%2C00.html/

2 https://themobmuseum.org/blog/the-commission-trial-lifted-the-lid-on-the-new-york-mafia/

3 https://themobmuseum.org/blog/the-commission-trial-lifted-the-lid-on-the-new-york-mafia/

4 https://themobmuseum.org/blog/the-commission-trial-lifted-the-lid-on-the-new-york-mafia/

5 https://themobmuseum.org/blog/the-commission-trial-lifted-the-lid-on-the-new-york-mafia/

6 https://themobmuseum.org/blog/the-10-week-long-commission-trial-played-to-full-courtrooms/

7 Ralph Blumenthal, "Verdict Is Termed Blow to Mafia," *New York Times*, November 20, 1986, B8.

8 Jeffrey Sussman, *Big Apple Gangsters: The Rise and Decline of the Mob in New York* (Lanham, MD: Rowman and Littlefield, 2020), 190.

ABOUT THE AUTHOR

Jeffrey Sussman is the author of nineteen nonfiction books, nine of which are about boxing and organized crime. He lives in New York City.

* *Max Baer and Barney Ross: Jewish Heroes of Boxing*
* *Rocky Graziano: Fists, Fame, and Fortune*
* *Boxing and the Mob: The Notorious History of the Sweet Science*
* *Holocaust Fighters: Boxers, Resisters, and Avengers*
* *Big Apple Gangsters: The Rise and Decline of the Mob in New York*
* *Sin City Gangsters: The Rise and Decline of the Mob in Las Vegas*
* *Tinseltown Gangsters: The Rise and Decline of the Mob in Hollywood*
* *Back Beat Gangsters: The Rise and Decline of the Mob in Rock Music*
* *Mafia Hits, Misses, Wars, and Prosecutions*

BIBLIOGRAPHY

Herbert Asbury, *The Gangs of New York*, Alfred A. Knopf, 1928.
Lee Bernstein, *The Greatest Menace: Organized Crime in Cold War America*, UMass Press, 2002.
G. Robert Blakely and Richard N. Billings, *Fatal Hour: The Assassination of President Kennedy By Organized Crime*, Berkley Publishing, 1992.
Alan Block, *East Side-West Side: Organizing Crime in New York, 1930–1950*, Transaction Publishers, 1983.
Bill Bonanno, *Bound by Honor: A Mafioso's Story*, St. Martin's Press, 1999.
Joseph Bonanno, *A Man of Honor: The Autobiography of Joseph Bonanno*, St. Martin's Press, 2003.
Peter E. Bondanella, *Hollywood Italians: Dagos, Palookas, Romeos, Wise Guys, and Sopranos*, Continuum International Publishing Group, 2004.
Jimmy Breslin, *Breslin Essential Writings*, Library of America, Penguin Random House, 2024.
Jimmy Breslin, *The Good Rat*, Harper Collins, ECCO, 2008.
Jimmy Breslin, *A Life of Damon Runyon*, Ticknor & Fields, 1991.
Rich Cohen, *Tough Jews: Fathers, Sons, and Gangster Dreams*, Simon & Schuster, 1998.
David Critchley, *The Origin of Organized Crime in America: The New York City Mafia, 1891–1931*, Routledge, 2008.
Simon Crittle, *The Rise and Fall of Joey Massino*, The Berkeley Publishing Group, 2006.
Mike Dash, *The First Family: Terror, Extortion, Revenge, Murder and The Birth of the American Mafia*, Ballantine Books, 2010.
Frank Dimatteo, *Lion in the Basement*, Dimatteo, 20014.
John H. Davis, *Mafia Dynasty: The Rise and Fall of the Gambino Crime Family*, HarperCollins, 1993.
John H. Davis, *Mafia Kingfish: Carlos Marcello and the Assassination of John F. Kennedy*, McGraw-Hill, 1988.
Anthony M. Destefano, *King of the Godfathers*, Pinnacle Books, 2006.
Dennis Eisenberg, Uri Dan, and Eli Landau, *Meyer Lansky: Mogul of the Mob*, New York: Paddington Press, 1979.
Robert K. Elder, *Last Words of the Executed*, University of Chicago Press, 2010.
T. J. English, *Havana Nocturne: How the Mob Owned Cuba – and Then Lost It to the Revolution*, New York: William Morrow and Company, 2008.
Sid Feder and Joachim Joesten, *Luciano Story*, Da Capo Press, 1994.
Tom Folsom, *The Mad Ones*, Weinstein Books, 2008.
Albert Fried, *The Rise and Fall of the Jewish Gangster in America*. Holt, Rinehart and Winston, 1980.
C. Alexander Hortis, *The Mob and the City*, Prometheus Books, 2014.

Dean Jennings, *We Only Kill Each Other*, New York: Pocket Books, 1967.
Leo Katcher, *The Big Bankroll: The Life and Times of Arnold Rothstein*, Da Capo Press, 1994.
Paul R. Kavieff, *The Life and Times of Lepke Buchalter*, Barricade Books, 2006.
Murray Kempton, *Rebellions, Perversities, and Main Events*, Times Books, 1994.
Robert Lacey, *Little Man*, New York: Little, Brown & Company, 1991.
Salvatore Lupo, *The Two Mafias: A Transatlantic History, 1888–2008*, New York: Palgrave MacMillan, 2015.
Peter Maas, *The Valachi Papers*, Pocket Books, 1986.
Peter Maas, *Underboss*, New York: Harper Collins, 1997.
D. Mahoney, *Sons & Brothers: The Days of Jack and Bobby Kennedy*, Arcade Publishing, 1999.
Tim Newark, *Boardwalk Gangster: The Real Lucky Luciano*, Thomas Dunne books, Imprint of St. Martin's Press, 2010.
David M. Oshinsky, Allan Brinkley, and Davis Dyer, "Harry Truman," *The American Presidency*, Houghton Mifflin, 2004.
David Pietrusza, *Rothstein: The Life, Times, and Murder of the Criminal Genius Who Fixed the 1919 World Series*, Carroll & Graf Publishers, 2003.
Hickman Powell, *Lucky Luciano, His Amazing Trial and Wild Witnesses*, Barricade Books, Incorporated, 2015.
Frank Ragano and Selwyn Raab, *Mob Lawyer*, Scribner, 1994.
Thomas Reppetto, *American Mafia: A History of Its Rise to Power*, Henry Holt and Company, 1994.
Carl Sifakis, *The Mafia Encyclopedia*, Checkmark Books, 1999.
Mary M. Stolberg, *Fighting Organized Crime: Politics, Justice, and the Legacy of Thomas E. Dewey*, Northeastern University Press, 1995.
Jeffrey Sussman, *Big Apple Gangsters: The Rise and Declineof the Mob in New York*, Rowman and Littlefield, 2020.
Jeffrey Sussman, *Sin City Gangsters: The Rise and Decline of the Mob in Las Vegas*, Rowman and Littlefield, 2022.
Gay Talese, *Honor Thy Father*, World Publishing, 1971.
Evan Thomas, *Robert Kennedy His Life*, Simon and Schuster, 2000.
Robert Weldon Whalen, *Murder, Inc., and the Moral Life: Gangsters and Gangbusters in La Guardia's New York*, Fordham University Press, 2016.

FIGURE 1 Joe "the Boss" Masseria NYPD, 1922

FIGURE 2 Ed Diamond, Jack Diamond, Fatty Walsh, and Charles "Lucky" Luciano (l. to r.) [Ed Diamond, Jack Diamond, Fatty Walsh, and Charles Luciano, full-length portrait, standing, facing front]. Photograph. 1931. Library of Congress. https://www.loc.gov/item/95511484/

FIGURE 3A Al Capone. Al Capone- Alcatraz mugshot photos. FBI Records: The Vault. https://vault.fbi.gov/Al%20Capone/Al%20Capone%20Images

FIGURE 3B Al Capone. Al Capone- Alcatraz mugshot photos. FBI Records: The Vault. https://vault.fbi.gov/Al%20Capone/Al%20Capone%20Images

FIGURE 4A Thomas Dewey. The Miriam and Ira D. Wallach Division of Art, Prints and Photographs: Print Collection, New York Public Library.

FIGURE 4B Thomas Dewey. The Miriam and Ira D. Wallach Division of Art, Prints and Photographs: Print Collection, New York Public Library.

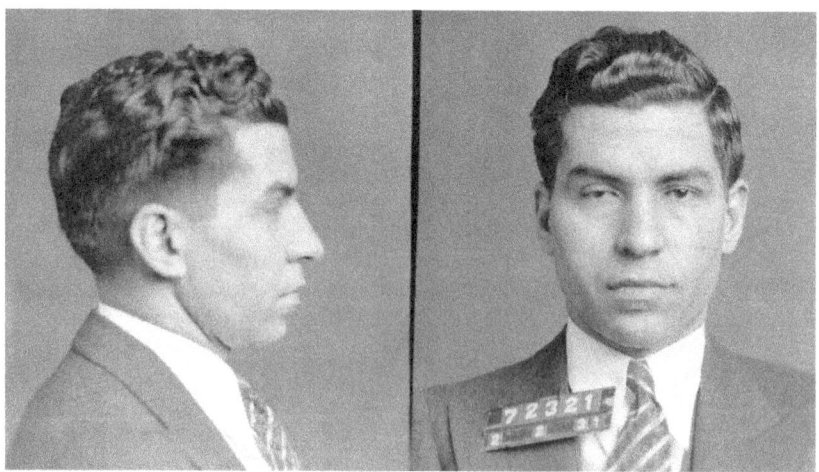

FIGURE 5 Mugshot of Charles "Lucky" Luciano. Mugshot of mobster Charles "Lucky" Luciano. Photograph. NYPD. 1931. https://www.fbi.gov/image-repository/luciano-mugshot-1931.jpg/view

FIGURE 6A Lepke Buchalter on his way to prison Aumuller, Al, photographer. [Louis "Lepke" Buchalter handcuffed to guard, getting into van]. Photograph. World Telegram & Sun *c*. 1939. From Library of Congress: Miscellaneous Items in High Demand. https://www.loc.gov/pictures/item/95511436/

FIGURE 6B Lepke Buchalter, arrested Aumuller, Al, photographer. [Louis "Lepke" Buchalter, center, handcuffed to J. Edgar Hoover, on the left, with another man on the right, at entrance to courthouse]. Photograph. World Telegram *c.* 1939 or 1940. From Library of Congress: Miscellaneous Items in High Demand. https://www.loc.gov/pictures/item/2004676730/

FIGURE 7 Bugsy Siegel, Hollywood and Vegas Celebrity Highsmith, Carol M., photographer. 'r Benjamin "Bugsy" Siegel, who built the Flamingo Hotel. Photograph. Las Vegas, Nevada. From Library of Congress: Highsmith (Carol M.) Archive. https://www.loc.gov/pictures/item/2011634441/

FIGURE 8 Meyer Lansky Ravenna, Al. photographer. [Meyer Lansky, half-length portrait, facing front] / World Telegram & Sun. Photograph. 1958. Library of Congress. https://www.loc.gov/item/98506512/

FIGURE 9A Albert Anastasia [Albert Anastasia, bust portrait, facing front]. Photograph. 1951. From Library of Congress. https://www.loc.gov/item/95511461/

```
POLICE DEPARTMENT      | No.
CITY OF NEW YORK       | B 57939

Name    Albert Anastasio
Alias
Residence  337 Clinton Street
Crime   Vagrancy
Age  34              Height 5'-9"
Weight 202           Build Stocky
Hair Dk. Chest.      Eyes Brown
Color White          Com Dark
Born     Italy
Occupation  Oil Salesman
Date of Arrest  10-21-36
Officer   O8Connor  M.O. Bklyn
Remarks



F.R. CLASS
```

FIGURE 9B Albert Anastasia NYPD Police Crime Report Police Department, City of New York black-and-white mug shots of Albert Anastasia. Head and shoulders portraits, facing front and facing left. Gallery number B 57939. 1936. Burton Turkus Papers, Special Collections, Lloyd Sealy Library, John Jay College of Criminal Justice/CUNY. https://dc.lib.jjay.cuny.edu/index.php/Detail/Object/Show/object_id/7153

FIGURE 10 Frank Costello, glowering at US Senate Committee Aumuller, Al, photographer. [Frank Costello, half-length portrait, seated, behind microphone, testifying before the Kefauver Committee investigating organized crime]. Photograph. World Telegram & Sun c. 1951. From Library of Congress. https://www.loc.gov/pictures/item/98506867/

FIGURE 11 Vito Genovese, boss of the Genovese Crime Family Stanziola, Phil, photographer. [Vito Genovese, half-length portrait, standing, facing right]. Photograph. World Telegram & Sun c. 1959. From Library of Congress: Miscellaneous Items in High Demand. https://www.loc.gov/pictures/item/99471743/

FIGURE 12 Vincent "The Chin" Gigante, arrested for the shooting of Frank Costello Stanziola, Phil, photographer. [Vincent Gigante, three-quarter length portrait, seated, facing front]. Photograph. World Telegram & Sun *c.* 1957. From Library of Congress: Miscellaneous Items in High Demand. https://www.loc.gov/pictures/item/99471566/

FIGURE 13 Senator Estes Kefauver. Senator Estes Kefauver in the Presidential Exhibit room of the Harry S. Truman Presidential Library. Harry S. Truman Library. 1963.

FIGURE 14 Joseph Bonanno wanted poster Joseph Bonanno on wanted poster, bust portrait, facing slightly right. Photograph. 1964. Library of Congress. https://www.loc.gov/item/99471741/

FIGURE 15A Robert F. Kennedy Leffler, Warren K, photographer. [Attorney General Robert F. Kennedy speaking with a bullhorn, in front of the Department of Justice, responding to African Americans at a demonstration organized by the Congress of Racial Equality CORE against discrimination and in response to the death of Medgar Evers, Washington, D.C.] / WKL. Washington D.C, 1963. Photograph. From Library of Congress. https://www.loc.gov/item/2022640449/

FIGURE 15B President John F. Kennedy, J. Edgar Hoover, and Attorney General Robert F. Kennedy (from l. to r.) Meeting with Attorney General Robert F. Kennedy (RFK) and J. Edgar Hoover (JEH), Director of the Federal Bureau of Investigation (FBI), 10:12 a.m.. Photograph. White House Photographs. 1961. https://www.jfklibrary.org/asset-viewer/archives/jfkwhp-1961-02-23-a#?image_identifier=JFKWHP-AR6372-A

FIGURE 16 Joey Gallo NYPD, 1961

FIGURE 17 John Gotti, strolling outside his social club Surveillance photo of mobster John Gotti, walking down a street in 1980s in New York City. Photograph. New York, New York. Federal Bureau of Investigations Multimedia https://multimedia.fbi.gov/item?type=image&id=1751

FIGURE 18 Salvatore "Sammy The Bull" Gravano. Mugshot of Salvtore Sammy "The Bull" Gravano, henchman of Gambino family's John Gotti, whose eventual cooperation with the FBI and NYPD helped build a case against the "Teflon Don." Photograph. New York, New York. Federal Bureau of Investigations Multimedia c1990. https://multimedia.fbi.gov/item?type=image&id=807

FIGURE 19 President George W. Bush is greeted by New York City Mayor Rudolph Giuliani, left, and New York Gov. George Pataki Friday, Sept. 14, 2001, upon arrival at McGuire Air Force Base in Wrightstown, N.J. President George W. Bush Visits New York, 09/14/2001. President (2001–9: Bush). Office of Management and Administration. Office of White House Management. Photography Office. US National Archives' Local Identifier: P7370-26.

INDEX

Abbandano, Frank "the Dasher"   7, 59
Abbatemarco, Frank "Frankie
    Shots"   159–60
Abraham the Just   13
Abrams, Hyman   46
Accardo, Tony   25
Adamo, Michael "Mike"   191
Adler, Polly   68
Adonis, Joe (formerly Antonio Doto)   4,
    34, 35, 102
  at 1946 Havana Conference   87
  Broadway Mob   50
  deportation   85–9, 94
Albertson, Jack   69
Aloi, Benedetto   204
Amato, Baldassare   195
Amato, Gaetano   158
Amato, Joseph   146
American Communist Party   146
Amuso, Vittorio "Little Vic"   244
Anastasia, Albert   34, 54, 63, 75, 76,
    137
  as CEO of Murder Inc.   57
  as Earthquake   119
  as Lord High Executioner   51, 57, 73,
    119–26
  as Mad Hatter   4, 6, 35, 51, 119, 122,
    123
  as One-Man Army   119
  role in Murder Incorporated   51
Anastasio, Tough Tony   53
Anguilo, Gennaro   220
Anslinger, Harry J.   21, 85, 139
anti-Semitism   46
Apalachin Conference of 1957   127, 186,
    187
Apalachin disaster   127–34

Ashcroft, John   213
Assassinations Committee   9–10
associates   18, 36, 45, 51, 52, 54, 70,
    74, 102, 110, 120, 130, 132, 154,
    158, 175, 176, 178, 180, 182, 197,
    205–7, 209, 210, 220, 235, 236,
    243
Atkinson, Brooks   69
Atlanta Federal Penitentiary   131
Attell, Abe   14–15
Aurelio, Salvatore "Toddo"   202
Avelino, Salvatore   237

Bagel, Sally   205
Baird, Bruce A.   176
Banana Wars   185–96
Bando, Dominick   111
Barbara, Joseph "the Barber"   127
Beck, Dave   106, 108, 109
Becker, Edward   9
Bender, Tony   138
Berman, Davey   44
Berman, Otto "Abbadabba"   40
Beverly Club   99
Big Al   30, 31
*Big Apple Gangsters: The Rise and Decline
    of the Mob in New York*   226,
    243–4
Big Bankroll   13
Biller, Hyman   18
Billings, Richard N.
  *Fatal Hour: The Assassination of
    President Kennedy By Organized
    Crime*   95, 116
Bilotti, Thomas   202
Birns, Shondor   44
Black Sox Scandal   14

INDEX

Blakely, G. Robert
   Fatal Hour: The Assassination of President Kennedy By Organized Crime 116
Blakey, G. Robert 8–9, 235
   Fatal Hour: The Assassination of President Kennedy By Organized Crime 95
Blast, Kid 124
Blumenthal, Ralph 243
Bocchino, Joseph 125
Boccia, Ferdinand 52, 83
Boggiano, Anna 138, 139
Boggiano, John 138
Bonanno, Joe 5, 68, 129, 185–95, 205–8
   Man of Honor, A 39, 178, 185, 209, 235
Bonanno, Salvatore "Bill" 189
Bones, Billy 205
Bonventre, Cesare 195
Bork, Robert 94
Boston Police Department 221
Brancatto, Joseph "Joey" 170
Brando, Marlon 100
Breslin, Jimmy
   Good Rat, The 213
Broadway Mob 50
Brown, Florence "Cokey Flo" 68
Brown, Sidney "Fats" 59, 60
Buchalter, Louis "Lepke" 6, 39–41, 44, 51, 59, 61, 62, 121, 241
   as CEO of Murder Inc. 57
   fried in Old Sparky 73–8
   relationship with Adonis 87
Bugs and Meyer Gang 50, 51, 57
Bulger, James Joseph "Whitey" 215–17, 219–25
Bulger, Whitey 10
Burg, Yosef 92
Burke, Fred "the Killer" 25
Burroughs, William
   Last Words of Dutch Schultz, The 41
Busa, Amy 206
business of murder 57–63

Buttons, Red 69
Byrd, Lawrence 227, 228

Café Geiger 47
Café Wienecke 47
Callahan, John B. 224–5
Camilla, Frank 24
Campagna, Louis 25
canary sang 135–44
Cantarella, Richard (Shellackhead) 210
Cantellops, Nelson 131
Caplin, Mortimer 146
Capone, Al 2–3, 24, 25, 27, 28, 30, 31, 83
   deportation 89
Capone, Louis 59
capos 5, 36, 82, 101, 116, 137, 159, 161, 168, 174, 175, 178, 180, 182, 189, 192, 195, 197, 202, 204, 208–12, 226, 235, 237, 243
Carbo, Frankie 51, 59, 60
Cardinale, Tony 222
Carfano, Anthony 132
Carr, Howie 223
Castellamarese War 3–6, 33–41, 159
Castellano, Paul 197, 198, 202, 237
Castellitto, Anthony 113
Cataldo, Dominic 176
Catena, Jerry 129
Chaney, James 226, 227
Chertoff, Michael 238
Chicago Crime Commission 113
Chicago White Sox 15
Childers, Gil 238
Church, Frank 105
Cianelli, Eduardo 68
Coffey, Paul E. 222
Cohen, Mickey 48
Cohen, Philip "Little Farvel" 59
Coll, Vincent "Mad Dog" 5, 37
Colombo, Joe 164, 165, 187
Colombo Trial 174
Colombos 167, 169, 170, 173–84
Colosimo, Big Jim 23, 24
Commission Trial of 1985 195, 196

Concrete Club 237
confidential informers 10, 193, 197, 219, 220, 229
Connolly, C. I. 220
Connolly, John "Zip" 219, 222, 224
consiglieri/consigliere 5, 36, 161, 167, 178, 189–91, 202, 204, 237, 238
Copacabana Nightclub 168
Coppa, Frank 204–8
Coppa, Marguerite 207
Corallo, Anthony "Tony Duck" 111, 112, 237, 238, 240, 242
Corleone, Don Vito 93, 100, 159
Costello, Frank (formerly Francesco Castiglia) 4, 13, 34, 52–4, 63, 98–101, 103, 125, 127, 128, 194
   deportation 84
   slot machines 65, 66
Croswell, Edgar D. 130
Cusick, Jack 31
Cutler, Bruce 202

Dalitz, Moe 44, 45, 127
Dallas Police Department 10
D'Ambrosio, Salvatore "Sally" 163
D'Amico, Joseph (Joey the Mook) 210
Dan, Uri
   Meyer Lansky: Mogul of the Mob 131
Davis, John H. 116
   Mafia Dynasty 128
Dawson, Samuel 238, 239
De Britaine, William 177
De Vito, Maria 88
decapitation 235–45
DeCavalcante 155
DeChristopher, Fred 175, 176
DeCologero, Paul 223
DeGregorio, Gaspar 189–91
Dellacroce, Aniello 59, 60, 237
DeLuca, Bobby 222
Democratic Party 97
deportations 81–95
Depp, Johnny 207
DeRoss, John J. 176

DeSimone, Frank "One Eye" 187
DeVecchio, Lin 229
   We're Going to Win This Thing: The Shocking Frame-up of a Mafia Crime Buster 231
Dewey, Thomas E. 1, 10, 39, 52, 58, 62–3, 66, 70, 71, 74, 75, 77
   decapitation 240, 242–3
   deportation 54, 82, 86, 123
Diapoulas, Pete "The Greek" 168, 169
DiBella, Thomas 176
DiBernardo, Robert 202, 203
DiBono, Louis 202, 203
DiFilippi, Joseph 191
Dio, Johnny 106–7, 109, 111
DiPalermo, Joseph 133
DiPietro, Anthony 183
Dirksen, Everett 99
Dodge City 44
Dollinger, Michael 238
Don, Teflon 94, 204
Donnie Brasco 207
Doto, Joseph Antonio 89
Doto, Michele 88
Dragna, Jack 45
Drucci, Vincent 27–9
Drug Enforcement Administration 221
Ducks, Tony 112
Duvalier, Francois 189

Einstein, Albert 97
Eisenberg, Dennis
   Meyer Lansky: Mogul of the Mob 131
Eisenhower, Dwight D. 97–8
Epstein, Joe 102
Essary, Sina 168
Evola, Natale "Joe Diamonds" 191
Exner, Judith Campbell 149

Falanga, Frank 176
Farnsworth, Marjorie 103
Farvel, Little 60
Faye, Joey 69

INDEX

FBI informants   62, 120, 121, 140, 143, 179, 193, 197–213
FBN, *see* Federal Bureau of Narcotics (FBN)
Federal Bureau of Narcotics (FBN)   21, 85, 139, 140
Federal Interstate Wire Act of 1961   146
Federal Narcotics Laws   139
Feraco, James   59, 61
Ferri, Charles   122
Fifth Amendment   15, 87, 106, 112, 113
FIREs, *see* flippers, informants, rats, and explainers (FIREs)
Fishman, Steve   183
Five Families   5
Flemmi, Stevie "The Rifleman"   220, 222–5
flippers, informants, rats, and explainers (FIREs)   197–213
Florida State Prison   225
Four Deuces   24
Fox, Louis   46
Fox, Max   45
Franconia Hotel   44
Franse, Steven   138
Fratianno, "The Weasel"   48
Furnari, Christopher "Christy Tick"   237, 238
Fusaro, Vincent   158, 178

Gaffney, George   131
Gagliano   36
Galante, Carmine   84, 129, 130, 192, 193, 195
Gallo, Albert "Kid Blast"   157, 160, 161, 170, 174
Gallo, Joey   125, 160, 166, 168–70, 185
Gallo, Larry   157, 160–3
Gallo Wars   157–70
Gambino, Carlo   34, 85, 125, 128, 129, 166, 170, 186–8, 192
Garaufis, Nicholas   205, 212
Garfield Boys   160
Garland, Robert   69

Geas, Fotios ("Freddy")   223
Gene the Hat   205
Genna, Bloody Angelo   26
Genovese, Vito   4, 34–5, 37, 70, 123, 126, 127, 129, 132, 137, 192
   death of   133
   deportation   83–5, 89, 90, 94
   humiliation   129–31, 133
German-American Bund   46
Giancana, Sam "Momo"   129, 149–50
Gianinni, Eugenio   137, 138
Gigante, Vincent "the Chin"   123–4, 210, 244, 245
Gilbert, Dan   100
Ginsberg, Allen   218
Gioielli, Joseph "Joe Jelly"   160
Giuliani, Rudolph   1, 10, 41, 235–8, 240, 241, 243
Gleeson, John   203
Glimco, Joey   111, 113, 114
Godfather, The   162, 165
Godfather I   242
Godfather II   242
Goldberg, Jay   226
Goldstein, Martin "Buggsy"   7, 59
Goldwater, Barry   105
Goodman, Andrew   226, 227
Gophers   16
Gordon, Waxey   45
Gotti, John   37, 202–4, 237, 240, 245
Gottlieb, Sidney   217, 219
Grancio, Nicholas (Nicky Black)   178
Grant, Cary   86
Grateful Dead   218
Gravano, Sammy 'the Bull'   10, 202–4, 244
   Our Thing   204
Great Depression   30, 74
Greenbaum, Gus   45, 85
Greenbaum, Isadore   47
Greenberg, Harry "Big Greenie"   44
Greene, Graham   68
Greig, Catherine   222, 223
Guccia, Bartollo   128

Gurino, Vito "Socko" 59, 60
Gusenberg, Frank 2
Gusenberg, Peter 29
Guzik, Jake "Greasy Thumb" 100

Harrington, Edward F. 224
Harris, Mildred 68
Hazelton Federal Prison 223
Healy, Dan 28
Helfant, Edwin 198
Hill, Virginia 86, 102–3
Hoff, Boo Boo 45
Hoffa, Jimmy 9, 94, 106–9, 112, 113, 115
Hoffman, Harold G. 98
Holtz, Curly 44
Hoover, Herbert 19
Hoover, J. Edgar 10, 103, 104, 129, 145–8
Hostage Rescue Team of FBI 203
Hudson Dusters 16
Hundley, William G. 140
Hunt, Sam "Golf Bag" 28
Hunter, Robert 218
Hyman, William 21
Hynes, D. A. Charles 158, 180

Immigration and Naturalization Service (INS) 90–1
Indelicato, Anthony "Bruno" 242
INS, *see* Immigration and Naturalization Service (INS)
International Longshoremen's Association 107
Irish Winter Hill Gang 215, 219–21, 223, 225
Irvin, Sam J. 105
Israel Day Parade 7
Italian American Civil Rights League 165
Italian Americans 23
Italians 43–8

Jack, Black 205
Jackson, Marie K. 143, 144

Jelly, Joe 162
Jews 43–8
Joey, Crazy 124
John, Giovann 9
Johnson, Jerome A. 166
Johnson, Lyndon 105
Jordan, Thelma 68
Justice Department 8, 88, 89, 92–5, 104, 115, 121, 140, 148, 149, 153, 186, 197, 213, 229, 236

Katcher, Leo 15
Keenan, John F. 177
Kefauver Committee 97, 98, 106, 115
Kefauver, Estes 87, 102, 105
Kempton, Murray 203
Kennedy, Bobby 140, 148, 155
Kennedy, Caroline 141
Kennedy, Ethel 141
Kennedy, John F. 115
Kennedy, Joseph P., Sr. 46, 108, 145
Kennedy, Papa 10
Kennedy, Robert F. 1, 8–10, 94–5, 106, 108, 113–16
  Federal Interstate Wire Act of 1961 146
  mafia nemesis 145–55
  Operation Big Squeeze 146
Kesey, Ken
  One Flew Over the Cuckoo's Nest 218
Kinzer, Stephen 217, 219
Kiss of Death 157
Kleine Konditorei 46–7
Kleinman, Morris 44
Kovalick, Philip 45
Kravits, Louis 44
Krieger, Albert 202
Kuhn, Fritz 47

La Guardia, Fiorello 21, 61, 65–71
  anti-crime mission 66
La Selva, Joseph 188
Lacey, Robert
  Little Man 92

INDEX

Landau, Abe 40
Landau, Eli
   Meyer Lansky: Mogul of the Mob 131
Landis, Kenesaw Mountain 15
Langella, Gennaro "Gerry Lang" 176, 237, 242
Lansky, Meyer 4, 5, 14, 39, 45–7, 82, 89, 127
   Bugs and Meyer Gang 50–1, 57
   as businessman 51
   in crime 49–55
   deportation 91–3
   friendship with Luciano 49, 52
   against the mob 65–71
   vs. the State of Israel (1972) 93
Lanza, Socks 52
Laster, Lee F. 175
Law of Return 91
Leavenworth Prison 30
Lee, Gypsy Rose 69
Lehman, Herbert 74
Leonetti, "Handsome" Phillip 198–202
   Mafia Prince 201
Levine, Sam "Red" 5, 37, 38, 44, 51
Liebling, A. J. 69
Lino, Frank 211
Linsey, Joseph (né Linsky) 46
Little Nicky Eyeglasses 205
LoCascio, Frank "Frankie Loc" 202–4
LoCicero, Charles "the Sidge" 161
Lonardo, Angelo 240
Long, Huey 66
Longworth, Alice Roosevelt 141
Lorelei Dance Hall 46
Lowell, Robert
   Memories of West Street and Lepke 78
Lucas, Scott 98
Lucchese, Thomas 186, 188
Lucchese, Tommy "Three Fingers Brown" 34, 37, 75, 112
Luciano, Charles 53
Luciano, Lucky 4–6, 13, 34–9, 45, 121, 122, 127, 136
   as businessman 51
   in crime 49–55
   deportation 81–8, 94
   friendship with Lansky 49, 52
   Operation Underworld 54
   sentencing 52
   testimony against 67–8
Luparelli, Joseph 169

Maas, Peter
   Valachi Papers, The 142, 144
MacArthur, Douglas 97
Madden, Owney 67
made man 138, 199, 209, 244
Maffetore, Anthony 7
Mafia associate 102, 175
Mafia Commission Trial 177, 185, 235, 238, 243, 246
Magaddino, Stefano "The Undertaker" 142, 187
Magliocco, Joseph (aka Joe Evil Eye) 161, 163, 187, 188
Magoon, Seymour "Blue Jaw" 59, 60
Mahan, Jim 109–10
Maione, Harry "Happy" 7, 59
Malpiso, James 158
Mangano, Venero 204
Mangano, Vincent 5
Maranti, Gandolfo 111
Maranzano, Salvatore 3–5, 33–9, 126, 185
Marcello, Carlos 9, 94, 111, 114–16, 127, 154
Marcu, Aaron R. 176
Mari, Frank 190, 191
Marked Woman 68
Massachusetts State Police 221
Masseria, Joe "the Boss" 3, 33–6, 39
Massino, Joseph 180, 196, 204, 205, 208–13
Maxi's Brauhaus 46
McCarthy, Joe 104–6
McClellan, John L. 104, 105, 108, 111, 113, 114, 140–1

Permanent Investigations
  Subcommittee 140
McClellan Committee 105, 116, 145
McGuire, Phyllis 149
McGurn, Jack 28, 30
McManus, George "Hump" 18, 20
Melli, Frank 176
Merlo, Mike 26
Mickey Mouse Mafia 45
Milito, Liborio 202, 203
Miller, John 158, 200
Mineo, Salvatore "Charlie Lemons" 167
Mississippi Burning 228
Mississippi State Sovereignty
  Commission 226–7
Mitchell, John 94, 165
MK-Ultra project 216, 217, 219
Mongelli, Daniel 211
Moran, George "Bugs" 2, 27, 29, 30
Moran, Jimmy 204
Moresco, Victoria 23
Moretti, Willie 4, 34, 98, 101–2
Morris, John 224
Mr. Arsenic 62
Mt. Sinai Health Systems 219
Mundt, Karl 141
Murder Incorporated 6–8, 47, 51
  modus operandi of 57

Napolitano, Dominick (aka Sonny
  Black) 207, 209
narcissism 37
Narcotics Bureau of New York 104, 131, 146
Nastari, Rosario 158
Natale, Ralph 51, 213
National Crime Syndicate 6, 14, 21, 45, 51, 58
  Commission of 75, 83
Nazism 46, 47
New York Fats 19
New York Newspapers Association 110
New York Police Department 143

New York Press Photographers
  Association 110
New York University Law School 236
Newark, Tim
  *Boardwalk Gangster: The Real Lucky
  Luciano* 37
Newspaper and Mail Deliveres Union 37
Newspaper Guild of New York 110
Night of the Sicilian Vespers 38
Nitti, Frank 30–1
Nitzberg, Irving 59
Nixon, Richard 105, 235
North Siders 27

O'Banion, Dion 25–7
O'Brian, Jack 91
O'Connor, Herbert 104
O'Dwyer, William 1, 7, 8, 76, 98
  as ambassador to Mexico 63
Old Sparky 73–8
On the Waterfront 52, 109
Operation Big Squeeze 146
Operation Underworld 54
Orbach, Jerry 167
Order of Saints Maurice 84
Orena, Vic 204, 228, 231
Orena, Victor 177
Outfit 23, 24, 26, 27, 30, 31, 33, 245
Overseas Press Club 110
Owen, Richard 239, 241, 242

Pagano, Pasquale 139
Pagano, Pat 137
Palma Boys Social Club 237
Parisi, Jack "The Dandy" 59, 60
Patriarca, Raymond L. S. 154, 164, 220, 221
Pendergast, Tom 8
Perlman, Nathan 47
Persico, Carmine "the Snake" 124–5, 173–84, 226, 237, 239, 240, 242
  death of 184
  leadership 174
  protective behavior 183

Philadelphia County Prison   120
Pileggi, Nicholas   9
Pilledsdorf, Gary   230
Pistone, Joseph D. (aka Donnie Brasco)   195, 207, 209, 210, 237
  Ceremony, The   224
Pitta, Vito   176
Pius XII, Pope   97
Plug Uglies   16
Polyclinic Hospital   19
Presser, Nancy   68
Price, Cecil   227
Prizzi's Honor   139
Profaci, Frank   161
Profaci, Joseph   5, 34, 36, 124, 129, 158–65, 173, 187
Profaci-Colombo Gallo Wars   5
Provenzano, Anthony "Tony Pro"   111–13
Purfield, Peter   17

Raab, Selwyn   9
Racketeer Influenced and Corrupt Organizations Act (RICO)   8, 41, 62, 113, 143, 155, 205, 212, 235, 236, 238, 244
Ragano, Frank   116
  Mob Lawyer   9, 95
Rastelli, Philip "Rusty"   191, 192, 194, 208
rats   197–213
Ratterman, George   146
Ravenite Social Club   37, 202
Raymond, Nigger Nate   18, 19
Reles, Abe "Kid Twist"   7, 51–2, 59, 62, 75
Rhody, Lou   45
Rice, Thomas   20–1
Rickles, Don   167, 168
RICO, *see* Racketeer Influenced and Corrupt Organizations Act (RICO)
Riesel, Victor   110, 111
Riggi, Giovanni   204
Rogers, Ralph   213

Rolfe, Louise   30
Roman Empire   37
Romeo Is Bleeding   78
Rosen, Harry   44
Rosen, Joe   58, 76–7
Rosen, Nig   45
Rosencrantz, Bernard "Lulu"   40
Rothenberg, Leslie B.   225
Rothkopf, Lou   44
Rothstein, Arnold   13–21, 23
Rudolph, Harry   62
Rupolo, Ernest   132
Russo, Andrew "Andy Mush"   180, 181
Russo, Joseph   175
Russo, Michael   192–3

Salemme, Frank   222
Salerno, Anthony "Fat Tony"   242
Salerno, Ralph   51, 132, 237, 240
Santoro, Salvatore "Tom Mix"   237, 238, 242
Santucci, Robert   244
Savarese, John   238
Scaglione, Pietro   88
Scalice, Frank   36
Scarfo, Nicodemo "Little Nicky"   198–201
Scarpa, Gregory "The Grim Reaper"   179, 215, 225–31
Schofield Flowers Shop   26, 28
Schultz, Dutch   39–41, 58, 61
Schuster, Arnold   73, 119, 120
Schuster, Lincoln   119
Schwerner, Michael   226, 227
Sciacca, Paul   190, 191
Sciascia, Gerlando   212, 213
Scimone, John   161
Scopo, Ralph "Little Ralphie"   176, 237, 242
Sebollena, Angelo   230
Sedway, Moe   51, 85
Senate Select Committee to Study Governmental Operations

with Respect to Intelligence
   Activities   105
Senate Special Committee to Investigate
   Crime in Interstate Commerce   87
Shapiro, Jacob "Gurrah"   44, 57, 61
Shargel, Gerald   203
Shiro, Linda   230
Siano, Fiore   137–9
Siegel, Bugsy "Bugsy"   4, 13, 14, 35, 39,
   44, 45, 102, 122
   assassination of   50, 51
   Bugs and Meyer Gang   50–1, 57
   deportation   85–7
   violent reaction to provocations   50
Sifakis, Carl   94, 100, 122–3, 143
Silver, Long John   205
Silvers, Phil   69
Sin City   146
Sinatra, Frank   98, 101, 165
Sing Sing Prison   7, 41, 51, 58, 76–8, 81,
   131, 136, 241
Smiley, Allen   99
Smith, William French   176
Smurra, Henry   178
soldier   5, 36, 38, 68, 70, 82, 101, 121,
   135, 137–9, 158, 159, 161–4, 178,
   180, 182, 188, 191, 195, 197, 202,
   210, 226, 235, 243
Solomon, Charles "King"   45
Speranza, Matteo   158
St. Valentine's Day Massacre   2–3, 23,
   29, 133
Stacher, Doc   44, 45, 89, 127
   deportation   90–1
Stacher, Joseph "Doc"   51
'Star Quest'   176
State Board of Mediation   62
Steinberg, David   167, 168
Stevenson, Robert Louis   205
Strauss, Harry (aka Pittsburgh Phil)   6,
   7, 57–9
Strollo, Anthony (aka Tony Bender)   132,
   137, 139
Sullivan, Big Tim   16, 17

Sullivan Act   16
Sunrise Club   24
Sutton, Willie "the Actor"   74, 119

Talese, Gay
   Honor Thy Father   188
Tammany Hall   16, 17
Tannenbaum, Allie "Tick Tock"   59, 60,
   77
taxi cab industry   107
Taylor, Tom
   Far Out   218
Teitlebaum, Harry   44–5
Telvi, Abraham   110–11
Tenuto, Frederick J. "The Angel"   120–1
Terranova, Ciro "The Artichoke King"   4,
   35, 69
Tetric, Stanley   110
Thomas, Evan   146
Thompson, Titanic   18
Three Brothers   204
Tobey, Charles   102
Tolson, Clyde   103
Top Hoodlum Program   129
Torrio, Johnny "the Fox"   23–7, 31
   deportation   89–90
Trafficante, Santos   9, 116, 129
Treasury Department   147
Tresca, Carlo   84
"Troutman St. Ambush, The"   190
Truman, Harry   8, 98
Tucker, Robert   44
Turano, Giuseppe   195
Turkus, Burton   1
   Murder Inc   62
Turner, Kathleen   139

underbosses   5, 35, 36, 60, 98, 101, 137,
   161, 163, 176, 181, 191, 192, 198,
   200, 202, 203, 210, 211, 220, 237,
   238, 240
United States House of Representatives
   Select Committee on
   Assassinations   8, 115

United States Medical Center for Federal Prisoners   133
United States Senate Select Committee on Improper Activities in Labor and Management   105

Valachi, Joseph   10, 121, 132
   canary sang   135–44
   Godfather II   135
Vanella, Robert   31
Virgilio, Nicholas "Nick the Blade"   199
Vitale, Salvatore   211–12

Warren, Fuller   99
Wasserman, Jack   115
Watergate Scandal   94
Wegman, J. Bertram   61
Weinberg, Bo   5
Weintraub, Benson   184
Weiss, Emanuel "Mendy"   40, 58, 59
Weiss, Hymie   27, 28
whack   130, 169, 174, 178, 240, 243

What's My Line?   97
Wheelchairs, Bobby   205
Wheeler, Roger   224
Widmark, Richard   157
Winchell, Walter   76
Winkler, Gus   25
Witness Protection Program   93, 170, 196, 197, 204, 212, 221
Wolensky, Morris "Moey Dimples"   75
Wolfe, Mark L.   222
Workman, Charlie "The Bug"   40, 58, 59
Workmen's Lunch Wagon Association   208

Yacovelli, Joseph "Joey Yack"   167
Yale, Frankie   24, 27

Ziegler, George "Shotgun"   25
Zurlo, Angelo   146
Zwillman, Abner "Longy"   39, 44, 51, 127, 128
   deportation   90